THE RETURN OF MITTELEUROPA: SOCIO-ECONOMIC TRANSITION IN POST-COMMUNIST CENTRAL EUROPE

THE RETURN OF MITTELEUROPA: SOCIO-ECONOMIC TRANSITION IN POST-COMMUNIST CENTRAL EUROPE

SOHRAB ABIZADEH AND ALLEN MILLS
EDITORS

Nova Science Publishers, Inc.
Commack, New York

Editorial Production: Susan Boriotti
Office Manager: Annette Hellinger
Graphics: Frank Grucci and John T'Lustachowski
Information Editor: Tatiana Shohov
Book Production: Donna Dennis, Patrick Davin, Christine Mathosian and Tammy Sauter
Circulation: Maryanne Schmidt
Marketing/Sales: Cathy DeGregory

Library of Congress Cataloging-in-Publication Data

Abizadeh, Sohrab.
The return of Mitteleuropa : socio-economic transition in post-communist Central Europe / Sohrab Abizadeh and Allen Mills.
p. cm.
ISBN 1-56072-643-1
1. Europe, Central--Economic conditions. 2. Europe, Central--Politics and government--1989- 3. Post-communism-- Europe, Central. I. Mills, Allen. II. Title.
HC244.A513 1998 98-51004
330.943'0009049--dc21 CIP

6080 Jericho Turnpike, Suite 207
Commack, New York 11725
Tele. 516-499-3103 Fax 516-499-3146
e-mail: Novascience@earthlink.net
e-mail: Novascil@aol.com
Web Site: http://www.nexusworld.com/nova

Printed in the United States of America

CONTENTS

PREFACE

The collapse of Communism after 1989 was an event of world-historical importance. Especially in Europe but throughout the world the fault lines of the cold war had run deep and wide. All that came to an end in 1989. The change was no more dramatic than in Central Europe. Czechoslovakia, Hungary and Poland were geographically closest to Western Europe and, culturally and historically, were part of Mitteleuropa (Middle Europe).

After 1989 this trio (now quartet) of states launched forth on the transition to political pluralism and market economies with special relish and enthusiasm. In Poland and Hungary the transition had already been underway before 1989. But the removal of Soviet hegemony evidently left the way ahead without obstacle and impediment. They could now unambiguously join Western Europe, politically and economically. In what follows we offer a sort of progress report on the state of the post-Communist revolution, ten years on, in this part of Central Europe.

The contributors come from a mixture of backgrounds; economics, history, political science and sociology. Their essays are the result of "field-work" in Central Europe as much as immersion in the abstract world of books and libraries. The essays evince a broad, multi-disciplinary perspective and a readiness to utilize both fact and theory in the pursuit of their subject. Their overall conclusion is that the transition to democracy and markets for these countries has been bumpier and longer than might have been expected in those heady days of ten years ago. Possessed of many cultural advantages to facilitate a rapid, advantageous transition, these have not been sufficient to achieve all that had been expected in the political and economic spheres. There is a sober, questioning quality to these essays; there is equally a tone of hopefulness that, nonetheless, the transition *is* proceeding, albeit more slowly and sometimes with more difficulty than was expected.

Part One consists of five chapters concentrating on the overall transition process in the countries of Central Europe, while Part Two deals with specific cases.

Chapter I, on the historical perspective of transition presents a detailed historical analysis of the events leading to the collapse of Communism.

Chapter II, using economic theory and historical data, performs an extensive comparative analysis of the economic performance of the Central European countries before and after transition. Following a detailed discussion on the overall economic performance of these countries, this chapter proceeds to deal with the specific issues of inflation, unemployment, government finances, the social safety net, and international trade. The predominant theme of this chapter is that when analyzing and evaluating the economic performance of these countries, the current models used in the capitalist economies of western countries are not readily applicable.

Chapter III focuses on the economic progress of the emerging market economies of Central Europe since 1989. The author argues that while economic progress generally has occurred the transition has not been priceless. This chapter provides some of the details of the macroeconomic developments in the sample countries and goes on to discuss the issues of privatization and the development of the banking and financial markets.

Chapter IV gives an analysis of the economics of mass media and their role in transition economies. While explaining the importance of free media, the author discusses how media can be used by governments and business alike to exert control over the people. Given that the countries of Central Europe are continuing their transition towards a market-oriented economic system, they are cautioned against blind imitation of media systems that dominate western cultures.

Chapter V reviews and analyses three perspectives on the growing role of information in advanced industrial societies. The author argues that while all these perspectives contain useful insight, none can be held to be exhaustive of the subject. This chapter then explores the utility of the information analogy or information model in providing an explanation of Central Europe's so far imperfect transition to market capitalism and political democracy. The author argues that the usefulness of the model is limited by the fact that the technological, occupational, economic and social factors associated with the development of the information society are still very much less evident in the east than they are in the west. For this reason, it is further argued, concepts developed in the west to describe the transition to information-based forms of activities should be applied only with caution to the east.

Chapter VI concentrates on Czech Republic's experience of the initiation of educational change since 1989. It claims that the Czech experience, a case of "sudden change", presents a unique opportunity to study the educational change process, particularly as it has been defined and understood by other scholars such as Fullan (1991). The fact that the phenomenon of educational transformation has been experienced within a more compressed time frame in Central Europe and under conditions of political revolution, suggests that the Czech experience provides a suitable "laboratory" for the investigation of educational change that is different from that experienced in North America where change occurs within a relatively stable socio-political context.

Chapter VII focuses on the status of women's employment in Poland. After presenting basic measures of macro-economic performance for the period 1990-1996, a comparison of women's employment in the labor market before and after transition is made. A discussion of the factors that might have been important determinants of women's labor force participation is presented. This chapter concludes that while the structural changes that have taken place since 1990 have adversely affected women and men alike, available evidence suggests that women have been subject to higher rates of joblessness than men.

Chapter VIII looks at the emerging market economy in Slovak Republic. The author points out that while this country faces some of the same problems that other countries in the region have had to confront (e.g., privatization methods, central bank independence, banking and capital market reforms), it has its own unique problems. It argues that, instrumental in the development of a market-oriented economy is an operational capital market and consistent sources of funds. This chapter discusses the progress made thus far in Slovak Republic's transition, with emphasis on the banking system, capital market development and the role for the National Bank of Slovakia.

Finally, Chapter IX discusses the Czech lands and juxtaposes their history to the theory of civil society of Ernest Gellner. The author suggests that, although Gellner claims that "civil society" first emerged in the specific historical circumstances of 17th century England, some of the reasons for its emergence there have possible "functional" continuities with the evolution of civil society in the Czech lands. He argues that the Czech lands have been a civil society, of a liberal kind, especially since 1918, and that Nazism between 1939 and 1945 and Communism from 1948 to 1989 only submerged and did not obliterate this cultural sub-structure. The chapter uses the condition of journalism in post-revolution Czech Republic as an example of the travails of change in a new civil-social order.

ACKNOWLEDGEMENTS

The original work on this volume began in early 1990 when a committee was formed at The University of Winnipeg to coordinate faculty research on the central and Eastern European transition to a market economy. The Social Science and Humanities Research Council of Canada (SSHRCC) had announced its intentions to provide research support in this area through its Aid to Small Universities Program. The present authors were successful recipients of part of a research grant under this program.

Subsequently, an international symposium on Mass Media in the Transformation of East-Central European Societies was organized by Dr. Gabriel Bar-Haim, then of the Sociology Department of The University of Winnipeg and a member of our research team and now at the Hebrew University of Jerusalem in Israel. The symposium was held in June 1992 in Bucharest, Romania. Some of the papers included in this volume are revised and updated versions of those presented at that symposium.

There are many to whom we owe thanks. We would like to thank SSHRCC and The University of Winnipeg Research and Travel Committee for funding this project.

Dr. Bar-Haim has been very instrumental in initiating the conference and getting us started on this volume. We thank him for his encouragement.

Many others have helped and encouraged us throughout this project. Special thanks go to Judi Hanson for her dedication and professional help in typing the original manuscript.

PART ONE:
THE REGION

CHAPTER 1

THE TRANSFORMATION OF CENTRAL EUROPE: AN HISTORICAL PERSPECTIVE

DAN STONE

I. INTRODUCTION

This chapter aims to introduce the reader to the central and Eastern European region, survey its development under Communism, describe the collapse of Communism, and examine its transformation after Communism's fall. Political and economic factors are emphasized along with some social and cultural trends. Within the central and Eastern European region, Poland is described first and longest because it was the leader in forcing Communism to liberalize and then to collapse. Although it is hard to generalize accurately, Poland may also have gone farthest in post-Communist transformation.

Since east and Central European developments did not take place in isolation, this chapter begins by providing a quick introduction to Communism and Communist systems as they were devised by the Soviet Union in the 1920s and 1930s. After World War II, the Soviet Union dominated Eastern Europe for forty-five years and forced the countries of the region to accept the Communist political, economic, social, and cultural system. Communism came to an end in Central and Eastern Europe in 1989 because the Soviet Union relinquished its hold and permitted domestic forces to assert themselves.

II. Regions in the Former Soviet Bloc

As Communism unraveled, the apparent monolith of the Soviet Union and the Soviet Bloc quickly broke into several regions with differing characteristics. The most successful region had enjoyed the closest links to Western Europe and shared the most common characteristics. Other regions had different historical experiences and faced different problems or more extreme problems as they transformed themselves from Communist states.

The Central European Region: Poland, Czechoslovakia, and Hungary entered the post-Communist world with the best chances of success. Ethnically homogeneous for the most part, each of these states enjoyed parliamentary traditions that began in the Middle Ages and continued into the nineteenth and twentieth centuries. They had long formed part of European political, economic, and cultural life, even when their geographic position and economies made them seem like poor cousins to the more prosperous West. Large émigré communities ensured plentiful contact with the West in the post-Stalin era. Despite the western orientation of these countries, geography, economics, and international affairs mark them firmly as central and Eastern European. Starting from a less developed base, forty-five years of Communist domination have left a more primitive economic system than even the most backward capitalist countries of the European Union and a fragile political system that is just beginning to strike deep roots in society. East Germany belongs to this region, but unification with West Germany has precluded consideration of it in this chapter.[1]

The Balkan Region: Romania, Bulgaria, Yugoslavia, and Albania have found transformation even more difficult. All but Albania possessed ineffectual parliaments in the nineteenth and twentieth centuries, and political activity was confined to a relatively small social elite. The economies were relatively backward and emphasized subsistence farming as their major activity along with some extractive industries. Non-Communist parties have failed to sink deep roots since Communism's collapse. Much of the former Yugoslavia has suffered devastating wars and civil wars, of course. The northernmost area, Slovenia, avoided involvement in the fighting and, as a result of long-standing ties to Austria, has maintained the highest standard of prosperity and democracy in the region. Croatia, also strongly western in its ties, has lagged as a result of militaristic policies and demagogic nationalism. The largest region, Serbia, has been devastated by militarism and western sanctions. Macedonia and Montenegro were very poor to begin with and made little progress. It is scarcely necessary to mention that Bosnia suffered greatly. Romania installed a former Communist who maintained much of the Communist political and economic system although he tolerated some dissent. Concern that the large Hungarian and Gypsy minorities might demand concessions has fostered authoritarianism until recently, when more substantial economic and political reforms were announced. Bulgaria was more successful in creating a functioning parliamentary democracy but it has not succeeded in effecting major economic change. The primitive and isolated state of Albania has moved backward since Communism's fall.[2]

The Ex-Soviet Region. The ex-Soviet republics, particularly Russia, Ukraine, and Belarus, have common political, economic, and cultural characteristics that distinguish them from the central and Eastern European and Balkan regions. Seventy-five years of Communist rule wiped out private industry, trade, and agriculture, and the Soviet Union emphasized the creation of heavy industry that was both capital intensive and difficult to modernize. The region lacks popularly-rooted parliamentary traditions and has long been isolated from world developments. Harsh governmental domination of political life prevented ordinary citizens from voicing their concerns and proposing solutions to pressing problems. Many of these characteristics formed under the Tsarist Empire before the 1917 Revolution. Transformation in this region has been particularly slow and painful.

There are many differences within the region, however. Russia contains both a strong nationalist movement that resists change and a government that has fostered change, even though much of that change rewards only some of its citizens. Ukraine has been open to western influence, particularly through the large Ukrainian diaspora, but it lacks a strong cadre of local reformers. The sense of national identity within Ukraine varies widely from west to east, and the large numbers of Russian speakers provide a ready-made excuse for intervention by the Russian state. Belarus suffers more than any other region from obsolete heavy industry and lacks a clear sense of national identity; its semi-dictatorial government looks towards re-confederation with Russia. The Baltic Republics (Lithuania, Latvia, and Estonia) entered the Soviet Union late (1940 and again in 1944 after the Germans were expelled) and achieved the highest level of development in the USSR. They have been hampered by Russia's desire to keep them under close surveillance and the presence of large Russian minorities (30-35% in Estonia and Latvia).[3]

III. The Emergence of Communism

The Bolshevik Revolution and Civil War installed Communism in Russia, Belarus, Ukraine, the Caucasus and other territories between 1917 and 1921; these territories formed the Union of Soviet Socialist Republics in 1924. 1921 to 1928 was a period of relative stability, but the Stalin Revolution (1928-34) fully nationalized the economy and imposed rigid Marxist-Leninist ideology in political and cultural life at the cost of at least 10 million lives during Collectivization (1930-2), Famine (1932-3) and Purges (1936-9). Stalin's tyranny resumed after World War II (1945-1953). Stalin's successor, Nikita Khrushchev (1953-64), ended mass terror and released millions from the concentration camps (Gulags) without changing the system fundamentally and his successors, Leonid Brezhnev (1964-82) and Konstantin Chernenko (1982-5) administered Communism more rigorously, jailing thousands and incarcerating others in psychiatric hospitals; several hundred dissidents went into foreign exile. The effort by Mikhail Gorbachev (1985-92) to overhaul the system through *Perestroika* (rebuilding) and *Glasnost* (openness) led to the collapse of the Soviet Union and the Soviet Bloc.

Stalin created the Soviet Bloc during and after World War II. He annexed the Baltic Republics in 1939-40, lost them to Nazi Germany, and reacquired them in 1944-5. The Baltic states joined a dozen other "Republics" (provinces/states such as Ukraine and Belarus) within the Union of Soviet Socialist Republics with limited cultural and self-governing rights exercised by Communists under Moscow's direction. After World War II had brought the Red Army to Berlin, the Soviet Union created a "Soviet Bloc" of formally independent states that it forcibly Communized: Poland, Czechoslovakia, Hungary, Romania, Bulgaria, East Germany, Yugoslavia, and Albania. Yugoslavia seceded from the Soviet Bloc in 1948 but remained Communist until it collapsed in 1992; its Communism underwent major reforms in the 1950s. Albania seceded from the Soviet bloc in the 1950s rather than accept Khrushchev's modest reforms and remained hard-line Communist until 1989.

IV. The Communist System

The defining elements of the Soviet Union and the Soviet Bloc of East European states were the One-Party Dictatorship, the official Marxist-Leninist ideology, and the Command Economy.

One-Party Dictatorship: The only legal party in the Soviet Bloc was the Communist Party (although some subordinated allies were tolerated, mainly in Poland) and the Party controlled the State. The Communist Party named state officials and other persons in high positions such as newspaper editors, heads of television stations, factory managers, and university presidents. Only the Communist Party's view could be expressed. To build a career in any field, Soviet Bloc citizens had to join the Party and mouth the party line. Only a few cultural and sports figures achieved fame and fortune without joining the Party.

The Communist state used terror ruthlessly to establish its hold in the Soviet Union (1917-21 and 1928-53) and in Eastern Europe (1944-52). Stalin and his East European lieutenants executed dissenters or sentenced them to long terms of harsh imprisonment. In addition, millions of innocent citizens were convicted of political offenses under transparent labels such as "sabotage" (lateness for work), "espionage" (contact with foreigners, including relatives), or "anti-state agitation" (grumbling). The reasons for this extraordinary reign of terror are obscure. The most plausible explanations mix Stalin's paranoia, efforts by Communist officials to find easy explanations for difficult problems, and squabbles within omnipotent bureaucracies.[4]

After Stalin, Communist governments generally restricted arrest to small numbers of genuine dissenters who urged reform. Most citizens could enjoy a peaceful life by avoiding public criticism of the system. However, even reform

Communists used violence on occasion as when Khrushchev ordered Soviet troops to shoot strikers in 1962 and when Polish troops shot Polish strikers in 1970. The Soviet army crushed the 1956 Hungarian Revolution with armed force and Soviet bloc forces intervened massively to halt the Czechoslovak Prague Spring of 1968.

Marxist-Leninist Ideology. The Communist Party and the Communist states subscribed to the Marxist-Leninist ideology that contended that Capitalism would inevitably fail as an economic system and that a workers' revolution would inevitably lead to Socialism. Marxism-Leninism claimed that economics determined existence so that political and cultural ideas mainly expressed class relations. Since all areas of public and private expression were politicized, censors evaluated books, newspapers, and lectures for their political content and suppressed dissenting views, often punishing their authors. At their worst, Stalinists even condemned as counter-revolutionary relatively innocent behavior such as playing jazz, painting in an abstract style, or drinking Coca-Cola.

Post-Stalinist Communist states gradually enlarged the area of politically neutral expression but even the most tolerant countries (Poland and Hungary) refused to allow anti-Communists to express their views. By the 1970s and 1980s, even Communist Party members' own adherence to Marxism-Leninism became a matter of form rather than conviction.

While Communist and western states treated each other as fundamentally hostile, Communist policies varied from anti-western antagonism to relatively amicable trade relations depending on the personalities of the leaders and the requirements of the day. After World War II, Stalin's fear of the West and expansionist policies caused inevitable cool relations to congeal in a "Cold War". Khrushchev sought peaceful coexistence and Brezhnev achieved Détente with the West, bringing closer trade and cultural relations even though he still proclaimed that no socialist state could ever secede from the Soviet bloc. East-West hostility increased when the United States President Jimmy Carter emphasized the Soviet Union's civil rights abuses and President Ronald Reagan denounced the Soviet Union as an "Evil Empire".

The fundamental glue holding the bloc together remained Soviet domination and the threat of military intervention by Soviet troops stationed in Warsaw Pact countries. Communist bloc unity was institutionalized through the Council of Mutual Economic Assistance (1948) and the military Warsaw Pact (1954).

Command Economy. The Stalinist Revolution developed the command economy in which the state owned all factories and trading operations. Most of the food was raised on collective farms (cooperatives) that operated under Party supervision and followed instructions from the Ministry of Agriculture. The Communist State organized all economic activity through multi-year plans (usually Five Year Plans) in which the state allocated resources according to its own priorities. Consumer demand for housing and clothing (not to mention cosmetics and audio equipment) went unfilled for the most part as the state concentrated on building factories, heavy machinery, and military equipment. Isolated from the international capital market, Communist states received little supplementary investment so that economic growth tended to be slow. Communist states achieved spectacular success in the early phases of development, but found it impossible to meet the increasing demands of technological change in the fifty years after World War II.

Post-Stalinist states put more emphasis on consumer goods and permitted modest amounts of private business activity to ease the rigidities of national planning. However, they restricted private enterprise to peripheral areas of the economy such as personal services, with the notable exception of Poland which never collectivized its agriculture. Even the Soviet Union allowed collective farmers to sell produce raised on their small private plots.

V. *PERESTROIKA* AND THE COLLAPSE OF COMMUNISM IN THE SOVIET BLOC[5]

Mikhail Gorbachev, head of the Soviet Communist Party, unwittingly let the genie out of the bottle and destroyed Communism by trying to reform it. Correctly diagnosing the causes of stagnation in the Brezhnev era as rigidity and corruption, Gorbachev introduced *Perestroika* and *Glasnost* to modernize and strengthen Communism. Within three years, the sputtering Soviet economy fell into a recession so that everyday necessities could scarcely be found. Efforts to break through bottlenecks by encouraging cooperatively-owned private enterprise led to the emergence of a two-tiered economy in which the large majority of the population got poorer while a minority flaunted its new riches. Gorbachev's policy of "openness" (*Glasnost*) permitted millions to voice their vehement disapproval over their declining standard of living. Others found that they could finally speak out about the crimes of the Stalin era and the injustices of the contemporary Communist bureaucracy. Soon, many Soviets citizens concluded that Communism itself was the problem.

Gorbachev found that he had little taste for holding the Soviet Bloc states of Eastern Europe in submission. At first, he encouraged Soviet Bloc leaders to reform in the mistaken belief that their populations would accept reformed Communism as legitimate. When the peoples of Eastern Europe showed that they wanted to end Communism, he had neither the means nor the desire to rein them in. Halting the secession of Soviet Bloc states could only have been accomplished by re-imposing Stalinism at home and re-kindling the Cold War with the West.

As the Soviet Union relaxed its hold, Communism collapsed in central and Eastern Europe in 1989-1992 for several fundamental reasons:

1. The citizens of the Soviet Bloc (especially Poland, Czechoslovakia, and Hungary) never accepted their Communist governments as legitimate. Citizens saw

local Communists as Soviet hirelings and tolerated them only as long as the Soviet Union kept them in power. Several unsuccessful revolts and movements of fundamental dissent (Poland 1956, Hungary 1956, Czechoslovakia 1968, Poland 1980-1) illustrated central and Eastern Europe's hostility to their Communist governments.

2. Marxist-Leninist ideology gained few adherents in Soviet Bloc states, although the much longer life of Soviet Communism gave it a high degree of public acceptance. Genuine Communists, observing the difference between the high ideals of the movement and the tawdry or violent practices of Communist governments, tried to reform Communism. Failure made them abandon the ideology entirely. Most East European parties were filled with opportunists and careerists.

3. The Command Economy provided a low level of basic services to the population but failed to adapt to changing times. Growing prosperity in the West made the slow growth of the Soviet Bloc embarrassing and left its countries relatively backward in the vital military and industrial sector. Public morale was a factor and ordinary citizens could see that they led harder lives than their western counterparts. Efforts to catch up in the 1970s and 1980s by borrowing billions of dollars from western banks or by allowing more private business produced short-lived prosperity at the price of long-term instability. Foreign debts mounted astronomically in some countries and the allocation of resources became unbalanced in others so that the Communist Bloc fell into a downward spiral for which there was no remedy. Living standards declined throughout the Bloc in the 1970s and 1980s. Poor environmental controls created ecological disaster zones and some countries suffered overall declines in life expectancy.

4. Governmental propaganda from western countries played only a small role in the collapse of Communism but western-style consumerism played a large role. The peoples of central and Eastern Europe quietly demanded access to blue jeans, fast food, and fancy cars without understanding the price that they would have to pay to transform their economies and societies. Frustrated by governmental authoritarianism and poor economic prospects, east bloc intellectuals succumbed without a struggle to the siren song of free market economic theory that had become the conventional wisdom of the Thatcher-Reagan-Mulroney era.

VI. The Transformation of Central and Eastern Europe Since 1989

Since the fall of Communism, the nations of central and Eastern Europe have achieved stable parliamentary governments which assure democracy and civil rights throughout the region. There are no movements for charismatic authoritarian rule despite the inevitable difficulties in governing new state institutions, although apathy and voter cynicism have become an even greater problem than in the west. The break-up of the Czechoslovak state into Czech Republic and Slovak Republic is the only major political failure. The peaceful methods used and the lack of bitterness may equally be seen as the region's outstanding success, however.

Central and Eastern European states have also achieved a rapid transformation from command economy to market economy. Substantial privatization and the growth of new business have given the private sector a dominant position in national economies. Rates of economic growth are positive while both unemployment and inflation have declined to reasonable figures. Currencies are reasonably stable although subject to levels of inflation that would be unacceptable in the west. Nevertheless, large sectors of the population have suffered from unemployment and declining living standards during the readjustment, and the economies remain fragile.

VII. Communist Poland and Independent Poland

The Red Army liberated Poland from Nazi occupation and the Soviet Union imposed a Communist-dominated coalition government that recognized the Soviet annexation of the eastern third of pre-war Poland in exchange for territorial compensation in the west at Germany's expense. The Polish Communists gradually gathered strength, falsified the 1947 election results, subordinated their Socialist allies and, by 1949, created a Stalinist system. Polish Stalinism followed Bloc patterns except for its slow pace of collectivization and its hesitancy in launching an all-out assault on the Catholic Church.[6]

Khrushchev's de-Stalinizing reforms in the Soviet Union unleashed greater reforms in Poland. After rioting broke out in the city of Poznan, liberal Communists elected Wladysław Gomułka (1956-70), who had been imprisoned by Polish Stalinists, as head of the Communist Party in a fevered atmosphere of mass demonstrations. The new regime dismantled Stalinist terror, abandoned collectivization, allowed some private business, and came to terms with the Catholic Church. Gomułka's reforms fell far short of what some reformers desired and dissatisfaction grew throughout the 1960s, particularly as the economy stagnated. Party hard-liners took advantage of student demonstrations in March 1968 to launch an anti-Semitic campaign aimed at unseating Gomułka but only succeeded in chasing much of the small remaining Jewish community out of Poland. Price increases touched off wide-spread rioting in Baltic cities in 1970 that forced an ailing Gomułka to resign.[7]

Polish Communists chose Edward Gierek (1970-80), who had acquired a reputation for pragmatism as Communist Party secretary in Silesia, to assume national leadership. Gierek attempted to modernize Poland with capital borrowed from western banks and by loosening ideological constraints. Poland made rapid progress at first, but a combination of bad management, bad luck, and corruption left the economy incapable of repaying the foreign loans. An effort to stabilize the economy and halt growing inflation by imposing consumer price increases led to rioting by industrial workers in 1976 which the government repressed harshly. Dissident professionals and intellectuals (including some Communists) boldly challenged government policies by publicly reaching out to help persecuted workers. The need for good relations with Western governments and banks restrained the Communist response while the election of a Polish archbishop, Karol Wótyła, as Pope encouraged Poles to ignore or oppose the government. As economic problems spiraled out of control, shortages and new price increases led workers to form the Solidarity Trade Union in 1980. Starting in Gdańsk, Solidarity quickly enrolled over 10,000,000 members -- well over 75% of all employed adults -- and enlisted professional and intellectual advisors. Solidarity wisely adopted a self-limiting policy and sought to co-exist with Communism rather than replace it. After trying to tame Solidarity for 18 months, General Wójciech Jaruzelski (1981-90), the new head of the Polish Communist Party, suppressed it in December 1981 by invoking the War Measures Act and arrested thousands of activists.[8]

General Jaruzelski released the Solidarity prisoners within a year and tried to introduce a series of reforms, but the embittered population rejected all overtures, particularly when hard-liners responded by murdering the popular priest, Father Jerzy Popieluszko and several youths. As the economy went from bad to worse, the government tolerated Poland's transformation into a vast bazaar of petty trading as Poles quit their jobs to travel the globe in search of blue jeans and small appliances to sell at home. Extra-legal firms (*samizdat*) published and distributed with impunity everything from underground Solidarity manifestos to translations of anti-Communist western literature such as George Orwell's *1984*; anti-government street demonstrations erupted on patriotic anniversaries. Organized opposition had declined among the exhausted and discouraged population, however, and Jaruzelski's government sought to win acceptance by granting final amnesty to all Solidarity activists, enrolling respected non-Party figures in a Social Consultative Committee, and seeking admission to the International Monetary Fund in 1986. Economic stagnation forced the government to put a package of economic reforms to a national referendum in 1987. The people rejected it as too little, too late -- and offered by the wrong people.[9]

Jaruzelski capitulated and started Round Table discussions with Solidarity leaders that led to the re-legalization of Solidarity and parliamentary elections in June 1989. The agreement promised free elections for 35% of seats in the lower chamber of parliament and 100% of the seats of the newly-created Senate. An improvised Citizens' Committee (led by Solidarity) surprised even its own members by capturing every contested seat except one Senate post won by an independent. Jaruzelski won the presidency by a narrow vote in the Polish Parliament but Communist efforts to form a parliamentary government failed after two previously subservient political parties defected unexpectedly and Jaruzelski invited Tadeusz

Mazowiecki, a top Solidarity advisor and a Catholic journalist, to become Prime Minister in August. His cabinet boasted a non-Communist majority although Communist ministers held four significant portfolios including internal affairs (security) and foreign affairs. Jaruzelski continued to serve as president for another year.[10]

President Jaruzelski resigned in 1990, leaving the electoral field to the Solidarity leader, Lech Walesa, who encountered unexpected difficulties in defeating a previously unknown Polish émigré who garnered support in the popular vote from people who felt threatened by economic change. The unity of the Solidarity movement had also disintegrated during the presidential campaign as a result of rivalry between Prime Minister Tadeusz Mazowiecki, head of the Liberal-Democratic Congress, who advocated a continuation of the economic shock treatment, and Walesa, who demagogically denounced the government while still promising to accelerate reform. Walesa's supporters formed a Center Agreement Party and attacked their rivals for ties to the former Communist Regime. Trade-union activists from Solidarity seceded to form their own movement which resisted austerity measures. Popular opinion responded to political conflicts with anger or alienation leaving the door open for the Social Democratic Party (ex-Communists). Far from maintaining authoritarian traditions, the Social Democrats became a party of ex-Communist businessmen who ran privatized firms; some members also enjoyed Kremlin support until the collapse of Soviet Communism in 1991/2. Pope John Paul II encouraged the public to look at long-range trends but Polish Church officials contributed to the growing political malaise by supporting candidates who developed a specifically Catholic program based on measures such as outlawing abortion, introducing religious instruction into the schools, and employing religious symbolism in state functions. They also denounced their opponents for alleged Communist ties. Many Poles resented the Church's involvement in politics.[11]

Parliamentary elections held in Fall 1991 left a deeply fragmented parliament that needed at least five parties to form a government. The first post-electoral government was formed by Jan Olszewski of the Center Alliance who courted popularity by attacking alleged Communist influence on the state. After he lost a vote of confidence, President Walesa chose Waldemar Pawlak, head of the leftist Polish Peasant Party, to try and form a government. Pawlak failed to rally enough support, although he came to power several months later after another cabinet crisis. The most successful government was formed by Hanna Suchocka of the Democratic Union (ex-Prime Minister Mazowiecki's party), who pressed market reform very strongly in the face of constant strikes and demonstrations from workers and peasants who were particularly dissatisfied by competition from Western European produce. Despite serious conflict, parliament maintained a steady course of economic reform and passed the "Small Constitution" in 1992 which prescribed a parliamentary government and granted the president limited control over appointments to key ministries and passage of the state budget. Lech Walesa established the presidency as an office of significance by using his prestige to speak out forcefully on important issues. However, he antagonized many voters and parliamentarians by his eagerness to play a crucial role despite his limited powers.

Difficulties in maintaining a governing coalition forced another election in Fall 1993 that brought the collapse of the rightist groupings despite their very substantial popular support and the creation of a leftist government. Rightists fragmented badly and failed to reach the lower limit for proportional representation provided by the electoral law: 5% for parties or 7% for blocs. The Union of the Democratic Left (Socialists, mostly ex-Communists) emerged the clear victor with 20% of the vote followed by the Polish Peasant Party with 15%. Lech Walesa's presidential party collected only 5% of the vote.

A Socialist-Peasant coalition governed Poland from Fall 1993 until the Fall 1997 elections. The coalition maintained itself with difficulty because ex-Communists pushed market reforms strongly while the Peasant Party advocated using the state budget to support inefficient peasant agriculture. Despite economic liberalization, the ex-Communists attracted criticism because of their past and because their ranks included individuals whose reformist credentials were weak, particularly in provincial administrations. Disputes about the role of the Church and the role of the "Commune" (Communism) divided society sharply. Debate over enactment of the full Constitution in May 1997 proved heated as a self-proclaimed citizens' coalition demanded official recognition of Christian principles in the Constitution. Despite their failure to force change, their success in convincing 47.3% of the electorate to vote no in a national referendum foreshadowed a change in government. Substantively, the most important change in the new constitution was a minor reduction in presidential power.

The Solidarity hero and Nobel prize winner, Lech Walesa, continued to slide in popularity and eventually lost the presidency to a former Communist.[12] Walesa often opposed the governing leftist coalition but he lacked public and parliamentary support so that his opposition seemed more peevish than principled. His conflicts were greatest with Prime Minister Pawlak, whose fall from office he engineered by rejecting the proposed 1995 budget with its high social expenditures. The government of Józef Oleksy, a Socialist, in March 1995 prepared a more market-oriented budget. Walesa also rejected Pawlak's nomination of a minister of defense who did not seem wholeheartedly devoted to joining NATO. Socialist domination of the Polish political scene became complete when party leader Aleksander Kwaśniewski narrowly defeated Lech Walesa in the presidential election of 1995 with 51.7% of the vote. Walesa's popularity had fallen to 8% early in 1995 as a result of his unilateral actions, his maneuvering between left and right, and a perceived lack of dignity in fulfilling his office. Liberal and conservative parties unenthusiastically endorsed Walesa late in the electoral campaign. The transition between the two presidents was marked by scandal as a member of parliament accused Premier Oleksy of spying for Russia. Incoming president Kwaśniewski prevented a full airing of the matter which probably came from embarrassing but insignificant contacts with Russian agents in Communist days. On assuming office, Kwaśniewski resigned from the Left Socialist Union and made conciliatory gestures to the Catholic Church. The political domination by ex-Communists did not signify a return of Communism to power in Poland as in some of former East Bloc countries since Kwaśniewski supported market reforms, democratic practices, and NATO membership. Parliament remained supreme, electoral politics were secure, the economy was largely privatized, and the press remained completely free. Newspapers and magazines flourished, subject only to the censorship of the marketplace. Numerous private stations competed with state television and radio.

Growing economic prosperity caused the public to look with equanimity at scandals such as the use of insider information and political favoritism to enrich party members in privatizing firms like the Bank of Silesia. The government also ignored or whitewashed the crimes of the Communist regime in shooting strikers in 1970 and awarded veterans' benefits to Communist security agents. The government stayed on correct terms with the Catholic Church despite the abortion issue and its refusal to ratify a previously negotiated Concordat without changes.

After four years of leftist government, public opinion polls signaled declining public satisfaction with the government and a trade union based Solidarity Electoral Action bloc won the September 1997 election with 34% of the popular vote and 44% of the seats in the lower chamber of parliament (*Sejm*). This Solidarity Electoral Action bloc united almost 40 small nationalist and Catholic parties but differed surprisingly little from the its leftist predecessor in policy. Both sought to create a full market economy and integrate with the West through entrance into NATO and the European Union even if discrepancies could be seen in terms of tactics and timing. The major differences were Solidarity's harsh criticism of the former government's Communist past as well as its opportunism in office. Another difference in principle was Solidarity's endorsement of positions taken by the Catholic Church.

Solidarity gained a firm majority in parliament through a coalition with the Freedom Union, primarily an association of former Solidarity advisors from the intellectual and professional classes that had won 13% of the popular vote and contributed another 13% of the seats. Solidarity chose a long-time Solidarity activist, Jerzy Buzek, as Prime Minister; the Catholic Church endorsed Buzek even though he was a Protestant. However, the best known figures in the new government came from the Freedom Union such as Leszek Balcerowicz, Finance Minister and Deputy Prime Minister, and Bronisław Geremek, Foreign Minister. Solidarity registered itself as a regular political party after the election but it may still have trouble keeping united due to the varied backgrounds of its members and its potential differences with its more secularly-oriented coalition partner, the Freedom Union. However, the coalition has withstood its first challenge by voting together to ban sex education in the schools.[13] The government will also face serious difficulties in fulfilling its pledges to improve living standards and privatize state industries without rekindling inflation. In the first half of 1998, symbolic issues have continued to excite debate. The government created a judicial tribunal to investigate whether candidates for high office collaborated with the Communist security police and passed a resolution condemning Communist rule in Poland. The post-Communist Democratic Left Alliance and President Kwaśniewski opposed these measures as simplistic responses to a complicated situation.[14]

Economic transformation:[15] The post-Communist government of Poland took over an economy that suffered from negative growth, triple-digit inflation, and high foreign debt. In 1990-1, the GDP fell another 9%. Polish exports declined 1% and imports grew 39%, causing a balance of payments problem. On the positive side, private sector production increased 25% and several western countries rewarded Poland by forgiving half her debts; currency depreciation helped, too.

Poland accepted the arguments of Jeffrey Sachs, a Harvard professor, that shock therapy would produce less social dislocation than a gradual transformation.[16] Already in 1989, Mazowiecki's Minister of Finance, Leszek Balcerowicz, cut back sharply on expenditures on education, health care, and public sector salaries. Curtailment of industrial subsidies caused unemployment to double. Nevertheless, Poles adapted well, mainly by seeking new jobs in the private sector, and household income generally increased by 6%. The increase in private sector activity was particularly noticeable in sales and distribution. Transport, construction, and industry also grew substantially. After some wavering, Prime Minister Suchocka's government adopted strong austerity measures to push ahead with reform. She refused to make concessions to striking workers or impoverished pensioners and Poland's economic decline deepened in 1992, although signs of improvement could be seen towards the end of the year. The GDP grew slightly (0.5-2%). The private sector grew and industrial production increased; almost half of industrial workers worked in private plants. Foreign capital began to flow into Poland; foreigners bought majority interests in some large automotive and paper concerns. Exports increased faster than imports. Foreign debt decreased, again due to debt forgiveness by western countries. The government gained only limited success with the privatization of large state firms because the regime would neither cut the workers adrift nor turn the firms over to them.

Poland, however, had turned the corner and the economy began to develop rapidly in 1993. An official 4% increase in GDP (one of the highest in Europe) understated growth because the grey and black markets could not be included. Industrial production increased 6.2% and agricultural production climbed 2.2%. Effective administration of a new income tax and value added tax helped reduce the budget deficit and halt inflation. Progress was uneven, however, and many citizens did not share the gains. Unemployment increased slightly to 16% and approached 30% in some regions. Real pay fell slightly (2%) overall and declined more sharply among workers in education, health, science, and public administration. Pensioners also suffered disproportionately. Imports climbed faster than exports and devaluation was needed to keep the balance of payments deficit within reasonable bounds.

Poland achieved 5% growth in 1994 and has grown at around 7% since 1995, one of the highest growth rates in Europe. Industrial production climbed rapidly and unemployment fell slowly. Exports rose more quickly than imports in 1994; the favorable balance of trade permitted some accumulation of cash reserves. Some dark clouds remain on the horizon. Unemployment remains high (although declining), the currency continues to depreciate, and inflation remains a factor. Imports grew in 1995.

Despite these achievements, social confidence remains low because many people have suffered from the economic transformation. Birth rates are among the lowest in Europe; social pathologies such as alcoholism and drug addiction are high. Life expectancy is relatively low for Europe. Criminal activity is high (or seems high) and is widely reported. Apathy, cynicism and anger are general in society as the press reports numerous scandals at all levels. In 1994, 70% of those polled expressed disapproval of the president and 40% disapproval of parliament. Only 35% viewed the future optimistically; the figure improved slightly in 1995.

The period from 1995 to mid-1998, then, has been a growth period through not without difficulties. Poland recorded an overall economic growth rate of 8% (6.5% in 1997-8) and growth of stock market values of 5% (9% in 1997-8) in Polish zlotys. Industrial production rose 16% in 1996-7 but only 4% in 1997-8. Nevertheless, imports outpaced exports and the zloty continues to decline in value (if slowly) so that the government will have to lower its expenditures and curb imports to achieve stability. On taking office, Prime Minister Jerzy Buzek immediately announced that he plans to adopt an austerity budget despite the grave political risk of laying off trade union members who voted him into office.[17] The government has recently announced plans to privatize and restructure the transportation, coal mining, oil refining, and insurance industries; the process of privatizing banks will be concluded. Several hundred thousand jobs will be lost. Groups affected by these changes and others, such as farmers who are losing their markets to western competition, have protested.[18]

VIII. Communist Hungary and Independent Hungary

Hungary served as a Nazi ally until 1944. When it tried to withdraw from the lost war, Germany occupied Hungary and put a native fascist government in power. After the war, the Soviets installed a leftist coalition government in which the Communists gradually took full control. They did poorly in the 1947 elections and had to use extra-parliamentary threats to subdue their coalition partners. The fully Communist government of 1949 imposed a particularly harsh Stalinist system.[19]

Stalin's death led to a struggle within the Hungarian Communist Party between Stalinists and reformers. The latter gained enough strength to make Imre Nagy Prime

Minister in October 1956 but revolution broke out after Hungarian security police fired on a large demonstration and the crowd sacked security police headquarters. Nagy attempted to create a reformed Communist state. He also planned to withdraw from the Warsaw Pact, hoping that the Soviets would accept Hungarian neutrality as they had accepted Austrian neutrality in 1955. Instead, the Soviets sent in strong military forces that defeated Hungarian soldiers and civilians after pitched battles in the streets of several cities. Over 200,000 Hungarians fled the country as János Kádár, first secretary of the Communist Party, harshly purged all reformers.

Despite his part in suppressing the 1956 Insurrection, Kádár eventually returned to his roots as a liberal Communist whom Hungarian Stalinists had imprisoned. He gradually introduced reforms in the mid-1960s abolishing harsh police terror and allowing relatively free self-expression. By emphasizing the production of consumer goods and small-scale private enterprise he created "goulash socialism". After 1968, the New Economic Mechanism de-centralized the economy further by giving production and marketing autonomy to collective farms and many state industries. Workers could start their own businesses and even use state facilities after hours. As joint ventures with western firms multiplied, multiple exchange rates made Hungarian currency semi-convertible. Hungarians prospered at the high price of working long hours at two or more jobs. Male life expectancy began to decline in the late 1970s.

Communist reformers saw Soviet *Perestroika* as a license to go still further. The state instituted "socialist pluralism" (multi-candidate elections) in 1985 and a faction headed by Imre Pozsgay advocated holding multi-party elections as well as legalizing private business. Several political parties formed and discussed plans for reform with the Communist Party, which removed Kádár from power in 1988 and gave him the largely ceremonial post of President. The new Secretary of the Communist Party, Karoly Grosz, did not go along with the reformers either, although he was willing to continue discussions and make some changes.

After non-Communists took power in Poland, the Hungarian Communist Party struggled to remain relevant and took the initiative to share power at home. Dropping Kádár as President, they permitted the re-burial of Imre Nagy in a public ceremony attended by several hundred thousand Hungarians at which even Communist Prime Minister Pozsgay called the 1956 Revolution justified. A round-table agreement was negotiated in September promising free elections and parliamentary democracy. The Communist Party abolished itself in October, hoping to win seats as a reincarnated Socialist Party and proclaimed a new Hungarian Republic.[20]

The Communists failed to win political advantage from their course of radical political reform. They lost a national referendum over the timing of presidential elections and then fared badly in the parliamentary elections of March 1990. A right-center coalition dominated by the Hungarian Democratic Forum won a majority in parliament. The Forum had little mass support but voters seemed to prefer them because they expressed concern for Hungarian minorities living in Romania and

Slovak Republic where they remained subject to both Communist and national discrimination. The Forum and its largest opposition party, the Alliance of Free Democrats, exercised oligarchical power without referring matters to party membership. They appointed Forum president Jozsef Ántall as Prime Minister and Árpád Goncz, an historian and prominent member of the Free Democrats, as President. Other opposition groups (the Union of Free Democrats and the Hungarian Socialist Party) enjoyed little influence and little possibility of forcing new elections before 1995 even though they won municipal elections in 1990. Trade unions supported the Socialists but could mobilize little enthusiasm among their members for the first few years.

Faced with six national ballots in 1990, voters became apathetic and voter turn-out declined sharply. Some local elections had to be held six or seven times before the required 50% of the electorate voted for a single candidate. Parliamentary frustrations found expression in bitter public debates and name-calling. An important issue was the constitutional relationship among the president, parliament, and the highest court. The degree of subordination of the mass media (television, radio, and mass-circulation newspapers) to the government and to political parties was also hotly debated. More alarming was the emergence of a national wing within the Hungarian Democratic Forum led by István Csurka, one of six vice-presidents, who blamed ex-Communists for the slow pace of reform, and who suggested that international Jewish groups were ultimately responsible. His views found some popular support but the clear majority of Forum delegates rejected them and expelled him in 1993. Prime Minister Ántall died in December 1993 after a long illness. His successor, Peter Boross, had exercised his functions during Ántall's hospitalization and stepped into the breach easily.[21]

The punishment of former Communists remained a hotly debated issue. The Forum put a bill through parliament allowing prosecution of those who had committed war crimes and crimes against humanity during the 1956 revolution but it resisted demands to search for persons who had supplied information to the Communist security police. Among other reasons cited was the substantial destruction of security records by the Communists before they left office in 1989.

The former opposition triumphed in the elections of May 1994 which gave the Hungarian Socialist Party 54% of the seats in parliament (33% of the popular vote) while the previous ruling party, the Hungarian Democratic Forum, fell to 10% of the seats. The second largest party was the Alliance of Free Democrats, previously in opposition, which held 18% of the seats. The electorate was tired of sacrifice and irritated by the nationalistic, albeit moderate, tone of the previous government. The voters saw the Socialist Party as a continuation of the 1980s reformist Communists who liberalized the economy pragmatically, ignored Communist ideology, and handed over power in 1989-90 without resistance. Voters accepted claims of professional expertise from former state officials.

Despite its absolute majority, the Socialist Party brought the left-liberal Union of Free Democrats into the coalition in order to increase its majority for difficult votes on economic issues and to assure the public that it was committed to Europeanization, the market economy, and democratic methods (a Free Democrat became Minister of Internal Affairs). The Prime Minister, Gyula Horn, took the political middle ground between the liberal-oriented Minister of Finance and the trade unions, which wanted substantial government support.

The ex-Communist Hungarian Socialist Party imposed shock therapy at long last. The government decreased social expenditures, reduced the budget deficit, cut the balance of payments deficit, sped privatization, and increased tax revenues by attacking the black and grey markets. These measures touched off a wave of strikes and protests from their own constituents and some ministers resigned. Corruption from the privatization process also brought criticism. President Goncz actively mediated disputes within the government and helped hold the coalition together. Parliament rewarded him by reelecting him as President in June 1995. The government finally resolved the media crisis in December 1995 by opening the door to private commercial television and radio stations.[22]

A center-right coalition headed by the Federation of Young Democrats-Hungarian Civic Party (FIDESZ) won the elections held in May 1998. The Young Democrats won 41% of the popular votes and an agreement with the rightist Smallholders not to oppose each other in run-off elections gave the two parties 54% of the seats in parliament. After some hard bargaining, the two parties agreed to form a government under a Young Democrat, Viktor Orban, in which the Young Democrats held 13 of the 17 cabinet seats while the Smallholders received the agriculture and provincial development portfolios that were central to their interests. The two parties plan to cooperate in electing a new president in 2000 as well as in future parliamentary elections.[23]

Economic transformation:[24] Hungary entered the post-Communist world in a favorable position due to the Communist regime's market reforms although it had also run up a large foreign debt. All political parties from left to right promised the electorate protection against shock therapy. Minister of Finance Mihály Kupa finally brought in a program of modest reforms in 1991. Nevertheless, inflation remained relatively low (30%) and Hungary enjoyed a healthy balance-of-payments surplus although unemployment quadrupled to 8%, the budget deficit climbed, and industrial production declined. Privatization of existing firms had scarcely begun, although new private firms sprang up quickly. The Right seemed to be carrying out a post-Communist strategy dependent on strong state direction. The pace of economic decline slowed in 1992 and 1993. National statistics indicated that the Gross National Product declined by 5% annually and industrial production fell by 12% although the performance of smaller firms, not included in national statistics, was much better. New regulations on accounting and bankruptcy provided better reporting, too. More market-oriented practices led to higher unemployment, however. Some 12% of former state enterprises had been privatized by the end of 1992 and the government set much more ambitious targets for the next two years. Most of the 1992 privatizations involved joint-ventures with foreign capital. The state budget deficit grew as a result of the slow pace of market-oriented reforms and the IMF declined to provide the next installment of credits.

Paradoxically, it was the ex-Communist Hungarian Socialist Party that finally imposed shock therapy when it took power in 1994. The government decreased social expenditures, lessened the budget deficit, reduced the balance-of-payments deficit and sped privatization. As their real salaries fell, Hungarian workers, especially in railways, utilities, and schools, launched a wave of strikes and demonstrations. A Gallup poll found Hungarians the most pessimistic people in the world. The Hungarian economy finally achieved positive growth in 1994 (3%) and continued in 1995 (2%) while industrial production increased; unemployment and inflation fell marginally. Nevertheless, fundamental changes had not occurred and the budget deficit reached 10% of GDP in 1994. Foreign debt increased. Exports climbed, primarily to Germany, Austria, and Italy -- although imports climbed faster. The IMF withheld its accreditation due to the budget deficit but foreign capital found business conditions favorable and continued to invest. Further reforms met the satisfaction of the IMF in 1996 but the World Bank refused to extend credit. Reforms have been sufficient to allow Hungary to run a balance-of-trade surplus with the European Union in 1996 although there was no increase in GDP in that year.[25] After slow growth in 1997, the Hungarian economy grew at a rate of 5% in the first six months of 1998. However, stock values declined slightly and the forint depreciated by almost 20%.[26]

IX. Communist Czechoslovakia and its Independent Successor States

Czechoslovakia emerged from World War II with its pre-war government and system because President Edward Beneš made special efforts to assure Stalin of his willingness to accommodate Soviet foreign policy positions. However, the Communist Party won 38% of the votes in free post-war elections and it used its strength to stage massive demonstrations in February 1948 to gain control of the government. Once in power, the Czechoslovak Communist Party imposed Stalinism. Stalin's death changed Czechoslovakia little and Czechoslovakia ignored the examples of the Hungarian Revolution and the Polish Reform of 1956.[27]

Stalinism finally began to ebb in the mid-1960s and a reform movement headed by Alexander Dubček, a Slovak Communist, launched Prague Spring in 1968 to create "Socialism with a Human Face".[28] The government investigated Soviet behavior in Czechoslovakia and launched so many reform initiatives so quickly and with such overwhelming popular support, that the Kremlin and its Warsaw Pact allies feared for the stability of Czechoslovak Communism. In August, 500,000 Warsaw Pact soldiers invaded. Few Czechs and Slovaks lost their lives but a neo-Stalinist government came back into power under Gustav Husák (1969-89). Political and civil repression was moderated by improved personal prosperity in which many Czechs and Slovaks bought summer cottages and cars and lived their lives peacefully -- if they kept their mouths shut. However, prosperity came from moonlighting and illegal investment. Overall, investment lagged and the Czechoslovak economy slowed. Public debate was non-existent. Communism went largely unchallenged as the state energetically pursued participants of the Prague Spring and potential imitators of Polish and Hungarian reform. Some two hundred Czechs and Slovaks took a stand in the mid-1970s by drafting and signing "Charter 77" which called for the restoration of civil freedoms. Signatories and sympathizers went to jail, lost their jobs, and endured social ostracism by timorous fellow citizens. Gorbachev's reformism encouraged some Czechoslovak Communists to call for economic changes and small groups of citizens began to speak out. Pope John Paul II's support could be felt in public statements by the Czechoslovak hierarchy.

The "Velvet Revolution" overthrew Communism in Czechoslovakia after Poland and Hungary successfully abandoned Communism in November 1989. Demanding major reforms, students began a series of demonstrations in downtown Prague. When the police surrounded and savagely beat them, Prague workers and other citizens turned out in tens and then hundreds of thousands to join the students in eighteen nights of escalating protests that forced the Communist government to surrender. An improvised Citizens' Forum in Prague and a similar Slovak group, People against Violence, demanded free elections to a free parliament. Negotiations with the Communist government led to the appointment of a non-Communist government on December 10 by President Husák and his subsequent resignation.[29]

The overwhelmingly popular leader of Charter 77, Václav Havel, a playwright, was chosen president in 1989.[30] He presided over a Communist-dominated reform government that dismantled Communist state institutions and scheduled free parliamentary elections for June 1990. The elections produced clear victories for the Citizens Forum and its Slovak counterpart. These umbrella groups disintegrated after parliament opened and more than 20 parties won seats in parliament in the 1992 elections. Part of the reason for disintegration was the split between President Havel and Prime Minister Václav Klaus. Both were firmly committed to rapid transformation, but a variety of issues made it hard for them to work together. Havel hoped to maintain the Citizens' Forum as a grand coalition and intended to offer sage advice without getting involved in political maneuvering. He wanted to moderate the extremes of the economic transition, to seek compromise with the Slovaks, and to accept reformed ex-Communists (including several signers of his Charter 77) as working partners. Klaus preferred to work with a tightly organized political party, endorsed rapid economic transformation, and opposed allowing ex-Communists any role in public affairs. The Movement for a Democratic Slovakia, headed by an ex-

Communist, Vladímír Mečiar, aimed to moderate economical reform to conform to what he perceived as Slovak national character and economic conditions.[31]

While the Czechoslovak Republic made a smooth transition from Communism to a parliamentary state, national pressures led to its break-up into two independent countries: Czech Republic and Slovak Republic. Many Slovaks had been unhappy in the unitary Czechoslovak state and found the federative form adopted by the Communists in 1969 insufficient. The dominant Movement for a Democratic Slovakia, which came to the fore when the broadly-based People Against Violence declined in popularity, pushed to loosen the Czech-Slovak federation still further but the Czech politicians resisted and preferred to make Slovakia fully independent. Numerous meetings in 1991 failed to achieve a mutually satisfactory solution. Part of the problem was the Czechs' desire to implement radical market reforms and the reluctance of the Slovaks to follow suit due to the large number of obsolete heavy industries established in Slovakia by the Communists. However, the main reason for the break-up was ethnic and cultural differences between these two similar but distinct nationalities that had never been linked before 1919. The peaceful dissolution of Czechoslovakia into two separate states followed on January 1, 1993 without a referendum. Public opinion polls showed that a strong majority of both populations opposed splitting but no political movement emerged to force the politicians to find a solution to the constitutional difficulties. On its own, the Czech parliament considered and then rejected the possibility of providing autonomy for Moravia and Czech Silesia.[32]

The emergence of a popular anti-Communist crusade embittered public life and broke the feeling of national unity that the smooth transition had inspired, although there were reasonable grounds for concern that ex-Communist managers used their position to gain economic benefits from privatization. Anti-Communist zealots campaigned to remove from positions of authority anyone who had cooperated with the security police without making any allowance for persons who had genuinely changed their minds (including some signatories to Charter 77) or who had been forced into cooperating against their will. The enactment of a law threatening five years' imprisonment for "supporting and propagating Communism" seemed anachronistic and vindictive, as well. Communists and others complained to international agencies that the new government was violating democratic norms.[33]

Political transformation was accompanied by a vast expansion of the press and other mass media. Private television stations arose in the Czech part of the country and privatization of the state channel was promised. Slovak media remained a state monopoly. Many cultural and scholarly publications failed to meet market requirements and disappeared.

The decline of state authority permitted a serious rise in criminal activity. Official statistics indicate that crime grew by 40% in 1991 compared to the previous year and another 20% in 1992. Financial problems and the need to retrain police officers made it difficult to control the rise. Many Czechs and Slovaks incorrectly blamed the Gypsy minority for the increase (which had many causes) and anti-Gypsy sentiments have become widespread. The need to find scapegoats also identified the small Jewish minority for allegedly exerting disproportionate influence.

Czech Republic: Václav Havel resigned rather than preside over the dissolution of Czechoslovakia and he won election as President of Czech Republic despite the quiet opposition of Prime Minister Václav Klaus who considered Havel too pro-Slovak and insufficiently anti-Communist. Nonetheless, Klaus controlled the Czech government firmly even as party fragmentation made governing more difficult. Klaus's party also won local elections in 1994 since economic prosperity and responsible parliamentary government made Klaus and his associates popular. The adoption of a "List of Rights and Freedoms" followed international guidelines and was to be guaranteed by a fully independent judiciary. Klaus's Civic Democratic Party won 30% of the votes in the June 1996 parliamentary elections but the opposition Social Democrats followed closely behind at 27%. Voters showed their discontent over low budgetary expenditures on health, education, and the environment; the continued rise of crime was a factor, as well. Klaus's government was a coalition of the Christian Democrats and ODA.

The Klaus government fell in December 1997 as a result of a party financial crisis and a growing sense that the government had lost its sense of direction. The outgoing Prime Minister, Václav Klaus, came under attack for accepting the gift of a summer house from a businessman but retained his leadership of the Civic Democratic Party; stories of sweetheart privatization deals circulated widely. President Havel designated a non-party representative, Josef Tošovský, governor of the Czech National Bank, as a caretaker prime minister with the support of all major parties.[34] Miloš Zeman's Social Democratic Party (32%) won a narrow victory in the June 1998 elections over Klaus (28%), whose fortunes revived to a surprising degree. The Communists won 11% of the vote but several parties of the extreme right failed to win any seats. Zeman failed to form a majority coalition and negotiated an agreement with Klaus which would allow the Social Democrats to form a minority government. The implications of this tacit coalition are unclear at this point.[35] President Havel underwent major operations for lung cancer in 1996 and a perforated colon in 1998 (as well as several post-operative corrective procedures), and his declining health threatens Czech stability. He was able to take a constructive role in the recent political changes, however.[36]

Slovak Republic: The new Slovak state (it effectively ruled itself after July 1992 although legal independence only came on January 1, 1993) pursued aggressively nationalistic policies.[37] Prime Minister Mečiar declined to guarantee language rights to the substantial Hungarian minority and refused to reconsider a project to build a hydroelectric dam on the Danube in the face of domestic and Hungarian environmental protests. Mečiar blunted criticism at home by limiting the deliveries of newsprint to opposition newspapers and by replacing most of the governing board of Slovak television with his own nominees. Strong measures taken against the Gypsies also aroused international protests. His government seemed increasingly arbitrary and undemocratic and Mečiar lost his parliamentary majority. He fell from power in March 1994 but won the Fall 1994 elections after a demagogic campaign. His new coalition partners worked together despite disagreements on fundamental issues such as European integration, privatization, and minority rights. These disagreements led to Mečiar's replacing many of the leading politicians with persons loyal to himself, creating the impression of a dictatorial government. An extensive purge of the Slovak media gave additional reality to that impression. Mečiar ran into strong criticism from his former close associate, President Michal Kovač, whom Mečiar tried unsuccessfully to dismiss. The abduction of the president's son to Vienna on embezzlement charges (he was eventually released on bail) and attempts to dismiss one of Mečiar's parliamentary critics have led to renewed accusations of undemocratic conduct and have persuaded both NATO and the European Union to leave Slovak Republic out of the current round of expansion.[38]

The Hungarian minority question became heated at this time. Almost 600,000 Hungarians live in southern Slovakia, adjacent to Hungary, in a region that includes an equal number of Slovaks. The Hungarians protested plans for gerrymandering new local districts. Under international pressure, Mečiar signed an agreement with the Hungarian state recognizing existing international borders and guaranteeing civil rights. Mečiar's government, particularly ministers from coalition partners, refused to submit the agreement to parliament for ratification, and insisted on pressing Hungarian students to speak Slovak in school and dismissing recalcitrant Hungarian school directors. Anti-Hungarian sentiments grew among the Slovak population.

These aspects of Slovak political life have earned the censure of the European Community and are partly responsible for postponement of Slovak Republic's admission to NATO. The scheduling of new elections in September 1998 did not resolve the doubts. The United States called for international supervision and Slovak Republic rejected the demand.[39] The elections brought the defeat of Mečiar and the arrival of a new center-right, broad coalition government.

Economic transformation:[40] Post-Communist Czechoslovakia enjoyed small foreign debt, low inflation, and stable finances. It moved slowly on privatization of major enterprises, but auctioned off many smaller businesses to the highest bidder. Though economically successful, this caused political problems because many purchasers were former Communists who had acquired private means. New legislation in 1991 made it easy to start new businesses and legislation enabled thousands of citizens to reclaim small businesses that the Communists had nationalized after 1955. Large-scale enterprises had been nationalized during World War II by the Nazis and remained in state hands. In the Czech area, employment rates remained high as a result of continuing state support; unemployment was only 4.1% In Slovakia, however, unemployment rose to 11.2% because its industrial economy depended heavily on exports to the Soviet Union which declined rapidly.

Czechoslovak economic decline continued in 1992, mainly in Slovakia, although the decline eased somewhat. Some 12% of former state enterprises had been privatized by the end of 1992.

The Czech government set much more ambitious targets through "coupon" or "voucher" privatization. All Czechoslovak citizens received stock in a basket of 400 privatized state industries for a payment of about two weeks wages (1,035 crowns); they had some choice. "Coupon" industry stock traded on a separate stock exchange from other enterprises and these state industries continued to receive some subsidies despite falling production. Such unreformed industries did little to modernize the Czechoslovak economy, but coupon privatization at least encouraged foreign investors to expand the real private sector. By 1992, Czechs eagerly traded in their coupons for real stock after careful analysis of the worth of the companies that they had chosen. The Czech economy improved in 1992 from foreign investment and from the cessation of subsidies to obsolete Slovak industry. Unemployment fell to 2.5% and inflation fell to 12%, although the Gross National Product declined by a further 13%. Living standards fell throughout the period and more than 50% of Czechoslovak citizens reported a decline in real income.

By 1993, the fully-independent Czech economy seemed to be adapting to post-Communist conditions smoothly. Economic decline ceased and unemployment remained low (4%) although inflation went up to 20%. Economists suspected that low unemployment came from hidden state subsidies for uneconomical firms. The state pursued privatization actively as over 900 firms traded their shares on the stock exchange which opened in April 1993. Private enterprise now made up more than 50% of the Gross National Product. Nevertheless, the break-up of Czechoslovakia caused a decline in trade that hurt both Czechs and Slovaks although the Czechs recovered more quickly. Foreign tourists brought enormous benefits to the Czech economy while foreign investment declined slightly although more than 7,000 joint ventures operated in Czech Republic as well as another 5,000 foreign firms. A policy of wage controls for firms employing more than 25 workers was installed to hold down inflation and attract foreign capital. The controls were lifted in 1995 without much effect.

The Czech economy grew by 3% in 1994 and almost 5% in 1995 with the help of relatively low inflation and unemployment. Private property's share of the national economy increased to 70% and counted for two-thirds of industrial production. Foreign investment and foreign tourism contributed to banking stability along with the low external debt. The most impressive single transaction was the sale of 27% of the shares in the state telephone firm to a Dutch-Swiss consortium for US$1.5 billion although, overall, Germany was the leading investor with 30% of overall foreign investment.

Nevertheless, the Czechs had unduly postponed significant reform and the weakened economy underwent a currency crisis in 1997. The banks, which themselves were waiting for government assistance, could no longer carry numerous state firms and newly-privatized firms that were losing money because they had not been restructured. The government had to take over eleven banks that had collapsed by mid-1997 under charges of fraud. The withdrawal of state funds caused the banks to waver and the currency to depreciate rapidly in Fall 1997. Even scandal-free firms privatized by the distribution of "coupons" lacked the pressure of involved stockholders and delayed making hard choices. Sweetheart deals between politicians and businesses came to light amid charges of widespread fraud and corruption. Foreigners withdrew capital, unemployment rose slightly, and the Czech crown fell 12%. The Czech Government has promised to enact regulatory reforms and sell its bank stock in 1998 in the hope that the banks will become profitable and, more important, that industry will make itself self-supporting.[41] The Czech economy shrank by 1% in 1997-8 although industrial production increased 3%.[42]

To the surprise of international observers, the Slovak economy responded well to independence. It grew by 5% in 1994 and 7% in 1995. Inflation was low and unemployment declined. Mečiar's government followed IMF recommendations and reduced budget deficits by cutting social expenditures. Privatization was rushed and achieved 80% success, although major industries remained in state hands. The Mečiar government committed many irregularities such as selling firms at low prices to political favorites. The short-lived Moravčik government succeeded in canceling some of the transactions but Mečiar's return to the premiership revived political favoritism in privatization. Concerns about political democracy have kept foreign investment low, but the Slovak economy is expected to outperform the Czech economy in 1997.[43]

X. Foreign Relations in Post-Communist East-Central Europe[44]

The transformation of East-Central Europe could not have taken place without the withdrawal of the Soviet Union from its East European Empire. As head of the Soviet Communist Party, Gorbachev supported liberalization by East European Communists and accepted the dismantling of Communist rule. The Soviet Union gradually withdrew from Eastern Europe between 1985 and 1989 because 1) Mikhail Gorbachev and the reform faction naively expected the Soviet Bloc countries to accept reformed Communism, 2) the political success of reform in the USSR required reducing the influence of the imperial faction of military and conservative forces, 3) the Soviet Union lacked the economic resources to subjugate Soviet Bloc countries, and 4) Gorbachev needed good relations with the West.

Since throwing off Communism, central and Eastern European states have successfully gained western support and avoided conflict with their neighbors, including the Soviet Union and post-Soviet states. Their efforts have been rewarded by agreements with the Council of Europe and the Common Market in 1991,

"Partnership for Peace" with United States 1993, and, finally, the promise of membership in NATO in 1997. Slovak Republic has not been admitted at this time because it failed to satisfy NATO's standards for democracy and economic progress. NATO membership will provide military security for the foreseeable future and guarantee the peaceful evolution of the region although it also opens thorny questions such as the nature of NATO's mission, the status of the ex-Soviet states abutting NATO's new eastern border, and NATO's capacity for cohesion. Western leaders acknowledged Russia's concerns and elicited her grudging approval but Russian opposition forces remain displeased by NATO's eastern progress. The prize of membership in the European Union (Common Market) appears finally to have fallen into the grasp of the central and Eastern European countries, although the terms have not yet been determined. In addition to concern over structural and legislative difficulties, countries within the present European Union are also worried about lowering trade and immigration barriers to low-wage competitors since they already suffer from high unemployment and surpluses. The European Union barred the import of Polish dairy and meat products in November-December 1997 citing dubious health grounds, for example; Poland retaliated by blocking EU meat exports to Poland and in transit to former Soviet bloc countries.[45]

NATO admission was eased by regional peace and security. Central and Eastern European states have abandoned all claims to neighboring territories based on historical, economic, and ethnic ties. For example, individual Poles flock to visit Vilnius (Lithuania) and Lviv (Ukraine), but the Polish state has cultivated good relations with Lithuania and confined its concerns about language rights for the large Polish minority to diplomatic channels. Also, Poland was the first state to recognize Ukrainian independence in December 1991. Similarly, Hungary is deeply concerned about the large Hungarian minorities in Slovakia and Romania but it has made its case diplomatically and avoided saber-rattling. Hungary also took its objections to the planned hydroelectric dam on the Danube to the World Court and promises to respect a recent decision in Slovakia's favor. Poland, Czechoslovakia, and Hungary formed the Vishegrad Group for regional coordination in 1991 which created a free trade zone but accomplished little in foreign policy, primarily because Czech Republic preferred to approach NATO by itself instead of in coordination with its neighbors. Hungary and Poland have undertaken to speak up for its less successful neighbors in relations with the European Union and NATO.

Relations with the Soviet Union and successor states have been surprisingly good. All parties have avoided making claims against each other. The Soviet Union (Russia after 1992) withdrew its troops from central and Eastern Europe with relatively good grace and relatively quickly. Both Mikhail Gorbachev and Boris Yeltsin made symbolic gestures acknowledging Soviet crimes against Central and Eastern European countries by the release of documents on the Katyń Forest massacre of Polish officers in 1940.

Poland has made special efforts to heal the wounds with the Jewish community and Israel. President Lech Walesa's visit to Israel in 1991 was generally successful and Israeli Prime Minister Yitzhak Rabin attended the fiftieth anniversary of the Warsaw Ghetto Uprising in 1993. Pope John Paul II helped solve a dispute over a Carmelite convent in Auschwitz and the prime ministers of Israel and Poland shared a platform at a 1998 Auschwitz commemoration. Despite persistent anti-Semitism among elements within their populations, all three Central and Eastern European states have given the remaining Jewish communities legal standing and have come to some agreements regarding Jewish property confiscated during World War II by the Nazis. Only Slovakia continues the pre-war attitudes of resentment towards Jews as illustrated by laying claim in July 1997 to gold that was identified in the Czech National Bank to have been confiscated from Slovak Jews by the Nazis; Czech Republic donated its portion of the gold to the Jewish community.

XI. Conclusion

The states of Poland, Czechoslovakia and Hungary emerged as independent states from the wreckage of the Russian, German, and Austro-Hungarian Empires in 1918-20. They suffered wars, civil wars, and revolutions before establishing stable political systems. Poland and Hungary became semi-dictatorial states with weak parliaments; Czechoslovakia maintained parliamentary democracy more successfully. The Polish and Hungarian economies had great trouble adapting to the post-1918 boundaries; Czechoslovakia prospered. Poland and Czechoslovakia suffered from conflicts between a dominant nationality and large minorities leading to separatist movements and terrorism. Hungary's irredentist claims against several neighbors brought her into the Nazi camp. Ignored and neglected by the West, Poland and Czechoslovakia fell prey to Nazi and Soviet conquest.

In sharp contrast, the states of Poland, Czechoslovakia (Czech Republic) and Hungary have emerged from the wreckage of the Soviet Imperium in relatively good shape and with excellent prospects for the future. They have established effective parliamentary institutions and have managed the transformation to a market economy successfully. They have solved their international problems peacefully and won western acceptance in less than a decade. The West's commitment has taken concrete form through advice, bank loans, and membership, prospectively, in such organizations as the Economic Union and NATO. Slovakia has made progress but has not managed the political and economic transformation as successfully.

Success is real but should not be overstated. Gross Domestic Production (GDP) declined in the former Czechoslovakia and Hungary between 1986 and 1995; Polish economic improvement mostly reflects the low bench-mark of prolonged depression starting in the 1970s. Unemployment and inflation are relatively high. Political alienation is rife. As in the West, intellectuals and clergy decry the violence and greed depicted endlessly in mass culture. Nevertheless, central and Eastern Europe has made remarkable progress in its first decade of post-Communist independence and the future promises continuing slow improvement.

Future problems appear to stem mainly from the possibility of world-wide economic depression and the loss of NATO cohesion. The Great Depression of the 1930s made many European countries adopt authoritarian solutions to unemployment and social unrest; another Great Depression might well do the same. Ethnic tensions have been greatly reduced since the 1930s but sufficient tensions remain (Hungarian-Slovak, Polish-Lithuanian, Czech-Slovak) to cause trouble. The revival of Russia under a nationalist leadership that is keen to seek revenge against a West that brought Communist Russia to its knees is the most dangerous scenario for central and Eastern Europe and the world at large. NATO membership is designed to protect Poland, Czech Republic, and Hungary against this eventuality but east Europeans who endured western abandonment at Locarno, Munich, and Yalta may well wonder whether they will be any better protected now than they were in 1939.

ENDNOTES

1. For recent historical views, see Wandycz (1993) and Longworth (1994).
2. Goldman (1997), pp.83-112, 265-390. See also Wandycz (1993) and Longworth (1994).
3. *Europa World Year Book*, (1997) pp.1988, 1215. See individual countries for general summaries.
4. See Rothschild (1989).
5. See, for example, Goldman (1992).
6. Dziewanowski (1977), pp.145-172.
7. Dziewanowski (1977), pp.173-209.
8. Dziewanowski (1977), pp.210-32; See Ash (1991).
9. Stokes (1993), pp.102-21.
10. Stokes (1993), pp.121-30; Ash (1993), pp.25-46.
11. Goldman (1997), pp.228-40, 247-51 covers the transformation period.
12. Walesa (1991) discusses the author's earlier experiences.
13. Radio Free Europe: September 19, September 25, October 16, October 21, and December 12, 1997.
14. Radio Free Europe: May 14, June 18, and June 19, 1998.
15. Goldman (1997), pp.240-47.

16. See Sachs (1993).

17. *The Economist*, 15 November 1997: 116; Radio Free Europe: September 24 and December 11, 1997.

18. Radio Free Europe: April 21 and May 15, 1998.

19. For the Communist period, see Hoensch (1994), pp.163-278.

20. For the transition period of 1989-90, see Ash (1993) pp.47-60; Hoensch (1994), pp.279-309ff; Stokes (1993), pp.78-101; Goldman (1992), pp.181-94.

21. The politics of the post-Communist state are discussed in Kiràly, (1995), Hoensch (1994), pp.293-342, and Goldman (1992), pp.194-203, 207-11.

22. *Europa World Year Book* (1997), p.1564; Radio Free Europe: September 25, 1997.

23. Radio Free Europe: May 25 and May 26, 1998.

24. See Goldman (1997), pp.203-7.

25. *Europa World Year Book* (1997), p.1566; Radio Free Europe: December 11, 1997.

26. *Economist*, July 4, 1998: 102.

27. Communist Czechoslovakia is discussed in Szulc (1971) and Korbel (1977), pp.218-320.

28. See Skilling (1976).

29. Ash (1993), pp.78-130. See John F.N. Bradley (1992).

30. See Havel (1990).

31. See Stokes (1993), pp.148-57; Goldman (1992), pp.113-27.

32. Goldman (1997), pp.135-45; see also Young (1994).

33. For the political transformation see Goldman (1977), pp.131-2, 149-52.

34. Radio Free Europe: December 1, December 15, and December 17, 1997.

35. Radio Free Europe: June 22 and June 23, 1998 and Radio Prague: July 5, 1998.

36. Radio Free Europe: May 6, 1998.

37. Goldman (1997), pp.146-9.

38. *Europa World Year Book* (1997), p.2914.

39. Radio Free Europe: June 23 and June 24, 1998.

40. Goldman (1997), pp.127-30

41. *Economist*, November 15, 1997:79-80 and December 6, 1997, pp.51-2; *Europa World Year Book* (1997), p.1066.

42. *Economist*, July 4, 1998: p.102.

43. *Europa World Year Book* (1997), p.2915; *Economist*, December 15, 1997:110.

44. Goldman (1997), pp.42-51, 134-9, 148, 194-7, 211-6, 251-63; Radio Free Europe: November 28, 1997.

45. Radio Free Europe: December 2, December 9, and December 12, 1997.

REFERENCES

Ash, T.G., (1993), *The Magic Lantern. The Revolution of '89 Witnessed in Warsaw, Budapest, Berlin and Prague,* New York: Random House.

Ash, T.G., (1991), *The Polish Revolution: Solidarity*, London: Granta Books.

Bradley, J.F.N., (1992), *Czechoslovakia's Velvet Revolution*, Boulder, Colo.: East European Monographs.

Dziewanowski, M.K., (1977), *Poland in the Twentieth Century*, New York: Columbia University Press.

Economist, various issues.

Europa (1997), *World Yearbook*, London, England: Europa Publications Ltd.

Goldman, M.I., (1992), *What Went Wrong with Perestroika*, New York: Norton.

Goldman, M.F., (1997), *Revolution and Change in Central and Eastern Europe*, Armonk. N.Y: M.E. Sharpe.

Havel, V., (1990), *Disturbing the Peace. A conversation with Karel Hvižďala*, transl. Paul Wilson, New York: Vintage.

Hoensch, J.K., (1994), *A History of Modern Hungary*, trans. Kim Traynor, 2nd edition, New York: Longman.

Király, B.K. ed., (1995), *Lawful Revolution in Hungary 1989-94*, Boulder, Colo.: Social Science Monographs.

Korbel, J., (1977), *Twentieth Century Czechoslovakia*, New York: Columbia University Press.

Longworth, P., (1994), *The Making of Eastern Europe*, New York: St. Martin's Press.

Radio Free Europe: WWW.RFERL.ORG/NEWSLINE.

Radio Free Europe: WWW.RFERL.ORG/NEWSLINE/INDEX.HTML "Europe: Has the West Embraced the East?", 28 November 1997.

Radio Prague: CR@WERICH.RADIO.CZ.

Rothschild, J., (1989), *Return to Diversity*, New York: Oxford University Press.

Sachs, J., (1993), *Poland's Jump to the Market Economy*, Cambridge, Mass.: MIT Press.

Skilling, H.G., (1976), *Czechoslovakia's Interrupted Revolution*, Princeton, N.J.: Princeton University Press.

Stokes, G., (1993), *The Walls Came Tumbling Down. The Collapse of Communism in Eastern Europe*, New York: Oxford University Press.

Szulc, T., (1971), *Czechoslovakia Since World War II*, New York: Viking Press.

Walesa, L., (1991), *The Struggle and the Triumph. An Autobiography*, New York: Arcade.

Wandycz, P.S., *(1993), The Price of Freedom*, New York: Routledge.

Young, R.A., (1994), *The Breakup of Czechoslovakia*, Kingston, Ont.: Queen's University Institute of Intergovernmental Relations.

CHAPTER 2

TRANSITION ECONOMIES: A TEMPORAL COMPARATIVE ANALYSIS*

SOHRAB ABIZADEH

I. INTRODUCTION

Much has been expected and written about central and Eastern Europe in recent years and the transition of Central Eastern Europe overall and Central Europe (CE) in particular.

CE countries were not only expected to transform their economies but were challenged at the same time by the ever changing and dynamic world around them. They needed to reform and catch up at the same time. Yet, it may be argued that transition economies were advantaged by the timing of globalization and freer trade and their acceptance in the international community. Globalization made it easier for these countries to join, and at the same time take advantage of growing worldwide opportunities. Globalization allowed these countries to take advantage of capital mobility, larger markets and foreign capital, and access to foreign expertise and more developed financial markets.

The debate over economic reform in CE has taken many dimensions. One is the question of the speed of change. Some have proposed the "big bang" approach, others have supported the "gradual" model while some have chosen to support the middle-of-the-road approach. Unanimity on this issue has not been easy and so each country has followed a combination of approaches, depending on the prevailing social, political and economic circumstances at the time of change and during the transition.

Some economists such as Olson (1995) are disappointed at the slow pace of progress in these countries while others such as Rosefielde (1995) disagree. Yet, according to Murrell (1996) "Eastern European progress acts as a beacon to those ex-republics of the USSR that are still mired in deep transitional recessions." This, he calls "a testimony to the turnaround in Central Eastern Europe . . ." (p.26).

What is clear is that over the past eight years or so, the transition economies of CE have had to deal with unprecedented and hard challenges to transform their command economies to free market systems and to integrate their economies into the global economy. Meanwhile, transition economies face many problems that are traceable to their past. Some of these are a lack of a tradition of market-based institutions, underdeveloped financial structures, and political rigidities.

Now that we are more than eight years into the new era in CE, we can use the available information to do some meaningful comparative analyses of the past and present. This is the main objective of the current chapter. I have organized it as follows. First, I analyze the overall economic performance of the designated countries (Poland, Hungary, Czech Republic and Slovak Republic). Next, a detailed discussion on inflation, unemployment and output trends will be given in section III. Section VI will deal with general trends in government finances while section V will compare the state of social programs in these countries. International trade issues will be discussed in section VI followed by summary and conclusions in section VII.

II. Overall Economic Performance

To set the stage for further detailed analysis of transformation, I start with an overall review of the economic performance of CE before and after 1989. Table 1 reports on the historical data for real GDP in millions of national currencies for these countries. Table 2 provides information on real GDP in US Dollars. Table 3 uses index numbers to explain the trends in GDP using 1990 (the first year after transition) as the base year. Table 3 also reports the rates of growth of real GDP in these countries. Both the index numbers and the rates of growth in output show the trends in real GDP in these four countries.

From Table 3, it is clear that Poland has experienced a continued growth in output since 1984 followed by a sharp decline beginning in 1990. This trend was subsequently reversed in 1994. Hungary has enjoyed a relatively stable rate of growth in output since 1980 (except 1985) until 1990 when it began to follow a similar trend as Poland. Czechoslovakia had experienced a more unstable growth before 1989. However, unlike the other two countries, after 1990 its recovery began earlier. Its growth rate first declined in 1992 then picked up immediately in 1993 and continued with a good performance. This growth rate is due to impressive accomplishments in Czech Republic.

Figures 1 and 2 depict the growth rates and index numbers, respectively, for the sample countries over time. A clear pattern emerges from these charts. This pattern is particularly more pronounced during the transition period. When considering the growth of output after 1989, it is easy to observe from these figures that growth follows a U-shaped pattern. This is clear in Figure 2, where index numbers are used. Blanchard (1996, p. 117) considers the task of explaining this U-shaped pattern of output as a major theoretical challenge facing economists working on transition.

Olson, writing in 1995, and before observing the economic turnaround in most countries, was concerned about the lack of economic progress in post-communist countries of Eastern Europe. He notes " . . . there can be no doubt that economic performance in these countries after the collapse of communism has been dramatically below expectations" (p. 47). This is true when one looks only at the early years of transition. However, the poor performance of these economies at the early stages of transition should come as no surprise. When one applies a sudden shock to an economy, a slow down is inevitable. In particular, setting aside the problem of measurement, several reasons can be given for the decline in output during the early years of change in CE countries. Among them are; 1) the collapse of the political structure and its slow replacement; 2) the collapse of the financial system; 3) social uncertainty about the future; 4) lack of consumers' and investors' confidence in the economy; 5) the attempt by the 'old guard' to protect the status quo; 6) a wait-and-see attitude taken by foreign investors; 7) the sudden change in the economic system resulting in a high rate of unemployment, particularly an increase in the number of what can be called, to borrow from Friedman, "transitory" unemployed; 8) the collapse of the output and the subsequent rise in prices;[6] 9) the drop in government subsidies; 10) the disorganization and collapse of the existing structure for the supply of raw material and distribution;[7] and according to Blanchard (1996) "... the worse the initial shock and the higher the unemployment, the more opposition there is to restructuring" (p. 177).[8]

One of the most important impediments to growth is political uncertainty due to resistance by the old guard to change at the early stages of transition. This has not been emphasized enough in the economic writings thus far. The new establishment wastes much energy and resources fighting the supporters of the old system. These people generally hold on to their powerful political and bureaucratic positions for some time after the change has occurred. This is an important issue considering the fact that in two countries, Poland and Hungary, members of the old guard have managed to return to power, while in the case of Czech Republic the political uncertainty continues to date.

Table 1: Real GDP (1990) in Millions of National Currencies

Year	Poland	Hungary	Czech Rep	Slovak Rep	Czechoslovakia
1980	519.33	1755897.70			728064.52
1981	477.96	1806400.20			577576.88
1982	473.02	1857604.20			575398.13
1983	470.43	1871165.00			583897.91
1984	504.91	1920732.30			613804.60
1985	551.41	1915822.40			760730.34
1986	586.71	1962419.40			725899.44
1987	607.15	2036321.80			794536.31
1988	669.06	2149104.50			824938.68
1989	775.44	2164983.10			834697.47
1990	560.27	2089300.00			811310.00
1991	457.73	1840732.80			620012.68
1992	447.59	1784883.60			633923.15
1993	443.21	1770108.70	451294.64	196538.97	647833.61
1994	449.25	1821820.90	463120.43	206209.17	669329.60
1995	481.64	2166480.00	485533.11	221405.21	706938.32
1996			532800.00	235539.00	768339.00

Source: International Monetary Fund, *International Financial Statistics* (IFS CD-ROM 3/97) and for Slovak and Czech Republics IFS 1996 and January 1998 and United Nations *Statistical Yearbook*, 1994.

Notes: 1) For Poland, Hungary and Czechoslovakia real values were calculated by applying CPI to NGDP.

2) 1992 data for Czechoslovakia is an average and 1993-96 data are calculated by adding the data from the two republics.

Table 2: Real GDP (1990) in Millions of US Dollars

Year	Poland	Hungary	Czech Rep	Slovak Rep	Czechoslovakia
1980	117452.16	53974.01			51020.64
1981	93439.12	52642.79			43590.71
1982	55764.78	50711.88			41969.23
1983	51384.77	43850.82			41235.73
1984	44587.29	39980.10			36953.92
1985	37474.97	38225.17			44383.33
1986	33471.70	42817.53			48425.58
1987	22904.12	43353.17			58037.71
1988	15539.78	42629.79			57446.98
1989	5388.04	36653.41			55461.63
1990	589.76	33055.48			45198.33
1991	432.79	24630.00			21031.64
1992	328.47	22596.78			22431.82
1993	244.67	19254.30	15480.30	6387.44	
1994	197.71	17324.20	16088.90	6435.02	
1995	198.61	17237.87	18293.93	7451.35	
1996			19627.98	7683.86	

Source: See Table 1.
Note: Average exchange rates from IMF (IFS CD-ROM 3/97) were used to generate GDP in US$.

Table 3: Index Numbers and Growth Rates for Real GDP (1990)

	Poland		Hungary		Czechoslovakia	
Year	Index Number	Growth Rate	Index Number	Growth Rate	Index Number	Growth Rate
1980	92.69		84.04		89.74	
1981	85.31	-7.97%	86.46	2.88%	71.19	-20.67%
1982	84.43	-1.03%	88.91	2.83%	70.92	-0.38%
1983	83.96	-0.55%	89.56	0.73%	71.97	1.48%
1984	90.12	7.33%	91.93	2.65%	75.66	5.12%
1985	98.42	9.21%	91.70	-0.26%	93.77	23.94%
1986	104.72	6.40%	93.93	2.43%	89.47	-4.58%
1987	108.37	3.48%	97.46	3.77%	97.93	9.46%
1988	119.42	10.20%	102.86	5.54%	101.68	3.83%
1989	138.40	15.90%	103.62	0.74%	102.88	1.18%
1990	100.00	-27.75%	100.00	-3.50%	100.00	-2.80%
1991	81.70	-18.30%	88.10	-11.90%	76.42	-23.58%
1992	79.89	-2.21%	85.43	-3.03%	78.14	2.24%
1993	79.11	-0.98%	84.72	-0.83%	79.85	2.19%
1994	80.18	1.36%	87.20	2.92%	82.50	3.32%
1995	85.97	7.21%	103.69	18.92%	87.14	5.62%
1996					94.70	8.69%

Source: Table 1.

Figure 1: Growth Rate of Real GDP Over Time

Source: Table 3.

Figure 2: Index Numbers of Real GDP Over Time

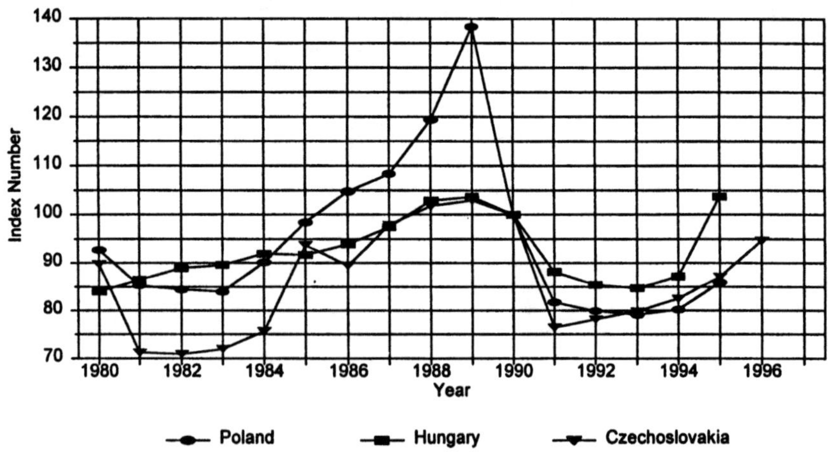

Source: Table 3.

Political fragmentation, in the form of large numbers of political parties, is an indication of political opposition and uncertainty that have prevailed for some time in transitional economies. Records show that the number of political organizations in Poland and Hungary rose from 4 to 13 and 4 to 11 between 1989 and 1990, respectively. For Czechoslovakia, this number fell from 11 to 10 for the same period.[9] However, by 1997, this number increased to 25, 20, 13 and 15, respectively, for Poland, Hungary, Czech Republic and Slovak Republic. Although increased numbers of political organizations is an indication of the introduction of democratic reforms, too many political parties will make the functioning of democracy more problematic. The best example is Italy in recent years, where it has become almost impossible to keep a government in power for any length of time.

Other reasons for the poor performance of CE countries, in the early years, can be attributed to the lack of some economic and political underpinning. For example, consider the views expressed by Olson (1995) where he compares the economies of West Germany and Japan after the War. He states that the success of these two countries after the war "owed a great deal to the fact that fascist governments and allied occupiers had largely eliminated their lobbies and cartels." After the defeat of communism in CE countries, by contrast, these societies "were dense with powerful lobbies of the large enterprises and industry associations inherited from the old regime." (p. 459). In addition, privatization was not a major issue in post war Japan and West Germany. Privatization has proven to be a serious economic and political concern for transitional economies. Furthermore, unlike transition economies after 1989, Japan and West Germany, after the War, did not have to deal with the introduction of a brand new economic system.

Another example is East Germany after 1989. A wealthy nation took over East Germany, "as tutor, benefactor, and disciplinarian" to borrow from Muller (1995). In his words " . . . this provides an ideal situation-an existing political system imparting credibility, a stable convertible currency, laws and institutions imported wholesale, a managerial and business class to facilitate privatization and restructuring, and the deep pockets of the rich country for a social safety net" (p. 165). Indeed, these are the very important underpinnings that were missing in CE countries in the early transition years. Thus, simply put, the relative decline in output at the early stages of transition was not only inevitable but predictable.

Following the early stages of transition, all indications are that CE countries have begun a journey to recovery. Although resolving some of the problems listed above has been instrumental in this recovery, in addition to the need to achieve a high degree of economic and political liberalization, two major economic events have further contributed to such an upturn. First, is the overall performance of the world economy in recent years, from Asia to North America (notwithstanding the so called 'Asian flu' which came about around the end of 1997) with the expected positive spillover effects into the CE countries. Secondly, there was the support and advice provided by the international community through the IMF and other organizations. It took some time before these supports could be planned, translated into action and carried out. Planning for and carrying out stabilization policies is a case in point. Recent political stability, the in-flow of foreign investment and the opening of the borders to freer trade have helped economic recovery as well.

III. Inflation, Unemployment and Output

When analyzing inflation and unemployment in CE countries, consideration must be given to the differing economic circumstances in these countries as compared with other market-based systems. Besides the traditional explanations given for other market oriented economies, we need to be aware of other unique social and economic issues that prevail and that can affect these two variables in the CE countries. With this in mind we proceed with the analysis of the twin problems of unemployment and inflation.

A. Unemployment

In transition economies, unemployment takes on a new meaning. Unemployment was a foreign term for planned economies since, by definition, unemployment was non-existent under the communist regimes. Unemployment was ideologically unacceptable and was even illegal in Bulgaria, Czechoslovakia and Romania. However, under-employment and disguised unemployment were prevalent in many CE countries (Ingham and Grima, 1994, p. 812).

Although transition economies have now introduced unemployment into their vocabulary, its determinants may not yet be the same as those for capitalist economies. Unemployment, at least at the early stage of transition, is not due to business cycle or other economic fluctuations since transition itself "... is not a cyclical downturn within a regular business cycle..." (Chu and Schwartz, 1994, p. 12). Once the communist system collapsed, unemployment came to be considered as "the natural outcome of the process of reallocation and restructuring in the economies in transition" (Blanchard et al., 1994, p. 6), at least during the early years.

Figure 3 shows the trends in rates of unemployment since 1990. As shown in Figure 3, Poland's unemployment rate began rising in 1990 and reached a peak of 16.5% in 1994 before beginning to decline. Hungary's unemployment rate rose to a peak of 12.3% in 1992 and has been stable or even declining since. The relatively sharp increase in the rate of unemployment for Czech Republic came in 1991 followed by, more or less, stable rates of around 3%. This is an exceptional performance by transition economies' standards. This "low rate of unemployment could indeed be the result of too little restructuring, but it could also be a signal that the labor market has been extraordinarily efficient in enabling laid-off workers to find jobs quickly in the private sector (in Prague's prosperous tourist industry, for example)" (Economist, 1994, p. 27). The lower than expected unemployment rate can be also due to a significant drop in labor force participation due to women leaving labor force, others taking early retirement, foreign workers returning home and out migration, among other things.[10] Slovakia's experience is significantly different from that of Czech Republic. Its unemployment rate began to rise in 1991 and peaked at 18.8% in 1994 before declining and then stabilizing in recent years at around 14%.

Figure 3 reveals that, except in Czech Republic, unemployment has followed an inverted-U pattern in these countries. The sharp increase in unemployment rates is relatively easy to explain. In addition to arguments made earlier, the collapse of communism and its institutions is the main reason. This resulted in the mass movement of the workers from the government sector of the economy to the private sector. Along with economic liberalization and restructuring a large number of people joined the structurally and frictionally unemployed group. At the early stages of transition, "unemployment would have been even higher if it were not for large flows out of the labor force, which partly reflects the reversal of the artificially high labor force participation rate-particularly women-that was a characteristic of a planned economy" (Blanchard et al., 1994, p. 7).

These relatively high rates are expected to remain. Once transformation takes hold, and the political and economic systems begin to stabilize, the unemployment rate is expected to either stabilize or decline slowly. Murrell (1996) observes that the typical pattern in Central Europe is first a rapid rise in the percentage unemployment rate to the mid-teens before stabilizing. "In a few countries, unemployment has begun to edge down, but there is no expectation of rapid fall" (p. 37). This is so because it will take many more years for these countries to complete their transition to a market economy. And so the rates of structural and 'transitional' unemployment will remain high. The moderate turnaround in unemployment observed in recent years is mostly due to the implementation of stabilization policies.

B. INFLATION

One main issue discussed in relationship to transition economies is the very high rate of inflation experienced in the early years of transition. For many decades before transition all prices, with minimal exceptions, were subject to strict administrative control. This control resulted in low and repressed measures of inflation.[11] Using 1990 as the base year, Table 4 and Figures 4a-4d[12] show that the rate of inflation was kept stable and low (around zero mark) for most of the 80s in these countries. Inflation began to rise during the late 80s and accelerated its rate of increase immediately after the collapse of communism. Marginal and rare cases of price increases before 1989 are due to the minimal market type activities sanctioned by the Communist governments at the time.

Figure 3: Unemployment Rates

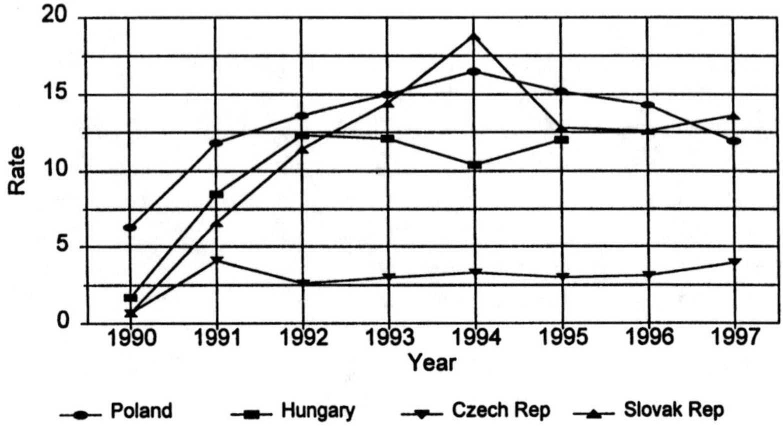

Source: International Monetary Fund, *International Financial Statistics,* different issues.
Note: Unemployment figures used for 1997 for Poland, Czech Republic and Slovak Republic are the averages of the first th quarters, the first two quarters and the figure from the first quarter, respectively.

Figures 5a-5d report on the rates of inflation in these CE countries since 1990, the first year after the change. Poland (Figure 5a) experienced the sharpest increase in prices in 1990 followed by a sharp decline in the rate of inflation in 1991 and steadily declining thereafter with a relatively respectable 20% rate of inflation in 1996. Hungary (Figure 5b) experienced the sharpest increase in prices in 1991, although 1990 also shows a high rate of 29%. In 1992 the rate of inflation dropped to 23% and continued the decline afterwards before rising again in 1994 and 1995. The 23.49% rate of inflation in 1996, although high by western standards, is respectable in this case. The lowest overall rates of inflation after 1990 are reported for Czech Republic (Figure 5c) and Slovak Republic (Figure 5d). The trend has been very similar for both these countries. This, of course, is because figures for 1980 to 1993 are those of the former Czechoslovakia. Inflation peaked in 1991 and has been declining since to a very respectable level of around 5 to 10 percent in recent years.

Table 4: Rate of Inflation (using CPI - Base 1990)

Year	Poland	Hungary	Czech Rep	Slovak Rep
1980	9.89%	9.26%	2.96%	2.96%
1981	19.13%	4.51%	0.82%	0.82%
1982	103.56%	7.02%	5.07%	5.07%
1983	25.53%	6.40%	0.95%	0.95%
1984	15.40%	8.65%	0.94%	0.94%
1985	11.52%	7.01%	2.28%	2.28%
1986	16.55%	5.29%	0.50%	0.50%
1987	26.38%	8.68%	0.08%	0.08%
1988	58.72%	15.79%	0.14%	0.14%
1989	244.55%	16.95%	1.38%	1.38%
1990	555.38%	28.97%	10.02%	10.02%
1991	76.71%	34.23%	57.71%	57.71%
1992	45.33%	22.95%	10.76%	10.76%
1993	36.87%	22.45%	20.46%	25.06%
1994	33.25%	18.87%	10.06%	13.41%
1995	26.80%	28.30%	9.10%	9.89%
1996	20.15%	23.49%	8.82%	5.81%
1997	14.41%	16.40%	7.04%	4.77%

Source: All data from 1997 IMF, *IFS Yearbook* (or CD-ROM 3/97). Czech Rep and Slovak Rep from 1980-1992 from 1994 Yearbook. All 1997 data found by averaging 3 quarters (2 in case of Slovak) of 1997 CPI data from Jan 1998 IFS monthly.

Figure 4a: Poland's Inflation Rate (1980-1997)

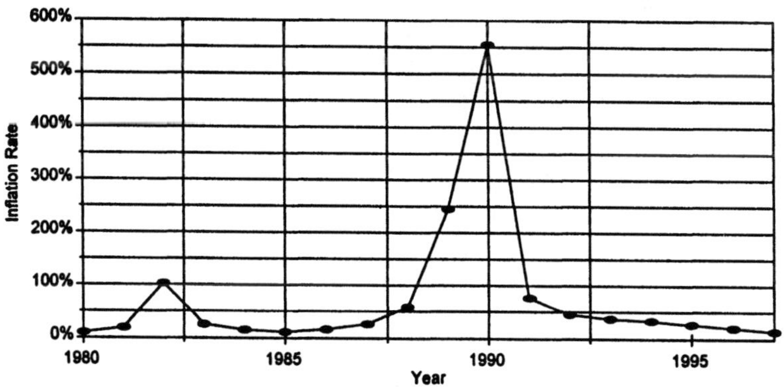

Source: Table 4.

Figure 4b: Hungary's Inflation Rate (1980-1997)

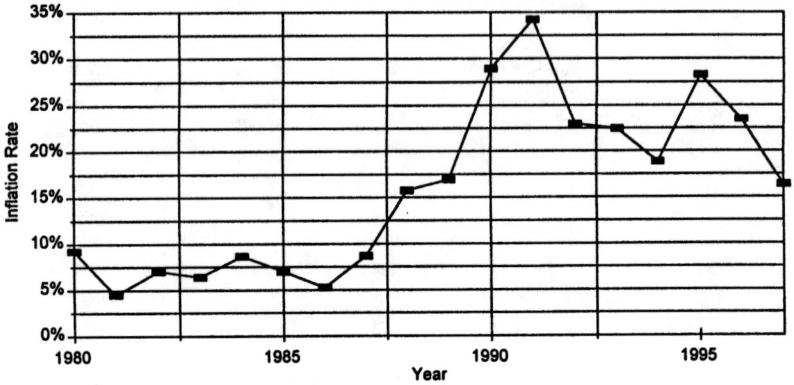

Source: Table 4.

Figure 4c: Czech Republic's Inflation Rate (1980-1997)

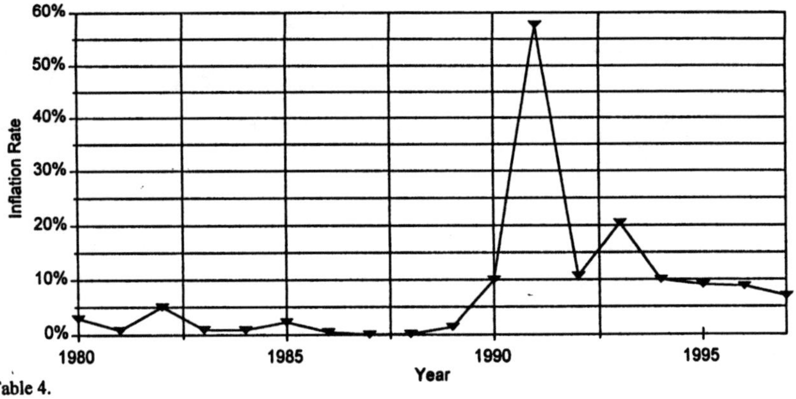

Source: Table 4.

Figure 4d: Slovak Republic's Inflation Rate (1980-1997)

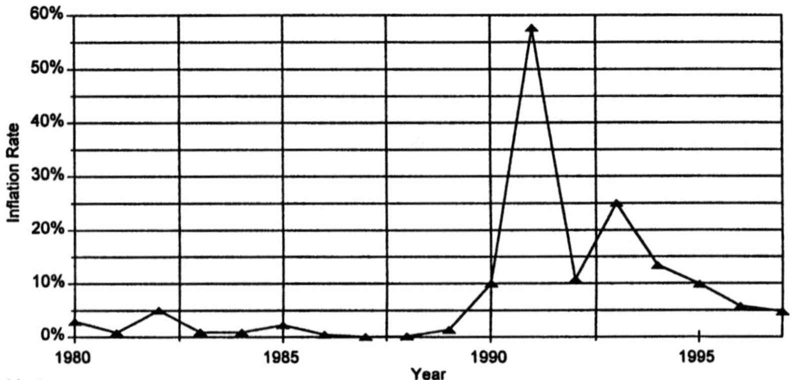

Source: Table 4.

Many factors have caused the very high and unexpected rates of inflation in transition CE countries. These factors can be divided into two distinct categories. One category includes factors present prior to the change and the other takes account of those particular to the post-communist era.

As shown in Table 4 and Figures 4a-4d, inflation in these countries began to edge up two or three years before 1990. According to Koen and De Masi (1997, p.7) the inflation pressure was, among other things, due to fiscal pressures that began in the late 1980s-early 1990s. More specifically, this initial high rate of inflation was mainly due to high government expenditures before the change. Communist regimes tried to bribe the public by pumping more money into the system in the hope that the trend of liberalization might reverse itself. For example, in Poland the budgetary deficit rose to 7.4 percent of GDP in 1989.[13]

As for the causes behind high rates of inflation in the post-communist era, several can be given. First, as just mentioned, the inflation pressures experienced by transitional economies were partly due to the flow through effects of policies carried out prior to transition. Once their systems collapsed, the inflationary pressures, which already existed, began to accelerate resulting in higher expected rate of inflation leading to even higher actual inflation rates. Second, according to Ghosh (1997, p.5), the governments of transition economies, faced with budget deficits and limited administrative capacity to tax, have had little choice but to resort to the 'inflation tax'.

Third, inflation is a complex phenomenon that can be attributed to several other factors once the transition and liberalization got underway. Enev and Koford (1996, p. 31), using Poland as a case, contend that price shocks, higher labor and other production costs, large credits to the state enterprises, the interest rate, the devaluation of currency, falling output, and increased unemployment have all played an important role in causing inflation. According to Koen and Di Masi (1997), money creation, the indexation of nominal incomes and the overall relative price adjustments contributed to these pressures as well (p. 8).[14] Finally, the sudden collapse of the system and the new ideology of a free market, along with price liberalization, have also contributed to the rise in prices. Recent relative decline in the rates of inflation is due to the various stabilization policies introduced in these countries with the help of international agencies such as the IMF.

Whatever the causes of inflation, economists have emphasized the negative and/or positive (if any) impact of inflation on the economy in general and those of CE countries in particular. Although the general debate, as applied to western industrialized countries continues,[15] there is some degree of unanimity achieved in the case of transition economies.[16] Fischer et al. (1996) argue that, in the transition economies, inflation stabilization is a prerequisite for the growth of output. Their results suggest that only when inflation falls below 50 percent will output growth occur. Leijonhufvud and Rühl (1997) share this view and believe that transition economies need monetary stability as a necessary condition for acceptable economic growth.

According to Ghosh(1997) there is some evidence that only those transition economies that have achieved at least some price stability have managed to grow. However, he contends that, with structural and other changes occurring simultaneously, this kind of relationship continues to be somewhat ambiguous, let alone causal. He sums up the debate by concluding that " . . . , there is mounting evidence that low and stable inflation is an important ingredient in sustained output

Figure 5a: Poland's Inflation Rate (1990-1997)

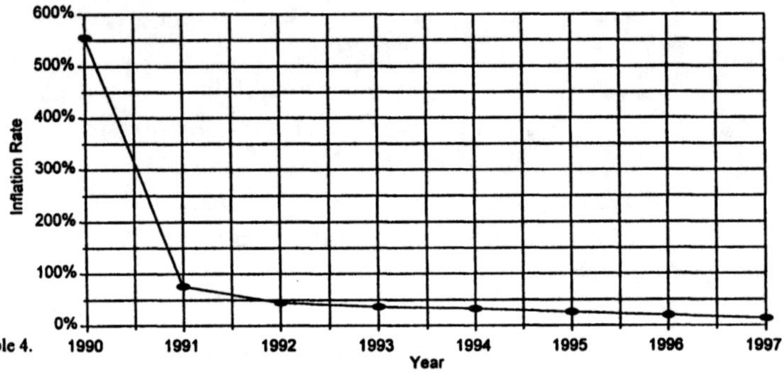

Source: Table 4.

Figure 5b: Hungary's Inflation Rate (1990-1997)

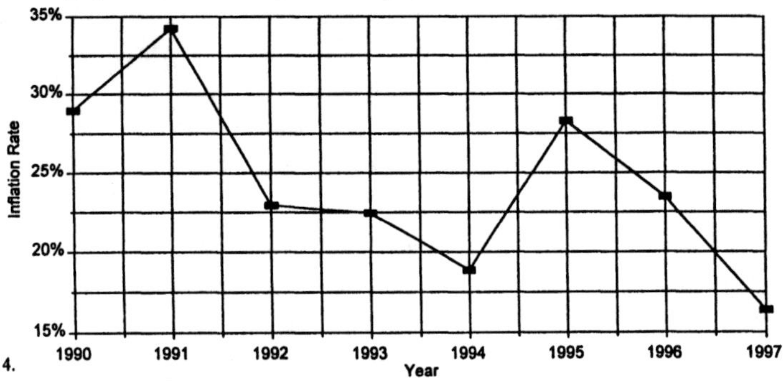

Source: Table 4.

Figure 5c: Czech Republic's Inflation Rate (1990-1997)

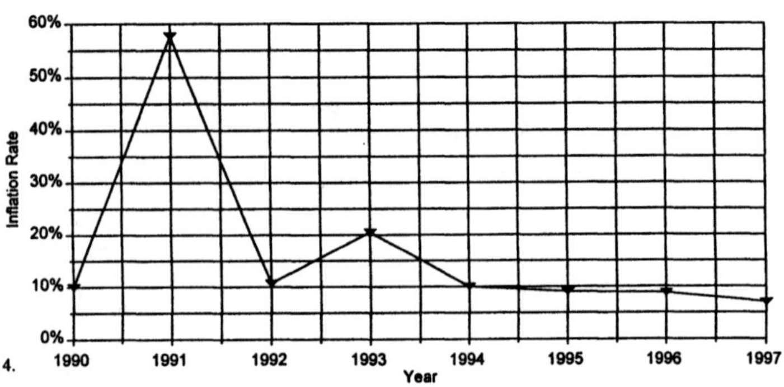

Source: Table 4.

Figure 5d: Slovak Republic's Inflation Rate (1990-1997)

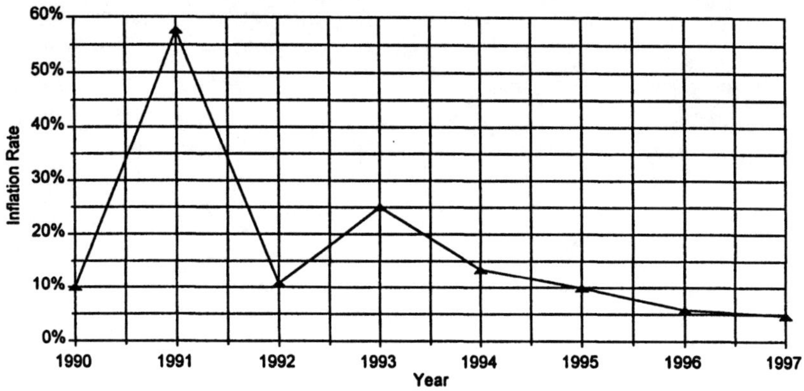

Source: Table 4.

growth. Naturally, there are exceptions to this rule - typically countries that are particularly open or that have been able to sustain export growth. Conversely, there are arguments - some peculiar to transition economies - for higher inflation. Given the costs of inflation, however, they may be less than fully compelling" (p. 26). Meanwhile he admits earlier (p. 25) that "there is thus the real possibility that these countries will continue with higher - but not critically high - inflation rates for several years to come" which suggests that the task of stabilization and economic growth continue to be a challenge for the transition economies in the immediate future.

Clearly, as long as high (or runaway) inflation prevails, enjoying the fruits of free market reforms would be extremely difficult for the citizens of these countries. No doubt, macroeconomic stabilization policies have resulted in a gradual control of inflation. There are weak signs that suggest that a declining trend in the rate of inflation may have already begun. Meanwhile, governments of CE have implemented different kinds of income policies to offset the possible adverse effects of inflation[17] Ghosh (1997, p. 25) claims that many transition economies continue to have administratively set prices for key consumer goods such as heat, communication services, fuels and the like, yet he recommends an increase in these prices to match true market prices. Finally, Fischer et al. (1996) support the policies of a fixed exchange rate and smaller fiscal deficits for reducing inflation and raising economic growth. It is my view that, as long as inflation remains high, thus adversely affecting fixed income earners and the poor, governments' price control policies are justified.[18]

C. The Phillips Curve

The above two sections show that immediately following the collapse of communism in the CE countries, both inflation and unemployment began to increase at an unprecedented pace. The traditional Phillips curve, without proper modifications, is no longer capable of explaining the relationship between inflation and unemployment. The twin high rates of unemployment and inflation remind us of the circumstances that prevailed in the late 1970s and early 1980s in North America that led to the introduction of the term 'stagflation' into economics textbooks. This familiar term and the subsequent introduction of expectation-augmented Phillips curve (EAPC) provide us with the theoretical tool necessary to analyze the twin problems of inflation and unemployment in CE countries.

As discussed above, it is recognized that the economic, social and political circumstances of CE are completely different from those that prevailed in North America during the 1980s. Nonetheless, the mixture of expected high inflation, wage-cost-push and unprecedented high unemployment properly fit into this theoretical framework. Using the expectation-augmented-Phillips curve (EAPC) we infer that there is an inverse relationship between the unemployment rate and the change in inflation.

Figures 6a-6d depict the expectation augmented Phillips curves by plotting the changes in inflation rates versus the unemployment rates for each year since 1990 for Poland, Hungary, Czech Republic and Slovak Republic, respectively. Figure 6a shows that, if 1990 is removed from the relationship, the EAPC reflects a relatively flat curve with a very mild positive slope for Poland. This is contrary to the theoretical underpinning of EAPC. Poland was the first country to introduce a fundamental reform in January 1990. They immediately removed government's control on almost all prices and implemented an aggressive macroeconomic stabilization plan (Blanchard, 1997, pp. 528-529). The effect of this 'big bang' approach was a sudden rise in prices, both actual and expected. This sudden rise in prices led to high inflation expectations causing even further price hikes. All this occurred, despite the sharp increase in the rate of unemployment. The combination of high expected inflation, leading to wage cost push inflation, particularly in the private sector and a high rate of unemployment are behind the shape of the EAPC for Poland.

For Hungary, Figure 6b depicts a downward sloping EAPC if 1995 is considered as an outlier. It follows that the initial transition shock in Hungary was not as severe as it was for Poland. In fact, generally speaking, the overall rates of inflation and unemployment have been relatively lower in Hungary than they were in Poland after 1990.

Figure 6c, for Czech Republic (ignoring 1991 as an outlier) gives a cluster of points with a downward trend. Czech Republic, particularly during prime minister Klaus's term in office, implemented aggressive market-oriented policies. This, among other things, led to the formation of high inflation expectations. However, for reasons elaborated earlier, the rate of unemployment did

Figure 6a: Poland's Adjusted Phillips Curve

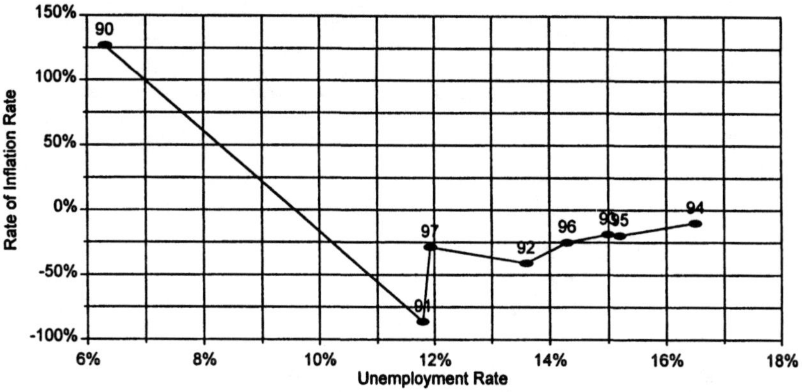

Source: Inflation figures from Table 4. Unemployment data source as for Figure 3.

Figure 6b: Hungary's Adjusted Phillips Curve

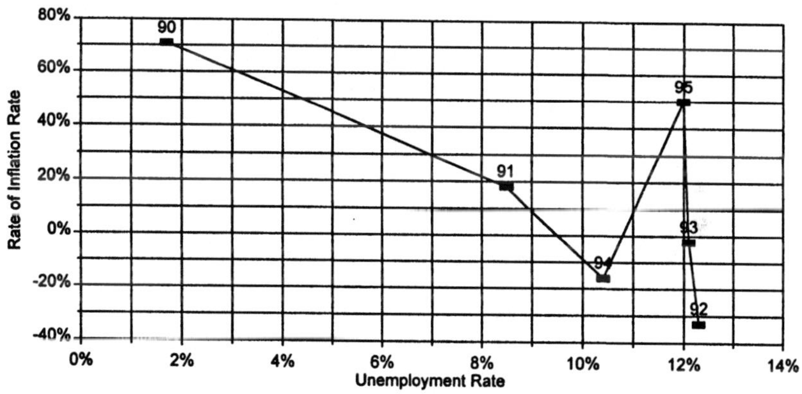

Source: See Figure 6a.

not rise as radically as was the case in Poland. Thus, the EAPC for Czech Republic represents the conventional trade-off between rates of inflation and unemployment.

Inflation and unemployment data for Slovak Republic produce a perfect EAPC (Figure 6d). This curve is downward sloping and very close to what theory tells us. This is an indication that Slovak Republic did not pursue economic reforms as aggressively as others did. At the same time, despite both high rates of unemployment and inflation, the trade-off between these two variables is most pronounced in the case of Slovak Republic.

Generally, with the possible exception of Poland, EAPC confirms that a short run trade-off between unemployment and inflation has prevailed in these countries. Whether there has been a shift in EAPC during the past nine years is difficult to assess. Unfortunately, we are limited by the number of observations available and the unreliability of data for the pre-transition era. In addition, an estimate of a comparable EAPC prior to 1990 may not be appropriate since neither inflation nor unemployment were market-driven in these countries.

Figure 6c: Czech Republic's Adjusted Phillips Curve

Source: See Figure 6a

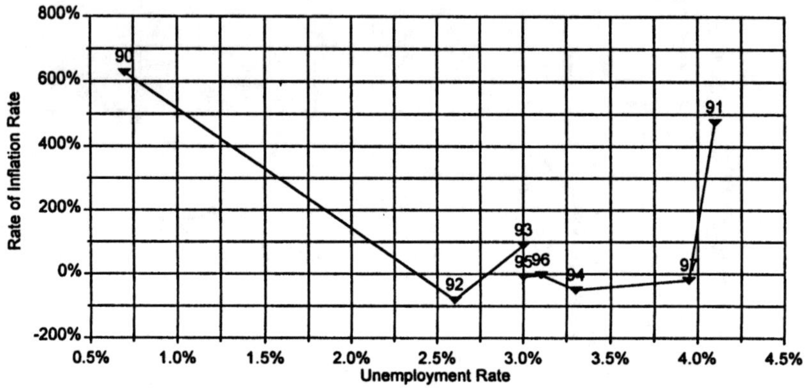

Figure 6d: Slovak Republic's Adjusted Phillips Curve

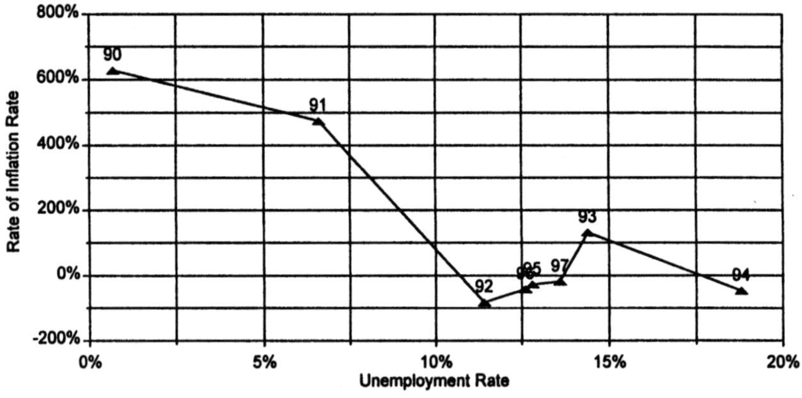

IV. General Trends in Government Finances

The main economic force in these countries before 1989 was government activity. All economic decisions including prices, distribution, and policies regarding labor market and financial institutions were made by the state. The government, under central planning, controlled resource allocation. "Public finance was all-encompassing and involved massive discretionary intervention in the economy through - among other things - direct transfers to non-financial, state-owned enterprises (SOEs), price subsidies, and social benefits. This intervention was financed by countless variable turnover taxes and payroll taxes, all differentiated by industrial activity or earmarked at the enterprise level" (Kopits and Offerdal, 1994, p.10). Economic liberalization has changed these leading to significant structural changes in government expenditures and taxes. Our data will show that the share of tax revenues and government expenditures to GDP have generally declined in these countries since 1990.

A. EXPENDITURES

The general theory of public expenditure growth explains that the ratio of government expenditures to GDP continues to rise with economic development and industrialization. However, once industrialization is complete, and the country enters its highly developed stage, this ratio may stabilize or even decline as the public sector becomes too large, making the public reluctant to accept any higher tax burden in support of a larger government sector relative to GDP.19 Clearly this is a theory more applicable to market economies and it cannot be readily applied to the case of CEE countries that have just abandoned communism and joined the market-oriented world.

With the desire to embrace capitalism, the CE countries became more interested in reducing the role of government in the economy by downsizing its operation. According to Chu and Schwartz (1994) "to create room for private initiatives, governments had to reduce the extent of state intervention in the economy. This meant reducing the size of government, raising revenues in a less distortionary fashion, and improving the expenditure mix" (p. 11). However, they conclude that "these reductions in government intervention manifested themselves in changes in institutional arrangements, and reductions in the share of government output and employment, but not necessarily in reductions in government expenditures and budget deficits" (p. 25). Table 5 shows that this conclusion holds, more or less, in the case of Poland. The share of government expenditures to GDP remained steady over the 1984-1995 period that includes the pre- and post-communism era. However, in all other cases a steady decline in the share of government expenditures to GDP is observed. This decline has been more pronounced for the Czech and Slovak Republics, particularly after separation which partially explains the very low ratios in recent years. However, not only has this ratio declined but there have occurred major structural shifts in the components of total government expenditures. Poland is a special case where changes in economic policy began well before the 1990 change in government. Given the most recent data reported in Table 5, it can be speculated that a downward trend in the share of government expenditures to total output may continue into the near future. Based on the minimum available data (not reported here) one obvious conclusion is that the structure of public expenditures has changed significantly in these countries after 1990 compared with the communist era.

Table 5: Government Expenditures as a Percentage of GDP

	Country			
Year	**Poland**	**Hungary**	**Czech Republic**	**Slovak Rep**
1984	44.29	53.09	64.08	64.08
1985	45.17	53.19	52.88	52.88
1986	41.85	58.46	52.68	52.68
1991	47.70	54.87	52.22	52.22
1992	50.00	55.30	----	----
1993	----	56.13	38.64	46.86
1994	44.08	54.95	35.96	36.71
1995	43.36	49.16	34.65	33.28
1996	----	----	33.99	----

Source: IMF, *International Financial Statistics Yearbook* 1997, IMF, *Government Finance Statistics Yearbook*, 1997 and *Europa*, different issues.
Note: Data for 1984-91 for the Czech and Slovak Republics are those of Czechoslovakia.

B. TAXES

A major preoccupation of the CE countries is that of broadening their tax base and creating new tax sources to raise revenues to reduce their deficits. Kopits and Offerdal (1994) have argued that the burden of budget deficit reduction was borne by decreased expenditures in these countries (pp.12-13). However, inevitably, there is a need for the introduction of a new tax system which is capable of supporting the rising levels of government expenditures that will be inevitable if economic growth is to be actively pursued. According to the IMF Survey (1998), "the move to positive economic growth with lower inflation in 1997 in many transition countries represent an important achievement. Many of these countries still need to reduce fiscal deficits by strengthening revenue collection and improving the efficiency of social security and welfare systems and government services more generally" (p.14).

Public finance literature clearly indicates that for a country to be able to diversify its tax base and achieve efficiency in its tax collection, certain levels of overall economic performance have to be maintained. As the economy develops and higher and higher levels of growth are achieved, more and more sources and varieties of tax revenues become available.[20] However, it is clear that the models developed to explain structural changes and trends in taxation based on capitalist systems are not readily able to explain the situation in CE countries. One obvious conclusion based on past studies is that, unless favorable economic and political circumstances and conditions prevail, it would be difficult for the governments of these countries to engage in a meaningful process of tax reform for improving efficiency and raising higher revenues. As Leijonhufvud and Ruhl (1997), when dealing with Russia, contend "Modern tax systems are not built in a day. The totalitarian state has been followed by a state lacking the authority to collect its taxes. In 1996, Russian governments may collect about 65 percent of taxes due (including those paid with 'commodity credits' and promissory notes!). The central government's revenue was running at less than 10 percent of GNP in the first half of 1996 - hardly enough to run a nightwatchman state at today's prices" (p. 344).

Kopits and Offerdal (1994, p.12), talk about the two stages that tax reform in these countries can follow. The first stage includes the reduction of the number of turnover tax rates followed by the introduction of a value-added income tax and harmonizing payroll taxes for social security. The goal is to convert a wide range of non-tariff barriers into relatively low ad valorem import duties. During the second stage, they point out, the reform will focus on the move toward a market-oriented tax system which includes the introduction of traditional taxes in western countries such as a progressive personal income tax, value-added-tax and others. This view finds much support in the public finance literature alluded to earlier.

Table 6 reports on the percentage of total tax revenues of GDP for our sample countries. What is clearly evident from Table 6 is the sharp decline in the ratio of total tax revenues to GDP in all four counties after the collapse of communism. This is not surprising. A comprehensive and well-defined system of taxation, as it is known in other market economies, was non-existent under communism. With the sudden collapse of this system came a period of chaos and disarray in regards to identifying different sources of tax revenues, defining the tax base, establishing the appropriate government departments for tax collection and creating an infrastructure for a tax system needed to match that of a market oriented economy. The majority of these problems prevail to date. Witness, for example, the issues related to tax collection in Russia which prompted the government to take drastic measures in Spring of 1998. In short, the fall in tax revenues has more to do with the lack of an infrastructure than an attempt by the governments to adapt a tax system more relevant to market economy and reducing the role of government in economy. In Murrell's (1996) word, "In many countries, the fall in tax collections goes beyond the reformers' goals of slimming the economic role of government; it is a process more akin to starvation than dieting" (p. 30).

V. Social System Trends

When it comes to the issues of social programs, we are told that under communism full employment was guaranteed and not one able person who could work would be unemployed. This is problematic since efficiency and productivity would have been compromised, leaving the central planning authorities with fewer resources to share with the population. That is, all the citizens, essentially, shared what the system could produce with no poverty at all. Before 1989, the governments of these countries ran the economy based on pre-approved plans and control of all economic variables, including guaranteed employment and universal pension and other social programs, for their citizens.[21] Murrell (1996) explains that "The system (of social protection) was inefficient, using little targeting and few incentives to keep down costs, but it worked better than many other aspects of the centrally planned economies" (p. 35).

Table 6 : Government Tax Revenues as a Percentage of GDP

	Country			
Year	**Poland**	**Hungary**	**Czech Republic**	**Slovak Republic**
1984	41.49	48.03	64.38	64.38
1985	41.63	44.13	53.13	53.13
1986	38.60	49.24	53.07	53.07
1991	----	----	50.05	50.05
1992	----	----	----	----
1993	----	----	39.30	22.23
1994	37.35	33.31	38.00	23.94
1995	36.78	32.57	35.64	25.45
1996	----	----	35.94	----

Source: See Table 5.

Clearly, in attempting hastily to bring about economic reforms to show impressive economic growth, social reform was, and is largely, being ignored. A common problem now shared by all transition economies is the collapse of their social programs with no properly defined plan to replace them. The social safety net gave way with change and those most affected are left to take care of themselves. According to Chu and Schwartz (1994), "while the process of transformation required creating new safeguards in the form of cost-effective social safety nets, these often came as additions to the old system, leaving the old system still in dire need of reform" (p. 23). Murrell (1996) argues that because of the fact that the centralized system worked relatively well "and because reformers saw higher priorities elsewhere, the redesign of the system of social protection received little attention. This relative neglect, combined with the spillover effects of privatization, liberalization and recession spells deep crisis in the forthcoming years" (p. 35) Chu and Gupta (1995) argue that financial constraint, unemployment and underemployment, distorted benefit structure and information deficiencies have led to the worsening of the situation in transition economies and a decline in their ability to establish an acceptable alternative social safety net.

Table 7: Expenditure on Social Welfare as a Percentage of Total Expenditures

	Year								
Country	**1984**	**1985**	**1986**	**1991**	**1992**	**1993**	**1994**	**1995**	**1996**
Poland	1.14	1.27	1.36	----	----	6.88	6.92	9.74	----
Hungary	19.61	20.35	19.54	15.51	25.27	24.06	----	----	----
Czech Rep	26.54	26.85	26.90	31.28	----	26.30	28.15	28.81	24.99
Slovak Rep	26.54	26.85	26.90	31.28	----	----	----	----	----

Source: *Europa* 1994, 1995, 1997 and 1988, for Poland and Hungary. IMF, *Government Finance Statistics Yearbook*, 1995 and 1997 for the Czech and Slovak Republics.
Note: Figures for Poland are expenditures on social welfare, for Hungary expenditures on social security, and for the Czech and Slovak Republics are expenditures on social security and social welfare.

Milanovic's (1995) findings, reported by Murrell (1996, p. 39), show that out of a total of 320 million, for a set of transition countries, 100 million are now considered poor, compared to 15 million people before the fall of communism. Persistent and continued high unemployment and the lack of a viable social program structure can lead to more social problems for these countries. For example, the overall crime rates have increased significantly in these countries. The number of crimes reported per 100,000 population for 1989 was 1460, 1479 and 1092 for Poland, Hungary and Czechoslovakia respectively. These rates jumped to 2311, 3287, 1911 and 1982 for Poland, Hungary, Czech Republic and Slovak Republic respectively in recent years.[22]

Unfortunately, economic progress alone cannot rectify these problems. While economic prosperity may improve the lives of a minority, there is no guarantee that such benefits will spill over to the less fortunate segment of the population, In fact, the opposite may occur. The trickle down economy did not work for western economies and will not solve the social problems of transition economics either. An IMF survey (1998, p. 14), emphasizes that while the recent move to positive growth with lower inflation represent an important step in these countries, more needs to be done to improve the efficiency of the social security and welfare systems. It is also recognized that market reforms by themselves, without a comprehensive social plan, are unable to cure a country's social and economic ills. Studies show that recent improvements in output have not translated into improved social services in these countries. For example, a drop in the birth rate, and increased death rate and infant mortality and lower life expectancy has led to a worsening of the health situation. According to Murrel (1996, p. 39), "coronary diseases, cancer and social ills such as suicide, alcoholism and murder are prime culprits," for the dramatic increase in mortality rates among middle-age men in Russia. Elsewhere, Murrel (p. 35) states that "health care is increasingly quasi-private, usually through the rise of corruption rather than as a result of privatization."

Kornai (1997, p. 339) claims that " there is complete agreement among researchers studying the post socialist transition that one key task is radical reform ... of the welfare system." Chu and Gupta (1995) propose that, increased revenue power, reform in social programs, strengthening of budgetary expenditures discipline and effective targeting mechanisms for the provision of benefits are important steps towards resolving some deficiencies in social programs.

Contrary to those who thought simple market reforms would solve all economic ills, at least concerning social programs, governments' involvement is obviously justified and called for in these countries. That the current changes have resulted in more inequities and relatively higher poverty for some than before is clear and supports the need for more government involvement in the establishment of a fair social safety net.[23] This amounts to governments' distorting market prices by implementing price control of different kinds (e.g., food and shelter) until they are able and can afford to replace the old system with a more developed social welfare program, similar to those in place in western countries.[24] Czech Republic is a prime example. Although they followed the so-called "big bang" approach in their economic policies, this mostly successful transition economy has given up its rent and energy price control policies gradually.

Information on social expenditures in the CE countries is incomplete and inconsistent. Data sources used have changed their definitions several times. Table 7 provides scattered information on expenditures on social welfare and security as a percentage of total expenditures in these countries. Because we have used different definitions it is difficult to either interpret the data or make a meaningful comparative analysis. What Table 7 shows is that the percentage of expenditure on social welfare or social security or both has increased, following the collapse of communism, in Poland and Hungary. However, for Czech Republic this figure has remained steady with minimal fluctuations. No consistency is observed in the data to allow for any meaningful comparison or analysis. Further research is needed in this area. In a way, the fluctuation in these figures as well as continued changes in the definitions is a reflection of the state of chaos in the area of social policy in these countries. This calls for a comprehensive plan for social welfare programs in the CE countries.

VI. International Trade

To strengthen their market and benefit from freer trade, CE countries have focussed on trade liberalization and trade diversification. This includes their desire to attract foreign direct investment and capital inflow.[25] Table 8 reports on direct foreign investment in the CE countries over time. Once again the numbers for Poland are most revealing. Between 1988 and 1990, direct investment in Poland only increased about five-fold. More recently, direct investment in Poland has increased by about fifty percent between 1990 and 1996. Hungary experienced a rate of growth of thirty-five percent in direct investment between 1991 and 1996, still an impressive performance. Meanwhile, Czech Republic and Slovak Republic show an increase of more than one hundred percent and forty percent in direct investment between 1993 and 1996, respectively. Clearly, Czech Republic, as in many other areas, has outperformed Slovak Republic. In general it can be concluded from the data reported in Table 8 that these economies have been successful in attracting investment after the transition.

Table 8: Foreign Direct Investment in CEE Countries (Millions of US Dollars)

	Year					
Country	**1988**	**1990**	**1992**	**1993**	**1994**	**1996**
Poland	15	89	678	1715	1875	4498
Hungary	----	----	1479	2350	1144	1982
Czech Rep	----	----	----	654	878	1435
Slovak Rep	----	----	----	199	203	281

Source: International Monetary Fund, *Balance of Payments Statistics Yearbook*, 1994 and 1997.

Besides their desire to attract foreign investment, data for transition economies shows a significant change in the direction of trade for these countries. Tables 9a-9d provide statistics on the direction of trade for the sample countries. Soviet-bloc in these tables refers to the former Soviet-bloc countries plus Turkey, Cyprus and Malta. Given that the percentage of trade between CE countries and these last three countries is negligible, we use the figures for Europe as proxies for the Soviet bloc. The group of industrial countries, on the other hand, includes the OECD countries.

Figures in Table 9a show that Poland's volume of trade was almost equally split between Europe and industrial countries in 1988 (42 and 44 percent of the total trade, respectively). Immediately after transition, in 1990, the direction of trade changed significantly in favor of industrialized countries. Since then Poland has continued to increase its trade with the industrialized countries. Most recently, 73 percent of its total trade is with these countries. Meanwhile, the share of trade with the former Soviet bloc countries has dropped from the high of 42 percent to 21 percent of the total trade by the end of the period reported in Table 9a.

A very similar pattern of trade is observed for Hungary as that of Poland. Table 9b shows that trade with Soviet-bloc and Industrial countries made up 45 and 40 percent of Hungary's total trade in 1988. In 1990, a relatively significant shift in the direction of trade occurred. Trade with the Soviet-bloc dropped to 32 percent of the total while trade with industrial countries rose to 55 percent. Since 1990 the proportion of trade with the former Soviet bloc countries has continuously declined while the reverse has occurred in trade with the industrialized countries. As of 1996,

Hungary's trade with the industrialized countries makes up 70 percent of its total trade, a very significant proportion. Meanwhile, trade with the former Soviet bloc countries has stabilized at around 20 to 25 percent range of the total trade.

Tables 9c and 9d report on the direction of trade for Czech Republic and Slovak Republic, respectively. Before the division of Czechoslovakia, 56 percent of total trade was with the Soviet- bloc countries; the highest among our sample countries. However, this percentage was reduced to 44 percent in 1990 while trade with the industrialized countries rose from 36 percent of the total in 1988 to 48 percent in 1990. After the division of Czechoslovakia in 1993, the two newly formed countries followed a somewhat differing pattern of trade. While Czech Republic managed to increase its trade with the industrialized countries of the west (61 percent of total trade in 1994 was with this group), the data for Slovak Republic point to a trend toward more trade with the former Soviet-bloc countries. In 1994 Slovak Republic's share of trade with the newly formed market economies rose to 56 percent of the total trade while the same percentage for industrialized countries dropped to 39. Although the situation has somewhat reversed in 1996, Slovak Republic is still one of the transition economies that has more reliance on trade with the former Soviet-bloc countries as compared with the rest of the industrialized world.

The observed difference in trade directions for the two newly formed republics requires further elaboration. This observed divergence can be partly explained in terms of differing industrial base, political and economic circumstances and the level of overall regional economic growth and performance prior to separation. Slovak Republic inherited a large number of obsolete factories and industries, mainly in military hardware production. This type of industry was structurally connected to a pro-Soviet foreign policy that Czechoslovakia rejected after 1989. Czech Republic, on the other hand, enjoyed the advantage of many functional industries such as banking, tourism and smaller industries. All these have helped Czech Republic in expanding its trade with the industrialized countries. As a result, Czech Republic has managed to enjoy a relatively higher rate of economic growth since 1993.

These significant shifts in the direction of trade for CE countries should come as no surprise. These are mostly due to the desire on the part of western countries to ensure economic success for the CE countries. For example, Pollard (1994) states that "as these countries undertook political and economic reforms, the United States reduced its tariff restrictions on their products" (p. 25). Meanwhile, the transitional economies, in turn, " . . . liberalized their trading environments by eliminating quotas, harmonizing tariffs, and permitting the convertibility of their currencies" (p. 36). Other developed countries, following the United States' lead, have reduced their trade restrictions with CE countries thus facilitating higher trade with western countries since 1990. All these along with the collapse of the Soviet-bloc caused a significant shift in the direction of trade for the CE countries.[26]

Based on the foregoing, the following general observations can be made. First, before transition, the CE countries relied heavily on trade with then Soviet-bloc countries. Second, this reliance was reversed immediately after 1990 and trade volumes with industrial countries began to rise at the expense of the Soviet-bloc nations. Third, although not reported here, since the beginning of transition, the shift in the direction of trade from the Soviet-bloc countries has resulted in a relative increased trade with other non-industrialized countries and developing nations as well.

Openness, defined as the total exports and imports divided by GDP, has long been used as a variable representing the degree of economic development and growth. Abizadeh and Yousefi (1985) observe that the trend in the international sector of a country "is an obvious indicator of the economic well-being of a country. A higher volume of international trade has been treated favorably in economic development literature" (p. 739). Openness is also used as an index of international trade volume.

Table 10 provides statistical information on the international trade sector for our sample countries. Specifically, Table 10 gives information on the degree of openness defined as the ratio of total of exports and imports as a percentage of GDP. Concentrating on the openness ratio for Poland, an interesting story emerges. This ratio was at its peak (54%) in 1980. It dropped to around 30% for most of the period prior to transition and rose immediately in 1990 (the year the transition took place). It has remained at that high ratio and showed some strength in 1995 (the last year data are available). Clearly, Poland would have been in a position during the 1980s to expand and benefit from its trade with the rest of the world. However, restrictions imposed by the Soviet-led regime not only discouraged freer trade but imposed such limitations that it reduced reliance on trade during the 1980s. Once these restrictions (political and economic) were lifted, Poland took advantage of its potential and engaged in a more aggressive international trade policy.

Table 10 shows, more or less, a similar pattern of international trade for Hungary as the one for Poland. Here too, the peak of the openness ratio was reached in 1980 (80%) followed by a decrease until 1991, then the trend was reversed with minor fluctuations. The figures reported for Czech Republic and Slovak Republic in Table 10 show that the openness ratio during the 1980s reached its peak in 1984 and then, more or less stabilized before beginning to decline until 1990. Right after the transition, in 1991, the ratio began to rise. The ratios reported all point to a significant rise in openness for both countries after transition and later after separation.

The foregoing suggest that, in addition to their desire to attract investment and a deliberate attempt to expand trade in their quest for trade liberalization as a prerequisite for market reform, transition economies have experienced increased overall trade. This is particularly due to: a) the collapse of the Counsel for Mutual Economic Assistant (CMEA) because of market pricing and the settlement of accounts in convertible currencies instead of currencies tied to the Soviet ruble; b) the need for western capital and technologies; and c) access to foreign exchange desperately needed to import western know-how.[27]

The general observation is that under their old systems of government, CE countries did not take full advantage of their ability to exploit the benefits of trade. Once transition got underway, with the help of the international community, these countries have managed to promote their trade by opening up their borders and lifting unnecessary restrictions. Although data for most recent years are not reported yet, it is speculated that this reliance on trade will continue to grow for several reasons. First, these countries are in need of more western technology and know-how to continue

Table 9a: Direction of Trade for Poland (in millions of US Dollars)

Year	Region	Exports(X)	Imports(M)	(X+M) Region	(X+M) Total	(X+M)Region as % of Total (X+M)
1988	**Soviet-bloc**	**5519**	**5911**	**11430**	27378	**42**
	Ind. Countries	6057	6070	12127		44
1990	**Soviet-bloc**	**3418**	**2509**	**5927**	22040	**27**
	Ind. Countries	8815	5722	14537		66
1992	**Soviet-bloc**	**2247**	**2598**	**4845**	29025	**17**
	Ind. Countries	9016	10596	19612		68
1994	**Soviet-bloc**	**2584**	**3096**	**5680**	38425	**15**
	Ind. Countries	12937	16139	29076		76
1996	**Soviet-bloc**	**5240**	**5942**	**11182**	53490	**21**
	Ind. Countries	17503	21452	38955		73

Source: International Monetary Fund, *Directions of Trade Statistics Yearbook*, 1995 and 1997.
Notes: Europe includes all the former Soviet bloc countries plus Turkey, Cyprus and Malta. Industrial countries includes all OECD countries.

Table 9b: Direction of Trade for Hungary (in millions of US Dollars)

Year	Region	Exports(X)	Imports(M)	(X+M) Region	(X+M) Total	(X+M)Region as % of Total (X+M)
1988	**Soviet-bloc**	**4529**	**3970**	**8499**	18821	**45**
	Ind. Countries	3694	3869	7563		40
1990	**Soviet-bloc**	**3284**	**2622**	**5906**	18171	**32**
	Ind. Countries	5050	4923	9973		55
1992	**Soviet-bloc**	**2690**	**3163**	**5853**	21803	**27**
	Ind. Countries	7381	7307	14688		67
1994	**Soviet-bloc**	**2255**	**3253**	**5508**	25171	**22**
	Ind. Countries	7575	10175	17750		70
1996	**Soviet-bloc**	**3242**	**3976**	**7218**	28582	**25**
	Ind. Countries	9065	11054	20119		70

Source: International Monetary Fund, *Directions of Trade Statistics Yearbook*, 1995 and 1997.
Notes: See table 9a.

Table 9c: Direction of Trade for the Czech Republic (in millions of US Dollars)

Year	Region	Exports(X)	Imports(M)	(X+M) Region	(X+M) Total	(X+M)Region as % of Total (X+M)
1988	**Soviet-bloc**	**8077**	**8323**	**16400**	29457	**56**
	Ind. Countries	4909	5655	10564		36
1990	**Soviet-bloc**	**5168**	**5762**	**10930**	24899	**44**
	Ind. Countries	5243	6626	11869		48
1992	**Soviet-bloc**	**3139**	**4021**	**7160**	23304	**31**
	Ind. Countries	7799	7872	15671		67
1994	**Soviet-bloc**	**4456**	**4270**	**8726**	29143	**30**
	Ind. Countries	8248	9415	17663		61
1996	**Soviet-bloc**	**6697**	**7535**	**14232**	48747	**29**
	Ind. Countries	13768	13493	27261		56

Source: International Monetary Fund, *Directions of Trade Statistics Yearbook*, 1995 and 1997.
Notes: Figures used for 1998, 1990 and 1992 are those of Czechoslovakia. Also see note in Table 9a.

Table 9d: Direction of Trade for the Slovak Republic (in millions of US Dollars)

Year	Region	Exports(X)	Imports(M)	(X+M) Region	(X+M) Total	(X+M)Region as % of Total (X+M)
1988	**Soviet-bloc**	**8077**	**8323**	**16400**	29457	**56**
	Ind. Countries	4909	5655	10264		36
1990	**Soviet-bloc**	**5168**	**5762**	**10930**	24899	**44**
	Ind. Countries	5243	6626	11869		48
1992	**Soviet-bloc**	**3139**	**4021**	**7160**	23304	**31**
	Ind. Countries	7799	7872	15671		67
1994	**Soviet-bloc**	**3729**	**3688**	**7417**	13085	**56**
	Ind. Countries	2552	2607	5159		39
1996	**Soviet-bloc**	**4547**	**5493**	**10040**	19128	**52**
	Ind. Countries	3906	4734	8640		45

Source: International Monetary Fund, *Directions of Trade Statistics Yearbook*, 1995 and 1997.
Notes: See Table 9c.

Table 10: Degree of Openness ((X+M)/GDP)

Year	Poland	Hungary	Czech Rep.	Slovac Rep.
1980	.54	.80	.59	.59
1982	.33	.76	.66	.66
1984	.30	.82	.72	.72
1986	.32	.78	.60	.60
1988	.39	.67	.58	.58
1990	.41	.55	.56	.56
1991	.40	.64	.63	.63
1992	.35	.58	--	--
1993	.38	.55	.83	.98
1994	.42	.60	.81	.95
1995	.42	--	.99	1.00

Source: International Monetary Fund (CD-ROM 1997). CD-ROM 1994 was used for Czechoslovakia.
Note: Figures for 1980-1991 for the Czech and Slovak Republics are those of Czechoslovakia.

their economic progress. Second, with economic progress and change will come a higher standard of living and more demand for foreign-made products, especially those produced in western countries, leading to increased imports. Third, as the economies of CE continue to grow, and their industries become able to benefit from economies of scale and decreasing cost due to trade, they will develop comparative advantage in those industries resulting in increased exports.

VII. CONCLUDING SUMMARY

This chapter focussed on a comparative analysis of pre- and post-communism in Central Eastern Europe (CE) countries using Poland, Hungary and Czechoslovakia and later the Czech and Slovak Republics as its sample countries.

When assessing the overall performance of these countries it becomes evident that while major economic indicators followed a more or less stable pattern during the communism era this stability was immediately disturbed after these countries abandoned communism and tried to join the capitalist club. The U-shaped pattern of the GDP growth rate since 1990 is most noteworthy. The main reason for the decline in the rate of growth is the collapse of the system while subsequent recovery can be mainly attributed to the opportunities brought about by globalization and the help received from international organizations such as the IMF.

Although traditional analysis of unemployment and inflation cannot be readily applied to these countries, nonetheless existing theoretical models can provide some helpful tools. The rates of unemployment and inflation will not follow a similar pattern as those in the capitalist world. During both pre- and post-communism, the economic and political circumstances prevailing in these countries make difficult the application of traditional, or even the expectation - augmented – Phillips - curve. However, with judicious application, some generalizations can be made. While unemployment was not recognized during communism, our analysis confirms that it followed an inverted U-shaped pattern during the post-communism era. Once again, this pattern can be explained by the collapse of the system followed by appropriate stabilization policies with the help of the international community. Of particular importance is the assistance of the IMF in reversing the trends of high unemployment in these countries.

While these countries enjoyed stable prices under communism, they experienced a significant level of price fluctuation right after the change. Since neither unemployment nor inflation were market-driven in these countries, the relationship between these two variables does not provide us with a concrete basis for theoretical analysis.

With the collapse of communism came the neglect and lack of interest in social programs in these countries. Governments, by concentrating on the goal of high growth, did not spend enough time or energy either to maintain the existing social programs or reform them to fit the newly established capitalist economies. As a result, much needs to be done in this area in order to prevent the total collapse of their "social safety net."

Economic transition began when the international community was embracing globalization and emphasizing global competition. This environment helps the transitional economies to readily join the expanding international trade market. Their attempt led to a significant inflow of foreign investment as well as expanded trade (imports and exports). Increase share of trade with the industrial countries has helped their economies and resulted in access to technical know-how needed for development and growth.

The overall increase in trade has been a major factor in the relative level of success enjoyed by these countries.

ENDNOTES

*I would like to thank my research assistants Paul Grower and Karen Buhr for their excellent work in compiling the data for this study.

1. See, IMF (1996) for further discussion on these approaches.
2. Note that the sharp decline in real GDP (US Dollars), reported in Table 2, is due to the devaluation of currencies immediately following transition and continuing thereafter. This supports the notion that exchange rates set by the governments under planned economic systems were artificially kept high and overvalued.
3. To maintain consistency, when calculating the numbers in Table 3, the GDP for Czech Republic and Slovak Republic were added for 1993 (the year when the two countries decided to separate) and then after. The average rate of growth for Czech Republic between 1993 and 1996 is understandably higher than the same for Slovak Republic by a small margin. See Table 1, columns 4 and 5.
4. There are many reasons given for the relative success of the Czech and Slovak Republics, particularly the former, compared with the rest of transition economies. Among them is a fortunate expansion of tourism. As a result, the average rate of growth for Czech Republic between 1993 and 1996 is understandably higher than the same figures for Slovak Republic by a small margin. See Table 1, columns 4 and 5.
5. For details on measurement issues, see, Chu and Schwartz (1994, pp. 10-11) and Blanchard (1997, pp. 535-36).
6. The two issues of unemployment and inflation will be discussed in details in the following section.
7. See Blanchard (1996, pp. 117-18) for detail.

8. Chu and Schwartz (1994, p. 4) also provide a comprehensive list of factors underlying the decline in output of transition countries.

9. Ideally, it would have been more helpful to use the number of political parties registered in these countries. This information was not readily available. For example, Poland has not registered its political parties after 1990 at all.

10. See Economist (1994, p. 27) for more details.

11. See Koen and De Masi (1997, p. 5). They provide a comprehensive and detailed analysis of price levels in transition economies.

12. Note that the figures used for the Czech and Slovak Republics from 1980 to 1993 are those of the former Czechoslovakia. This is true for Figures 5c and 5d.

13. See Mondschean and Opiela (1997, p.17) for details.

14. With liberalization of prices, lifting of trade barriers and the introduction of a market-oriented exchange rate, prices began to move toward international price levels in these countries. This convergence is not complete yet and it will take a while before prices, particularly for tradable goods, are essentially the same in transition economies as those in other western industrialized countries. See, Koen and De Masi (197) for details on this.

15. See Abizadeh and Yousefi (1998) for the review of literature. Also, see Bulir and Guldewolf (1995) and Fischer (1993) and Fischer et al. (1996) for differing points of view.

16. This, more than anything else, is due to the unique characteristics of CE countries and the extremely high rates of inflation at the beginning of their move toward liberalization.

17. For discussion of these policies see, Bogetic and Fox (1993) and Enev and Koford (1996).

18. This issue will be discussed in more detail later.

19. See Abizadeh and Gray (1985) for more detailed discussion on this issue.

20. See Abizadeh (1979) for support of these views.

21. See Chu and Gupta (1995) for more details on these programs.

22. See http://www.ifs.unirie.ac.at/~uncjin/profiles/ for reference. Murrell (1996, p. 39) gives support to this. A recent surge in petty and violent crimes in Prague is an obvious result of such neglect.

23. For further support, see Murrel (1996) pp. 35-36.

24. Note that the introduction of any social welfare system can result in some distortive effects in the market.

25. In order for the flow of capital to take place at an acceptable rate, CE countries not only need to establish a proper market structure but a clearly defined set of rules regarding property rights as well as some sort of guarantee protecting against the possibility of nationalization and other related risks. For a comprehensive analysis of property rights issues see Rapaczynski (1996).

26. Havrylyshyn and Al-Atrash (1998) provide a comprehensive and detailed analysis of trends in international trade in transition economies.

27. Pollard (1994) provides more details on these issues.

REFERENCES

Abizadeh, S., and M. Yousefi, (1998) "Deficit and Inflation: An Open Economy Model of the United States", *Applied Economics*, (forthcoming).

Abizadeh, S. and J. Gray (1985), "Wagner's Law: A Pooled Time Series Cross-Section Comparison," *National Tax Journal*, 38:209-218.

Abizadeh S. and M. Yousefi, (1985), "International Trade and Economic Development: An Empirical Analysis", *International Review of Economics and Business*, 32:735-749.

Abizadeh, S., (1979), "Tax Ratio and the Degree of Economic Development," *Malayan Economic Review*, 24:21-34.

Blanchard, O., (1997), *Macroeconomics*, Prentice Hall: Upper Saddle River, New Jersey.

Blanchard, O., (1996) "Theoretical Aspects of Transition", *American Economic Review, Papers and Proceedings of the Hundred & Eight Annual Meeting*, 86:117-122.

Blanchard, O., S. Commander and F. Coricelli, (1994), "Unemployment in Eastern Europe", *Finance and Development*, December: 6-9

Bogetic, Z., and L. Fox, (1993), "Income Policy During Stabilization: A Review and Lessons from Bulgaria and Rumania," *Comparative Economic Studies*, 35:55-64.

Bulir, A. and A. Guldewolf, (1995), "Inflation and Income Distribution: Further Evidence on the Empirical Link," *International Monetary Fund Working Papers*, WP/95/86.

Chu, K. and S. Gupta (1996), "Social Protection is Transition Countries: Emerging Issues," No. 96/5 in the *International Monetary Fund Papers on Policy Analysis and Assessment (PPAA) Series*.

Chu, K. and G. Schwartz, "Output Decline and Government Expenditures in European Transition Economies," *International Monetary Fund Working Papers*, WP/94/68.

Economist, (1994), "The Czech Republic: Bohemians," *The Economist*, October 2nd:23-27.

Enev, T. and K. Koford, (1996), "Income Policies in Bulgaria and Poland," Paper presented at the *Annual Meeting of the Eastern Economic Association*, March 15-17.

Fischer, S. (1993), "The Role of Macroeconomic Factors in Growth," *Journal of Monetary Economics*, 32:485-512.

Fischer, S., R. Sahay, and C.A. Végh, (1996), "Stabilization and Growth in Transition Economies: The Early Experience", *Journal of Economic Perspectives*, 10:45-66.

Ghosh, A.R., (1997), "Inflation in Transition Economies: How Much? and Why?" *International Monetary Funds Working Paper*, WP/97/80.

Havrylyshyn, O. and H. Al-Atrash, (1998), " Opening Up and Geographic Diversification of Trade in Transition Economies," *International Monetary Fund Working Papers*, WP/98/22.

Ingham, M., and K. Grima, (1994), "Regional Unemployment in Central and Eastern Europe," *Regional Studies*, 28.8: 11-817.

International Monetary Fund, (1997), *IMF Survey*, April 27.

International Monetary Fund, (1996), "From Plan to Market", *World Development Report*, Washington, DC.

International Monetary Fund, (various Issues of CDs and hard copies), *International Financial Statistics*, Washington, DC.

Koen, V. and P. DeMasi, (1997), "Prices in Transition: Ten Stylized Facts," *International Monetary Funds Working Paper*. WP/97/158.

Kopits, G. and E. Offerdal, (1994), "Fiscal Policy in Transition Economies: A Major Challenge," *Finance and Development*, December: 10-13.

Koranai, J., (1997), "The Reform of the Welfare State and Public Opinion," The *American Economic Review, Papers and Proceedings*, 87:339-343.

Leijonhufvud, A. and C. Rühl, (1997), "Russian Dilemmas," *American Economic Review, Papers and Proceedings*, 87:344-48.

Milanovic, B., (1995), "Poverty, Inequality and Social Policy in Transition Economies," *World Bank Research Paper Series*, No. 9, Washington, D.C., World Bank, April.

Mondschean, T. S., and T.P. Opiela , (1997), "Banking Reform in a Transition Economy, The Case of Poland," *Economic Perspectives*, Federal Reserve Bank of Chicago, March/April, pp.16-32.

Murrell, P., (1996), " How Far Has the Transition Progressed?" *Journal of Economic Perspectives*, 10:25-44.

Olson, M., Jr. (1995), "Why the Transition From Communism is so Difficult," *Eastern Economic Journal*, 21:437-461.

Paterson, D.M., (1996), "Reform in Eastern Europe: A General Equilibrium Model with Distortions in Relative Prices and Factor Markets," *Canadian Journal of Economics*, 29:457-72.

Pollard, P.S., (1994), " Trade Between the United States and Eastern Europe," *The Federal Reserve Bank of St. Louis Review*, 76: 25-45.

Rapaczynski, A., (1996), " The Role of The State and the Market in Establishing Property Rights," *Journal of Economic Perspectives*, 10:87-103

Rosefielde, S., (1995), "Eastern European Economic Reform: Transition or Mutation?," *Atlantic Economic Journal*, 23:323-332.

CHAPTER 3

THE ECONOMIC PROGRESS OF SELECTED TRANSITION ECONOMIES

KAREN S. VORST

I. INTRODUCTION

The emerging market economies of Central Europe have witnessed tremendous change since 1989. Their transition from Soviet-style economies to the market system has been both a burden and a blessing. Unemployment, especially in the industrial sector, has hurt many people, throwing them out of jobs that previously had guaranteed employment. Inflation hit record levels in the early 1990s and is still problematic for some countries. Governments had to find an effective way to transfer state-owned property to the private sector, write or rewrite the laws regarding private property rights and bankruptcy, and grapple with underdeveloped banking systems and capital markets. Issues regarding currency convertibility, balance of trade deficits, foreign competition, government budget deficits, and insufficient capital needed to be addressed.

Despite differing initial conditions in the transition economies of Central Europe and the problems they experienced, much progress has been made. The rates of both unemployment and inflation have tended downward. Economic growth turned from their initial negative rates to positive rates by 1994 in most of these countries. Progress has been made in the privatization process. The banking sector is emerging and stock exchange activities are growing.

This chapter discusses the economic progress of four selected transition countries: Poland, Hungary, Czech Republic and Slovak Republic. These countries have a long, established economic relationship and have traded with each other for centuries. Because of their location and established trade patterns, their economies inevitably affect one another. Some economists believe that these economies will be among the first to succeed in the transitional process. These countries have already positioned their economies to join the European Union (EU) and they are likely to succeed in being admitted in the near future.

Section II provides an update on the performance of each economy with the most recent information available. We analyze the privatization methods used by each country and indicate the progress made in various economic sectors in Section III. Section IV examines the changing nature of the financial systems in these countries and looks at capital market developments, including stock exchanges. Section V contains a summary and conclusions.

II. Macroeconomic Performance

First we should note that broad-based, macroeconomic numbers for these countries are not strictly comparable, since each country's economy was run somewhat differently under Communism, essentially making the initial conditions in 1989 unequal. For example, Poland's farms are mostly family-owned and, therefore, already privatized in 1989. This stands in stark contrast to the large, state-run collective farms in the former Czechoslovakia. Unlike other countries, Hungary had many private businesses that were allowed to operate before 1989. Each country adopted its own pace of transition and each has experienced problems along the way. Despite differing initial conditions at the beginning of the transition, it is useful to examine the macroeconomic numbers in order to understand the present state of each economy. A collection of these numbers is in Table 1.

Poland's economy has experienced considerable improvement from the early 1990s. Its real GDP growth increased every year since 1991 when it was -7.0%, reaching 7.0% in 1995 and 6.4% in 1997. The unemployment rate increased from 6.5% in 1990 to a peak of 16.4% in 1993 before falling to 10.7% in 1997. Poland's growth and continued progress in reducing unemployment made it the first emerging economy in the region to produce in 1995 beyond its 1989 level.

The Polish consumer price index decreased from its extremely high level of 640.3% in 1989 to a relatively modest 13.5% expected for 1997. This significant progress on inflation may be attributed to a monetary policy that has focused on inflation via controlling the money supply and to a decreasing need to assist in financing government programs. The government budget deficit has been 3.0% of GDP or less since 1992.[1] While both unemployment and inflation have been falling, they remain above the levels of the EU. However, the post-Communist regime of Aleksander Kwasniewski remains committed to the market system transition and further economic progress is expected.

Economic growth in Hungary has lagged somewhat behind that of some of its neighbors. It too experienced negative rates of growth during the 1990-92 period.

While the rates have been positive since 1993, the 1.0% increase in 1996 was the smallest of the group. The unemployment rate decreased from a peak of 13.2% in 1993 to 10.5% in 1996.

Contributing to slower growth and keeping the unemployment level in double digits was the ongoing significant restructuring of industries and agriculture. In addition, household consumption rates were negative or very near zero for most of 1990s thus far.

Inflation has been a continual problem in Hungary and little progress is visible. The inflation rate in 1991 was 35.0%, falling to 18.8% in 1994, but increasing again to 23.6% in 1996. Industry saw costs increase due to increasing nominal wages, higher energy costs and higher costs of imports. In addition, much of the cost of industrial restructuring was borne by the industries themselves as government subsidies were cut. The National Bank of Hungary continues to have inflation control as its main monetary policy goal and it uses exchange rates as its main tool.[2]

Table 1: Basic Macroeconomic Variables, Selected Central European Emerging Economies, 1989-1997

	1989	1990	1991	1992	1993	1994	1995	1996	1997
GDP (% change, real)									
Poland	0.2	-11.6	-7.0	2.6	3.8	5.2	7.0	6.1	6.4
Hungary	-	-3.3	-11.3	-3.1	-0.6	2.9	1.5	1.0	-
Czech Republic	1.4	-0.4	-14.2	-7.1	-0.9	2.7	5.9	4.1	-
Slovak Republic	-	-2.5	-11.2	-7.0	-3.7	4.9	6.8	6.9	6.0
Unemployment Rate									
Poland	-	6.5	12.2	14.3	16.4	16.0	14.9	13.2	10.7
Hungary	-	0.4	1.9	7.8	13.2	10.4	10.4	10.5	-
Czech Republic	-	1.0	6.6	5.1	3.5	3.2	2.9	3.5	-
Slovak Republic	-	1.6	11.8	10.4	14.4	14.8	13.8	12.4	13.1
Inflation Rate									
Poland (CPI)	640.3	249.3	60.4	44.3	37.6	29.5	21.6	18.5	13.5
Hungary	-	28.9	35.0	23.0	22.5	18.8	28.2	23.6	-
Czech Republic (CPI)	2.1	12.3	53.6	11.5	18.2	10.2	9.1	8.8	-
Slovak Republic (CPI)	-	10.0	61.2	10.1	23.2	13.4	9.9	5.8	6.1

Source:: *Poland: International Economic Report, 1995/96*, World Economy Research Institute, Warsaw School of Economics, 1996; p. 29; *Annual Report* of the National Bank of Hungary, 1996; *Annual Report* of the National Bank of Slovakia, 1995 and 1996; *Annual Report* of the National Bank of Czech Republic, 1995; and selected papers in *Financial Market Restructuring in Selected Central European Countries*, K. Vorst and W. Wehmeyer, eds., Ashgate Publishing, 1998.

The Czech Republic saw its rate of growth increase fairly steadily from -0.9% in 1993,[3] to the 5.9% increase in 1995, though estimates were 4.1% for 1996. The unemployment rate has remained fairly low relative to others in the region, inching down from 3.5% in 1993 to 2.9% in 1995, before increasing to 3.5% in 1996. This relatively low rate may be attributed in part to an effective government program that helped workers who were displaced due to market restructuring and privatization efforts to become re-employed in the private sector. However, it should be noted that the most recent growth rate and unemployment rate numbers were moving in ways that would be unacceptable if the trends continued and indications are that GDP will decline in 1997-98 and unemployment increase.

Consumer prices decreased dramatically from the high of 18.2% in 1993 to 8.8% at the end of 1996, despite rates of growth of the money supply that averaged over 20% from 1992-1995, and decreased to 14% in 1996. The Czech National Bank (CNB) attributes the lower inflation rates in part to a decrease in income velocity and to their policy of using a fixed exchange rate regime as their policy anchor. The CNB has not had to become involved in government deficit financing since, unlike other transition countries, Czech Republic has had a surplus or near-balance in its state budget.[4]

The Slovak Republic experienced a difficult first year of independence in 1993 but has seen much improvement since then. Economic growth was -4.1% in 1993, which really was a continuation of its early 1990's negative growth rates. In fact, from 1990 to 1993, its growth rate was -23.7%. Clearly, the 6.9% growth rate in 1996 and 6.0% in 1997 were good news, though the country in 1996 was still performing below its 1989 level. While growth rates recently have been between 6-7%, the unemployment rate has varied between 13% and 15% since 1993, due primarily to significant restructuring in the industrial sector.

Slovak inflation fell substantially from a high of 25.1% in 1993 to 6.1% in 1997, due in part to steep declines in food prices and to cuts in the basic rate of the value added tax in 1996. The National Bank of Slovakia (NBS) has inflation control as its main policy goal and uses a fixed exchange rate regime together with the monetary aggregates as its policy tools. The NBS has had trouble in the past controlling the monetary aggregates because of the role that the NBS must play in financing government deficits. The deficits in the state's budget, as a percent of GDP, have consistently been between 3% and 7%, with the 1996 deficit down to 4.4% of GDP. However, the NBS's share of the country's internal debt in 1996 was 21.8%, down from previous years.[5]

It should be noted that the first years of transition were the most difficult for these economies. Markets had to be established where they previously had not existed. Growth rates in all of these economies were negative in 1990 and, with the exception of Poland, remained negative until at least 1994. Employment and subsidies to industries were no longer immediately guaranteed in many sectors. After over 40 years of living in a centrally-planned economy, participants were not likely to adjust automatically and without difficulty to a new system. Unemployment was now a reality and, for those affected, it was a true hardship that left some asking, "Why do we need these changes? At least before 1989, we had a job."

Governments that experienced internal division over the direction taken or the methods and/or speed of advancement to a market system were likely to have the most problems in the transition. The Slovak government, for example, after participating in a first wave of coupon privatization initiated through a united Czechoslovak government, cancelled the second wave of coupon privatization in 1995. While this program was replaced by a bond program, there was indication that the privatization process had slowed considerably in 1997. The biggest Slovak banks have yet to be privatized. These actions have not helped the overall movement toward a market system. Even governments, such as those of Poland and Hungary, that were committed to the change were not exempt from facing significant difficulties. The inflation rate in both countries was close to 20% for a number of years.

In all of these countries, industrial output and/or real wages in 1995 were below, and in some cases significantly below, their 1989 levels. For example, industrial output in 1995 in Czech Republic and in Slovak Republic was 31.0% and 36.3%, respectively, below their 1989 levels. Real wages in 1995 in Poland, Hungary and Slovakia were 18.0%, 21.0% and 21.8%, respectively, below their 1989 levels. In 1995, Poland became the first transition economy in Central Europe to see its GDP level go above its 1989 level. While growth rates of GDP in the other countries have been positive and rising recently, the actual levels of GDP in 1995 were still below their 1989 levels: Hungary's 1995 GDP level was still 16.9% less, Czech Republic's 1995 GDP level was 15.9% less and Slovakia's was 18.0% less. On a more positive side, all countries in 1995 had higher levels of both exports and imports than they had in 1989 (*Poland, 1995/96*, pp. 31,37), though some have experienced trade deficits in recent years. Many of these numbers clearly indicate that these countries have suffered economic hardship, especially during the period 1989-1993. However, improvements clearly have been made since 1993. If current trends continue as expected, further advancements should be forthcoming.

III. Privatization: Methods and Issues

One of the most difficult tasks in the transition process was to find a way to transfer state-owned property to the private sector. There were various methods available and no one method was necessarily right for all countries. Most countries used a combination of methods and made changes in them as needed. Some countries faced a larger-scale privatization process than others. For example, the state's share of value added production in commercial and industrial operations amounted to 97% in Czechoslovakia in 1986, 81.7% in Poland in 1985 and 65.2% in Hungary in 1984 (Fischer, 1992, pp. 229-230). While all have made considerable progress toward their privatization goals, the transfer process is ongoing in all of these countries.

Poland's privatization plans employed a variety of methods. The sale of small-scale businesses was encouraged at the outset so that by early 1991 an estimated 70% of the small-scale retail and service outlets had been sold (Scott, 1992, p. 282). The medium- and large-scale firms, however, would take more time.

Beginning in 1991, large-scale enterprises (especially those in financial trouble and without ready buyers) were to be part of a mass privatization effort. Under this plan, groups of companies were packaged together and eventually run by one of fifteen National Investment Funds (NIF), that went into operation in 1994. There are 512 companies participating in the NIF program, representing about 8% of the sales and productive assets of the corporate sector.[6]

By the end of 1996, Poland had over 2 million individual private businesses, 87,100 domestic companies and 28,600 joint-venture business (with foreign capital), not including about 2 million private farms. Private firms accounted for 60% of Poland's GDP in 1996 and employment in these private businesses amounted to 65% of the total labor force (Pulawski and Rapacki, 1998, p. 26). While these numbers have been growing over the years and the state's share has been declining, it is clear that the state still contributed significantly to overall GDP.

In a sense, Hungary had a head start on the other countries with regard to privatization since the state owned a smaller percentage, 65.2%, of commercial and industrial operations in 1984. Reform Communists as early as 1968 began a slow movement away from the strict system of central planning and outwardly embarked upon a gradual path toward capitalism in 1987. However, Hungary's full-scale privatization efforts did not begin until after 1989 and this country, like many others, encountered problems along the way and progress was delayed intermittently.

The sale of small-scale shops by the government was greatly encouraged and much progress has been made. Hungary's initial success in privatizing large enterprises outpaced that in other countries. A total of ten large-scale companies had been privatized by the end of March, 1991, for a value of approximately $100 million (Scott, 1992, p. 286). So-called 'spontaneous' privatizations, which occurred quite frequently in Hungary, were usually initiated by the firm's managers, though outsiders could also initiate a privatization project. The key to such deals was to acquire sufficient additional capital for the firm, whether from the managers themselves or from outside sources (not government sources). Foreign capital investors were greatly encouraged to participate. Such arrangements initially resulted in questionable 'sweetheart' deals and negative public reaction slowed the process. This negativism was short-circuited by the establishment by the government of the State Property Agency that would oversee the process and instill integrity into the system by implementing regulations and by approving or vetoing proposals. This agency continued to be busy into 1996 with the privatization process, managing assets valued at approximately HUF 1 trillion, of which HUF 300-400 billion of assets are to be retained by the state in the long run (*Annual Report*, NBH, 1996, p. 42. HUF = Hungarian Forint).

The former Czechoslovak economy was very rigidly structured in the Soviet style of central planning. The state produced more than 95 percent of the nation's output including nearly all of its agricultural products. In 1989, over 60 percent of its exports, mostly heavy machinery and other industrial goods, went to Soviet-bloc countries (*Annual Report*, NBH, 1996, p. 287). These economies were definitely intertwined and the undoing of this relationship in 1989 presented unique problems, privatization being just one of them. By 1991, however, the government had in place a series of laws that specified the procedures for privatization, as well as those for bankruptcies and liquidations. A National Property Fund was set up to oversee the privatization process.

Many of the same methods available to other countries were put to use in the former Czechoslovakia, including public auction, direct sales, public competitions, conversions of state enterprises to joint stock companies and voucher privatization. Foreign participation in public sales or auctions was encouraged.

When the country officially split into Czech Republic and Slovak Republic on January 1, 1993, privatization continued in each country using essentially the same methods that were put into place in 1991. By the end of 1995, Czech Republic had privatized approximately 93% of all property slated for large-scale privatization and this process was expected to be completed in 1996. The state's share of GDP in 1995 was approximately 36.2%, down significantly from the high of 95% in 1989 (*Annual Report*, CNB, 1995, pp. 15-16). At the same time, the state contributed 35.1% to the GDP of Slovak Republic (*Annual Report*, NBS, 1995, pp. 19). While both countries have experienced unique problems associated with their privatization programs, these numbers would indicate that both have made considerable progress in this area.

IV. Banking and Financial Sector Development

The effects of the transition to a market system on the banking and financial sectors have been quite dramatic. More banks have been set up and now provide a wider variety of products and services. Privately-run investment funds and insurance companies are new to many of these countries and stock exchanges have been developed in each country. In this section, we review the many changes that have taken place in the banking sector and in the capital markets of the four transition countries since 1989.

A. Banking System Developments

In all of these countries, the banking system was to be changed from a mono-bank system with the state dictating the allocation of credit to a two-tier system headed by a central bank. New regulations and accounting methods were needed in order to guide the banks toward reputable banking practices and to conform to international banking standards. While the number of private commercial banks has increased in all of these countries and banks now are able to provide a variety of services, the growth of many banks has been slowed by the burden of bad bank loans and the lack of sufficient working capital. Hungary's system began its transition in January, 1987. The enterprise-financing aspects of the National Bank of Hungary were separated from the central bank and became the new responsibility of three independent commercial banks. Other banks were eventually set up to specialize in providing services for development, foreign trade and investment. The National Savings Bank in Hungary, as well as a large number of savings cooperatives, collected deposits and extended home loans. The state was not involved in this process but rather the loans were made from the resources of the savers.

The number of banks operating in Hungary totaled 41 in 1996, an increase of 15 from 1989. Of this total, 33 are commercial banks, seven are specialized financial institutions and one is an investment bank. The five largest banks controlled 60% of the market in 1996, which would indicate a relatively lower degree of concentration than some smaller European Union countries. In addition to banks, savings cooperatives provide savings alternatives across the country. Though these institutions are relatively numerous with 248 of them in 1995, they are very small, amounting to just under 5% of the total financial institutions balance sheet figures (Botos, 1998, p. 86; *Annual Report*, NBH, 1996, p. 116).

While domestic ownership was preferred, relatively few domestic investors came forward. Therefore, most of the investors were foreign. Hungarian banks had the highest ratio of foreign ownership in Europe with a foreign share of 14.9% of total bank capital in 1994, a 34.7% share in 1995 and a 48.1% share in 1996. The state's share of ownership decreased from 66.8% in 1994 to 28.8% in 1996 (*Annual Report*, NBH, 1996, p. 116).

The dismantling of the mono-bank system in the former Czechoslovakia began in January, 1990, and followed the established pattern of forming a central bank and three separate commercial banks (Komfercní banka, Investiční banka and Vseobecna Uverová banka). These three commercial banks, two savings banks (one Czech and one Slovak) and one relatively small bank that specialized in foreign exchange activities (Živnostenská banka) comprised the entire banking system and were completely owned by the state. This configuration would change considerably in the following years with the establishment of new banks, both with and without foreign capital assistance.

The expansion of the Czechoslovak banking sector increased rapidly in 1991 to include 33 institutions, up from 11 at the end of 1990. Further growth was seen in 1992 when the total increased to 45, of which only 3 banks remained owned by the state, though these banks were the largest. About one-third of the banks was partially or wholly-owned by foreign investors (Miroslav, 1995, pp. 70-71)

The split of the country into two separate republics did not slow down bank expansion. By the end of 1995, there were 55 banks and foreign bank branches operating in Czech Republic. Foreigners were part or full owners in 31 commercial banks and building societies and operated 10 foreign bank branches. Only 13 commercial banks, a little less than one-fourth of the total, were entirely owned by domestic investors. As in other countries, the few, large banks dominate the market and possessed nearly 74% of total bank assets at the end of 1995 (*Annual Report*, CNB, 1995, p.100). These continue to be effectively controlled by the state. (In the 1998 election, the Social Democrats took a position of slowing the process of bank privatization.)

In Slovak Republic, there were 24 banks and 5 foreign bank branches in business at the end of 1996. Of the total, two banks were state owned, five were 100% foreign controlled, and 9 others had some foreign-owned capital. The remaining banks were completely controlled by domestic entities. Foreign capital in the banking sector amounted to 39.6% of total capital, with Czech Republic being the largest contributor of foreign capital (*Annual Report*, NBS, 1995, p. 81).

Serious banking restructuring began in Poland in 1991 with the transformation of nine of the branches of the National Bank of Poland into nine joint-stock commercial banks. With price liberalization, the freeing of interest rates, and a liberal licensing procedure, the number of banks increased rapidly to a high of around 100 in 1992. However, without sufficient capital and/or banking expertise, many of these banks did not survive. By the end of 1996, there were 88 banking organizations reporting to the National Bank of Poland operating in Poland, together with over 1550 small cooperative banks. Foreign capital helped to support 33 of the 77 banks and generated 23% of total bank revenues in 1995. A *de facto* moratorium on foreign bank entry into the Polish banking sector was issued in the early 1990s. The government preferred foreign banks to take over existing, troubled Polish banks, rather than licensing them for new banks, effectively shielding Polish banks from foreign competition. However, legislation in 1996 allowed for bank consolidation into more efficient banks, preparing the way for their survival when foreign restraints are lifted.

The state still has a significant presence in the banking sector, controlling 14 of the biggest Polish banks. In 1996, these banks held 75% of aggregate bank assets (down from 90% in 1989) and made a large share of total loans, resulting in a highly concentrated banking sector.[7]

One of the most serious issues facing the banking systems in these countries early in the transition period was the proportion of non-performing loans on the books of commercial banks. Though partially due to economic downturns experienced in the early 1990s, problem loans in the transition economies were mainly the result of collapsed markets, reduced governmental subsidies and restrictive policies that raised interest rates and prevented firms from servicing their debts. Solutions had to be devised that were tailored to each country's satisfaction.

In June, 1993, bad credits amount to approximately 31% of total credits in the nine leading Polish banks, up substantially from 19.8% in 1992. The bad debt problem of banks was addressed by Parliament in 1993 when it passed the Acts on Financial Restructuring of Enterprises and Banks. The so-called "bank conciliatory procedure" would permit part of the debt to be sold, converted to equity shares, or refinanced at lower interest rates. The Treasury could reduce tax arrears and the National Bank could provide needed funds. This program, which ended in 1995, reduced substantially the bad debt problem in Poland and its banks are on much more stable financial ground.

At the end of 1991, Hungarian banking law set in place a rating system for credits. There were four categories: standard, substandard, doubtful and bad debts. Based upon these ratings, banks were required to keep an appropriate level of reserves to support its debts. In addition, capital standards were raised from 7.25% of assets in 1992 to 8% by January, 1993. The loan-loss reserves provision and the higher capital standards, though representing a movement toward more sound banking practices, were quite steep. As a result, many banks were not able to meet these new requirements as they were struggling with a total level of substandard, doubtful and bad debts of approximately HUF 305.8 billion, or 25.6% of total debt, in December, 1992 (Nyers and Lutz, 1995, pp. 139-140).

The Hungarian government initially guaranteed approximately one-half of the bad credit that banks accumulated before 1987, allowing banks some additional time to accumulate loan-loss reserves. Part of the government's 1992 loan consolidation plan was the takeover of the non-performing loans of banks by the Hungarian Development and Investment Company, a state-run institution. In exchange for the bad assets, banks received special treasury bonds that helped to clean up their portfolios and ultimately would make them more attractive for privatization. An additional program in 1993 encouraged banks to work with firms in restructuring the debt or even canceling it. By this time, there were a number of private organizations that could buy bad loans at a discount. Banks that participated in this program could get capital directly from the government, thereby further improving their capital positions and increasing their saleability. By the end of 1996, the proportion of qualified loans (those needing special attention, substandard, doubtful or bad) decreased to 11% of total loans (Botos, 1998, p. 93).

In the former Czechoslovakia, as in Poland and in Hungary, the bad loan problem was difficult to identify. So-called "bad loans' may refer to (1) a relatively narrow class of loans that were non-performing and that displayed little chance of payment recovery; or (2) a broader classification of "qualified' loans that included non-performing, doubtful or questionable in some way. In Slovak Republic and Czech Republic, problem loans are called 'classified credits' which includes doubtful, substandard and loss-generating loans.

Early in their reform period, the former Czechoslovak government dealt with the bad loan problem by creating the Consolidation Bank that would receive the bad loans from banks and attempt the recovery of funds. This procedure greatly improved the balance sheets of existing banks and newly-created banks were not saddled with these loans, at least not initially. Due in part to the collapse of markets, the recession experienced in the Slovak and Czech Republics in the early 1990s, the inexperience of bank loan officers, and the reluctance on the part of the government to end enterprise subsidies altogether, 'classified credits' continued to be a significant proportion of total credits. In Czech Republic, classified credits increased from 23.6% of total credits in June, 1994, to 38.5% in June, 1995 (Matousek and Hrncir, 1995, p. 12). In Slovak Republic, classified credits decreased from 41.8% of total credits at the end of 1995, to 35.9% in June, 1997 (Komínková and Mučková, 1998, p. 214).

B. Capital Market Development

The development of an active capital market is critical to the expansion and growth of the rest of the entire economic system. A market for securities and stocks in these countries needed to be developed either by resurrecting previously closed stock exchanges or by starting markets from scratch. The successful privatization of state-run enterprises and banks depended upon capital markets to bring buyers and sellers together and to promote an orderly transfer of ownership to the private sector. These markets are instrumental in providing an avenue for capital expansion for banks and in enhancing the government's ability to finance its debt. The initial start-up costs may be extremely high, not just in terms of training market participants and installing new equipment but also the legal framework has to be put into place so that the market can perform with integrity according to a set of rules. The latter, in some cases, took years to formulate and delayed the development process.

In Poland, the Warsaw Stock Exchange (WSE) has been in operation for several years. The WSE had a somewhat rocky start and as recently as 1994, it "... could not be efficiently used as a tool by companies who were looking to raise funds to finance development. Weak market demand left many new issues in the hands of underwriters" (*Poland, 1995/96*, p. 106). However, as of September, 1997, there were 132 companies listed on the WSE, an increase of over 40 from 1996, with a total turnover of PLN 29.0 billion. In addition, there were "...49 entities running a brokerage firm, as well as 10 trust fund companies operating 23 trust funds. There were over 1500 registered securities brokers and nearly 100 individuals registered as advisors in public trading of securities" (Pulawski and Rapacki, 1998; PLN=new Polish zloty).

After a relatively slow beginning in 1990, the Budapest Stock Exchange (BSE) in Hungary grew significantly. In 1990, only corporate stocks were traded with a turnover value of HUF 6.1 billion. As government securities, investment bonds, corporate bonds and other instruments started to be traded in subsequent years, volume and market values greatly increased. By the end of 1996, turnover on the BSE was valued at HUF 1,145.4 billion, up substantially even from the 1995 total of HUF 253.2 billion. Treasury bills and bonds constituted 54.5% of total trading volume on the BSE in 1996, down from 62.5% in 1995 (*Annual Report*, NBH, 1996, pp. 126-127).

Investment funds in Hungary have been increasing in popularity. In 1995, the number of funds quoted on the BSE increased from 16 to 36, at least partially due to favorable tax treatment of these funds. Open-end funds were allowed for the first time in 1995, and together with closed-end funds, the yields of investment funds in 1995 surpassed interest yields on bank deposits for the first time. Funds that were based upon government securities showed yields up to 36%, clearly making them an attractive investment.

The Bratislava Stock Exchange (BrSE) in Slovak Republic trades in securities and shares of over 500 companies. In the winter of 1993-94, the "monthly volume of trading began to exceed 30 million Slovak crowns (Sk)".[8] By the end of 1996, the total volume of stock traded was valued at Sk 114.1 billion, which was a 184.8% increase over 1995. The turnover in government bonds amounted to 27.2% of the total BrSE volume in 1996, up from 9.7% in 1994 (*Annual Report*, NBS, 1995, pp. 67-68; and 1996, p. 65).

The Czech capital market has continued to evolve since its beginning in 1993. Favorable economic results in 1995 and the establishment of the Czech Capital Information Agency that supplies investors with up-to-date information on market activity have helped to create investment opportunities. In addition, domestic investors and foreign capital inflow were encouraged by (1) a higher Standard & Poor's rating for the Czech National Bank in 1995, (2) a relatively low price/earnings ratio for many companies, (3) the external convertibility of the Czech crown and (4) the implementation of OECD standards. The Prague Stock Exchange (PrSE) witnessed the orderly transfers of shares from the first and second waves of voucher privatization and a growth in overall volume of transactions valued at CZK 124.9 billion at the end of 1995 (*Annual Report*, CNB, 1995, pp. 51-52. CZK=Czech crown).

Regional investment decisions can be made based upon the CESI, a joint stock index based upon the stock exchanges of Warsaw, Budapest and Prague. The CESI started with an initial index value of 1000 points on June 30, 1995, and was based upon 27 stocks (13 Polish, 8 Hungarian, and 6 Czech). This index may give investors, especially foreign investors, better information regarding investment opportunities in the region. In 1996, the CESI reflected the growth experienced in the region, increasing by 54.3% from 1995 (*Annual Report*, NBH, 1996, p. 128).

V. Summary and Conclusions

This chapter provides a macroeconomic overview of several transition economies in Central Europe, including Poland, Hungary, Czech Republic and Slovak Republic. Direct comparisons may be made across countries with regard to growth, inflation and unemployment data, for example, though such comparisons should be tempered with the knowledge that each economy started the transition process with a different set of initial conditions and each has been pursuing their individual goals at various speeds and with divergent priorities. Perhaps the best way to view these data is to focus on the movement in the macro variables over time toward their established goals and to concentrate on the progress made, not on the actual levels themselves.

Each country has pursued similar methods of privatization of state sector property, including mass privatization programs, direct sales and the establishment of joint-stock companies with the state retaining some interest. While governments generally remain committed to the goal of privatization and progress has been made, the process is not complete in any of the countries and is slowed at times by political maneuvering and lack of sufficient funding.

The banking and capital markets play an important role in the privatization process and in moving the economy toward a market system. Each country moved from the mono-bank system toward a system with a central bank and smaller commercial banks. While the number of commercial banks has grown, the process was slowed by (1) legislative and political delays in formulating regulations in the banking sector, (2) the reluctance on the part of some governments to give up complete control over the distribution of funds, (3) the existence of bad bank loans that threatened the capital position of banks, (4) the lack of sufficient bank capital or investors to supply the needed capital, and/or (5) the lack of banking expertise of individuals who suddenly found themselves in control but did not have sufficient training or experience to run a bank. Despite these problems, the condition of the banking sectors in these countries did improve over time, and should continue to evolve.

Each country too has seen some advancement in its capital market development. Stock exchanges and securities markets have been established. Both have assisted in the privatization process and have helped to attract investors to the market, both domestic and foreign. Improvement is needed in the further development of secondary markets, in the training of market participants and in the implementation of the latest technology.

The transition process is complicated. Political disagreements can and do delay forward movement. While a government may agree on the overall goal of moving to a market system for its economy, it may not always agree on the methods used to achieve this goal. The governments in Central Europe have chosen similar but distinct paths, have utilized different speeds of transition, have dealt with unique problems and have achieved varying degrees of success. It will take time to overcome all of the obstacles in the transition process. However, as long as forward progress continues to be made, there should be no doubt that the goal will be attained.

ENDNOTES

1. The numbers in this and the previous paragraphs were taken from *Poland, 1995/96*, pp. 39, 120; and Polanski,1998, pp. 8-9 .
2. The numbers in this and the previous paragraphs were taken from Vorst, 1998, p. 71.
3. The year, 1993, was chosen for both Czech Republic and Slovak Republic since that was the first year that the two countries were two independent states. Comparison before 1993 is more difficult as separate numbers for the two economies are not generally available.
4. The numbers in this paragraph and the previous one were taken from *Annual Report*, CNB, 1995, pp. 59-60; and from Frait and Tamarappoo,1998, p. 133.
5. The numbers in this paragraph and the previous one were taken from *Annual Report*, NBS, 1995, pp. 14-18, 36; and 1996, pp. 40-41; and Z. Komínková and V. Muková, 1998, p. 192.
6. For more details regarding privatization in Poland, see Pulawski and Rapacki, 1998.
7. Banking information was from Lamacz, 1995, p. 162; *Poland, 1995/96*, pp. 102-103 and 211; and Rutkowska,1998, p. 57.
8. "The Gradual Development of the Capital Market in Slovakia," in *Slovakia Today*, January, 1994. Sk = Slovak Crown.

REFERENCES

Annual Report, (1995), Czech National Bank.

Annual Report, (1996), National Bank of Hungary.

Annual Report, (1995/96), Slovak National Bank.

Botos, K., (1998), "The Status and Prospects of the Hungarian Banking System", in *Financial Market Restructuring in Selected Central European Countries*, K. Vorst and W. Wehmeyer, eds., Ashgate Publishing Co., 83-101.

Fischer, S., (1992), "Privatization in East European Transformation", in *The Emergence of Market Economies in Eastern Europe,* C. Clague and G. C. Rausser, eds., Blackwell: Cambridge, MA.

Frait, J. and R. Tamarappoo, (1998), "Macroeconomic Stabilization in Czech Republic", in *Financial Market Restructuring in Selected Central European Countries*, K. Vorst and W. Wehmeyer, eds., Ashgate Publishing Co.,131-149.

Kerous, M., (1995), "Key Issues in Czech and Slovak Banking: A Central Banker's Perspective", in *Financial Reform in Central and Eastern Europe*, S. Griffith-Jones and Z. Drabek, eds., St. Martin's Press: New York, 67-91.

Komínková, Z. and V. Mučková, (1998), "Restructuring of the Banking Sector in Slovakia", in *Financial Market Restructuring in Selected Central European Countries*, K. Vorst and W. Wehmeyer, eds., Ashgate Publishing Co.,191-216.

Lamacz, T., (1995), "Financial Sector Development and Macroeconomic Policy in Poland in 1990-3", in *Financial Reform in Central and Eastern Europe*, S. Griffith-Jones and Z. Drabek, eds., St. Martin's Press: New York,151-176.

Matoušek, R.and M.Hrnčíř,. (1995), "Banking Supervision and the Problem of Bad Loans in Czech Republic" ACE Project Workshop Paper, Institute of Economics, Czech National Bank, Prague, October.

Nyers, R. and G. Rosta Lutz, (1995), "Development of the Financial Sector in Hungary During the Transition Period", in *Financial Reform in Central and Eastern Europe*, Stephany Griffith-Jones and Zdenek Drabek, eds., St. Martin's Press: New York, 127-150.

Polanski, Z. (1998), "Polish Monetary Policy in the 1990s: A Bird's Eye View," In *Financial Market Restructuring in Selected Central European Countries*, K. Vorst and W. Wehmeyer, eds., Ashgate Publishing Co., 7-22.

Pulawski, M. and R. Rapacki, (1998), "Privatization and Capital Market Development in Poland", in *Financial Market Restructuring in Selected Central European Countries*, K. Vorst and W. Wehmeyer, eds., Ashgate Publishing Co., 23-43.

Rutkowska, I.. (1998), "Banking Institutions in Poland", in *Financial Market Restructuring in Selected Central European Countries*, K. Vorst and W. Wehmeyer, eds., Ashgate Publishing Co., 45-66.

Slovak Economic Sheet, (1995), No. 6, Center for Economic Development, Bratislava, Slovakia, December.

Slovakia Today (1994), "The Gradual Development of the Capital Market in Slovakia".

Thomas, S. (1992), "Political Economy of Privatization: Poland, Hungary and Czechoslovakia", in *The Emergence of Market Economies in Eastern Europe*, C. Clague and G.C. Rausser, eds., Blackwell: Cambridge, MA, 279-295.

Vorst, K. (1998), "Economic Progress in Hungary", in *Financial Market Restructuring in Selected Central European Countries*, K. Vorst and W. Wehmeyer, eds., Ashgate Publishing Co., 69-82.

World Economy Research Institute, (1996), *Poland: International Economic Report, 1995/96*, Warsaw School of Economics.

CHAPTER 4

THE ECONOMICS OF MASS MEDIA: WESTERN WORLD EXPERIENCE AND CENTRAL AND EASTERN EUROPEAN EXIGENCIES

SOHRAB ABIZADEH

I. INTRODUCTION

We live in the age of information revolution. Mass media or mass communication[1] are an integral part of this revolution. The mass media perform an important function in every society, and for that matter the whole world. So important are they that Schramm (1964, p. 114) refers to the role of mass media as the "agent of social change." He contends that "the specific kind of social change they are expected to accomplish is the transition to new customs and practices and, in some cases, to different social relationships." Other scholars like Lorimer and Wilson (1988, p. 25) call the mass media "a structuring force in organization of both economic and cultural life." Seymour-Ure (1974) goes as far as saying that without mass communication societies may find it difficult to function in the contemporary world.

The communication and dissemination of information have existed, in one form or another, ever since recorded history. However, the role of mass media in the political, social and especially economic life of people began to take its current form after the Second World War. According to Hook (1972, p. 7), war was responsible for the widespread changes that occurred in the control and use of the mass media. It was due to the emergence and development of new technologies and means of communication in the nineteenth century that, according to Schramm (1964, p. 91), "a great change in human life and society on several continents" occurred, leading to "political democracy, economic opportunity, free public education, the industrial revolution, and mass communication."

During the 1980s and early 1990s the mass media helped bring about social and political transformations never witnessed before. Most astonishing was the way these changes occurred with minimum bloodshed. In the early 1990s, the world witnessed decades of Soviet style socialism come to an abrupt end in central and Eastern Europe and the former Soviet Union. These changes could not have occurred if humanity had been deprived of the mass media's ability to provide information. The transition was sudden and abrupt, and these countries have a long way to go in their journey toward a new social structure. In particular, these countries are in the process of taking some critical steps toward political democracy, social restructuring, and modernizing their economy. It is argued in this paper that the mass media, as instruments of social, political and economic change, will have an important role in this process.

Social scientists have paid more attention than economists to the study of mass media , particularly in their modern form: "sociologists, psychologists and political scientists have defined a number of functions fulfilled by the media, . . . Among the social sciences, only economics has been silent concerning the impact of these important institutions" (Orr, 1987, p. 79).[2] Such a lack of interest can be partly blamed on the dominance of neoclassical microeconomic theory as related to the production, provision and dissemination of information by the mass media industry.[3]

We will argue that the role of the mass media during social, political and economic change requires a critical analysis, especially since the media act as a source of information. The use of this information, and the way it is produced and provided, are the central focus of our analysis.[4] While the production, provision and use of information entail many positive features, the possibility of their abuse is very great indeed. The western world has seen both positive and negative uses of information. Since the mass media, like any other institution, are linked with the type of social, economic and political systems that prevails in a country, when analyzing the mass media, one needs to examine them in context. For example, an autocratic system of government preaching free enterprise may exert an absolute control over the mass media. This is done to justify the government's goals, political or otherwise, no matter how right or wrong they may be. Chile under Pinochet is a case in point. In contrast, there may exist a more democratic government with less emphasis on a free market system that may not need to use the media for achieving its economic (or other) objectives. India is a good example here. With the new and vast changes in technology, selective targeting through the mass media for control becomes much easier to carry out.

A fundamental economic question dominating the discussion on transition in central and Eastern Europe is how fast and how far should changes go towards a free market system. This question becomes relevant when the issue of information disseminated through the media is of concern. Given the length of time necessary to prepare for such a critical leap (that of moving toward a free market system), it is argued in this chapter that steps toward a market type economy should be taken cautiously, after the establishment of fundamental infrastructures; and that an immediate and hasty duplication of the system of mass media modeled after western media, particularly those of the United States, may be too much for these central and Eastern European countries to absorb at the early stages of their transformation given their social and cultural differences with those of the western world. Even after these countries have prepared themselves for a leap, we should continue to remind ourselves of Rotstein's view, when he talked about cultural policies in Canada, that "the marketplace has no nationality, and does not observe borders and boundaries. Societies, on the other hand, have both a nationality and borders. It is to societies rather than markets that cultural expressions are, in the first instance, addressed and for whom they speak" (Rotstein 1988, p. 155).

In summary, my objective here is to outline and analyze the economic nature of the mass media and relate this to the process of change in central and Eastern Europe.

After providing a brief definition of the "economics of mass media," I will go on to consider the output produced/provided by the mass media — information. Next, information as a means of control will be discussed. The nature of information as a public good and the role of government in the provision of such a product will be presented and analyzed. A general discussion on the role of the mass media in the transformation of central and Eastern Europe will follow. The last section will summarize the discussions presented.

II. The Economics of Mass Media Defined

To conduct an economic analysis of the mass media, I begin with a simple theoretical definition of "the economics of mass media." The economics of mass media deals with the role of the mass media in providing ideas, cultural and social values and, in particular, information to consumers to satisfy their alternative needs and wants, given the availability of resources. This definition is based on economics in isolation. It involves, similar to any production activity, the use and allocation of an input for producing an output. This output is used as a consumer or capital good. This output takes the general form of "information" or service. The economics of mass media, in its theoretical sense, as Picards (1989) explains, are concerned with the basic questions that are paramount to all aspects of economic analysis. That is, given limited resources and unlimited wants in a capitalistic system, how are resources allocated in the most efficient way.[5] This kind of definition assumes that the mass media are privately owned and the owner's sole objective is to produce a product (information or entertainment or other services) based on the neoclassical assumption of profit maximization. This limited definition ignores the public good nature of the products produced by the mass media. It follows that, for my purpose, a broader view must be taken if the practical dimension of the mass media and their relevance to social and political changes and reforms are to be pursued and analyzed. Following Murrel (1991, p. 74), "in matters of economic reform, the skills and knowledge more usually associated with philosophers and the historian must supplement those of the economic theorists and the econometricians." The mass media, besides performing the task of producing private goods and services to satisfy private needs and wants, produce social goods and services. Thus, their impact reaches far beyond the realm of individuals' private utility maximization and the profit maximization motive of business firms.

Given this modified view of the economics of mass media, the tradition of subsidized newspapers, strong identification with political parties, and considering the desire by central and Eastern European countries for rapid reform, it is important to consider the impact of those changes before vital economic decisions are made.

III. Information as a Commodity

After World War II scholars and politicians began to pay special attention to information and the role it can play in the lives of people. Recent scholars have also echoed the importance of information. Schramm (1964, p. 240) contends that "information involves one of the fundamental rights of man, that of expressing himself and knowing what others are expressing." Later he concludes that access to information is one of the basic rights of humankind, "and an indispensable requirement for the freedom and dignity of the world's people" (p. 249).

According to the rational learning model, consumers/individuals view the mass media as a source of information to be used in their decision-making, be it economic or political. Another model of consumer/individual response is based on psychological theories of learning. This, in turn, is based on the repetition of simple stimuli that themselves originate as information.[6] Both models lead to decision making by individuals based on the information provided.[7] However, for the information to be provided it has to be produced first. The production of information takes form through the media. This happens no matter who owns and operates them, i.e., whether they operate privately or publicly.[8] If information is a product then its use must lead to an outcome. Mosco (1989, p. 20) asserts that "information itself is increasingly becoming a commodity as well as an instrument in a society-wide commodification and control process." Mosco emphasizes the idea of information as a "product," a product that, in his view, is a powerful means of social control (p. 28). The role of information in affecting the decisions of people is well documented in the writings of Nelson (1974) and Wildman (1982). According to Wildman, the response to advertising, which is the information provided to individuals as the specific consumer of goods and services, is generally affected by the individual's desire for information *per se*. "The intensity of this desire for information is in turn determined by the perceived benefits of making an informed choice . . . relative to the anticipated costs of acquiring and evaluating relevant information" (p. 6). It follows that information, as provided by the mass media, becomes relevant when it can help the users to make better choices - economic or political. This argument leads us to the use of information, as a consumer good for rational decision-making. According to the pure neoclassical economic theory, they assume perfect information as a prerequisite for efficient allocation of resources. In reality, even a neoclassical economist would agree that perfection is an ideal that may never exist.[9]

Information may be also viewed as a resource used for promoting economic development and change. As Mosco (1989, p. 24) points out. ". . . when we think of information as a non-depletable, strategic resource, arguments about the transition from an industrial society begin to make sense . . ." What steel and fossil fuel were to the transition from an agricultural to an industrial society, information is to the transition from an industrial to the post-industrial service or information society. Accordingly, information is viewed as a product that takes either the form of a capital good (resource) to be used to produce future products, or a consumer good to be used to satisfy the ongoing and current needs and wants of consumers by helping them make rational decisions.

Meanwhile, as mentioned above, information, as a product, can serve as an instrument of control. When information is provided to make rational economic and political decisions the result is positive. On the other hand information may lead to a negative outcome when abused by the providers (not necessarily producers) for deceptive purposes, e.g., deceptive advertising (Nelson 1974, pp. 749-751). The western world has seen both the positive and negative aspects of these roles that information has played.

IV. Information as a Means of Control

Information disseminated by the mass media can be used for three distinct purposes: first, as a consumer good used in the process of rational political and economic decision-making; second, as a capital good used for the purpose of economic and social development; and third, as a means of control by the provider, not necessarily the owner of the media organizations, of information. It is the third issue that I wish to discuss in this section.

Mass media and its outcome (information) can be used by either the private sector or the government as a means of control. This control can be carried out by government, the private sector in general and business firms in particular. The general objective of this control is to alter the consumers'/individuals' behavior in favor of the provider's product or political stance. Usually this control is carried out through the medium of advertising. This involves two types of advertising, market and political (Orr 1987, pp. 83-89). According to Mosco (1989), each of these advertising schemes can take two different forms – direct or indirect. Direct advertising includes those that directly promote a product or political platform, whereas, indirect advertising uses the information for the purpose of winning favors. The latter is usually done by the government and/or politicians. It follows, that there are two agents of control through advertising: one is government and the other is the private sector. Both have one major objective in common: that of control (not necessarily manipulation). Politicians may use this control to achieve their objective of vote maximization and/or staying in power, while private firms strive for profit maximization utilizing similar controls. The politicians do this by, among other things, providing information as social goods whereas private firms are solely in business to provide private goods. Orr (1987, pp. 90-91) sees a parallel between control by politicians and control by business firms. He argues that "when the dimension of political advertising as news is considered explicitly, a straightforward analogy between political competition and market competition disappears. Without that form of advertising considered, the appealing parallel would hold that politicians provide political services and public goods through government in exchange for votes while firms provide marketed private goods or services in exchange for dollars."[10]

Based on the rational learning model of advertising, consumers make their economic decisions based on information they receive through the mass media. If this model is extended to the role of advertising in the political arena, a similarity can be observed. That is, political advertising will directly affect the political behavior of individuals. Apart from the goals of profit and vote maximization, the degree of influence that advertising of this sort can exert is dependent upon the level of control sought by the agent. Similarly, if one applies the second model of consumer/individual response to advertising, which is based on learning in response to repetition of simple stimuli (Wildman 1982), and extend it to political advertising, like the rational learning model, parallel arguments could be made and identical outcomes could be observed. Thus, despite the theoretical model adapted, both business (run by managers) and government (run by politicians) can exert much influence, and thus control, over consumers/individuals through commercial and political advertising, respectively. The impact of these controls can be felt in social, political and economic circumstances.[11] The general objective of this control, as explained earlier, is to alter the consumer's/individual's behavior in favor of the provider's products or political stance. Whether such a control results in a positive or a negative outcome is subject to debate. If advertising is done for the sole purpose of informing, then more information helps the consumers/individuals in the process of making "rational" decisions.[12] However, if that information is supplied for the purpose of control, it may take the form of a misinformation and thus result in adverse outcomes both politically and economically.[13]

However, there is a distinct difference between just providing the information and allowing the user to decide how to use it and providing the information for the purpose of "manipulating."

When dealing with deceptive advertising,[14] Nelson (1974) points out that "deception requires not only a misleading or untrue statement, but somebody ready to be misled by that statement." In my view, those in control, government or politicians and business firms, can be and are always able to make "misleading and untrue statements" using the mass media. However, the extent to which they adhere to this approach and the effectiveness of it is very much dependent upon the level of access to varying and diverse viewpoints. If, for example, the level of social and formal education of the recipients of such information is not adequate then there will be more people who are ready "to be misled." This is particularly important when the government or business organizations who control the source of information, or wrongly command the respect of the population, use their powers. As Mickiewicz (1988, p. 300) states, "in general, media effectiveness is related to the credibility of source, the importance of what is covered for the audience, and the utility of the information." When the audience is not well educated, the importance of the source declines and the specific form and composition that the message takes will control the effectiveness and the kind of information that they disseminate. This is why Mickiewicz later states that "clearly, audience demand and interests are at the center of effectiveness . . . Those interests and demands can be and are shaped by the media themselves . . . But the initiative to meet information demands — and thus to achieve increased effectiveness — remains and will always remain in tension with the requirements of control."

Although the mass media can be used for control, a well developed and free mass media system may make it more difficult for the manipulations to succeed. The basic political and social impact of a free mass media system is to inform rather than to manipulate the people. (Schramm, 1964, pp. 36-38). When there is no freedom, control, particularly political control, stands a good chance. This calls for a balancing act on the part of the central and Eastern European countries. If the objective is to give their citizens the kind of information that results in promoting social objectives, then they should reduce their use of the media for manipulating.

There are circumstances where control may not come from within but it may be initiated from outside the country.[15] Central and Eastern European countries, given their current economic and political climate, are particularly vulnerable to this possibility. Given the many critical roles that information can play in a society and because of the concentration of wealth and power within a small group of countries and thus their ability to provide the kind of information that is best suited to their own political or economic agenda, the newly liberalized countries of central and Eastern Europe ought to be careful of receiving information that might be intended to result in control from outside their borders. This does not mean that the central and Eastern European countries should restrict the flow of information, but rather they should encourage and promote the type of information that can be used in helping them to flourish as independent nations. After all, their culture, values, and social norms are different from those who disseminate the information that crosses international borders. Unless these countries are after absolute coherence with the western world, which I think would be a great mistake, information coming from the west should be used only when it adds to their wealth of knowledge - technological and otherwise - rather than information that directly influences social and cultural values. As Rotstein (1988, p. 155) has argued, the marketplace has no nationality and is not restrained by borders and boundaries, whereas societies have their own nationality and borders. The market should not dictate the cultural values of societies. It is the society that should determine the cultural needs of its citizens.

One characteristic of central and Eastern European countries before the changes of the late 1980s was the absolute control of the mass media by the central authorities. According to Herman and Chomsky (1988, p. 1) "where the levers of power are in the hands of a state bureaucracy, the monopolistic control over the media, often supplemented by official censorship . . ." will become possible. More specifically, and as claimed by Volgyes (1975b, p. 18), Communist political systems used and relied heavily on mass media while placing "controls on these media in order to prevent their use as negative agents of political socialization." Later (p. 19) he admits that "the range and intensity of controls vary from country to country and there seems to be a direct correlation between the amount of control a government exercises over the entire polity and the intensity with which it uses the media for the purpose of political communication." It should be noted that governments have particularly exerted such political controls through broadcasting rather than the press.[16]

While the new liberal democratic countries may still be suffering from these phenomena, the fact that more political freedom has been the outcome of current changes means that there is a need for careful planning about the future role of the mass media. The ownership of the mass media, be it by the government or private sector, should not be intended to facilitate control but to make information (both as a consumer and/or capital good) available to speed up political and economic changes directed toward improving social conditions and economic progress.

V. Information as a Public Good

So far I have emphasized the importance of information and its use for control. Earlier, I argued that information is a commodity that is both used as a consumer good and a producer good. Whether a consumer or producer good, information, as a "good", can be further considered from two different perspectives. First, we can look upon information as a private good: a type of commodity that commands a market price and, once paid for, that establishes a property right. Second, information can be used collectively which will reflect the public good nature of information. A clear distinction between private and public goods will follow.

At the heart of the free market system are the theories of neoclassical economics. However, there are many reasons which suggest that markets may not function as perfectly as the neoclassical theory suggests. Markets may "fail" to lead the economy to what is known as the "optimal allocation of resources". Market failure will occur when a) externalities of different kinds exist, b) increasing return to scale leads to the formation of monopolies and c) the market does not provide some goods and services desired by the public.

Individuals and households are one of the three main economic agents. They do not only act but also interact with one another. In this process they may impose costs on each other or create benefits for each other. When these costs and benefits go unnoticed or when they are not accounted for in the transaction process an "externality" is said to exist. Thus externality refers to the harmful (costs) or beneficial (benefits) side effects created in the process of production, distribution and consumption of any product including information. When externalities exist market demands and supplies will reflect only the benefits and costs of the acting agents in the market; the benefits and costs that may fall on others will not be taken into account by the acting agents (consumers and producers). The exclusion of these benefits and costs (as externalities) lead to an inefficient allocation of resources and thus market failure. If any costs or benefits are not reflected in the market prices, there is no guarantee that individual decisions, which are aimed at maximizing their well being, will necessarily lead to maximizing the overall welfare of society.

Increasing return to scale can result in the formation of a monopoly firm. Since, here, the producer has market power and thus the ability to affect price, the result will be inefficiency.

The market system is dependent upon the signals received by the business firms from the households (consumers) who reveal their preferences in the market by casting their dollar-vote on the products they would like to consume. However, occasionally, although the consumption of certain products is desirable, consumers are reluctant, for one reason or another, to reveal their true preferences for some products and thus the product may not be produced at all. The reason that agents do not reveal their preference is that those goods are *nonrival* in consumption; with a given level of production, consumption by one agent does not necessarily reduce the quantity consumed by others. With private goods, once produced and purchased or acquired by an individual, that individual establishes a property right to the product and no one else has access to that particular product. However, social goods, once produced and provided, would be available to all in equal amounts. One individual's consumption or use of the product, theoretically, would not preclude others.[17] At the same time limiting the benefits of these goods to an individual or a certain group of individuals is impossible, or at least too costly, (once produced). *Exclusion* is inefficient in the sense that the additional resource cost of the additional user is zero.[18] It is also difficult to exclude anyone from the consumption and use of public goods, without incurring a high or prohibitive cost.

Efficiency dictates that as many individuals as possible should use a public good if the consumption by one does not decrease that of another. Since individual consumers cannot, and/or should not be excluded from consumption because of their unwillingness or inability to pay a price, there is no rationing mechanism such as the one prevalent in the market. These goods are usually indivisible and thus have to be consumed collectively. Goods with these characteristics are called public goods or social goods. Once produced, they cannot be divided up nor can each consumer purchase an amount consistent with his or her preferences and ability to pay.[19] Thus public goods are defined as those goods that are *nonrival* in consumption and where *exclusion* is either impossible or inefficient. Some kinds of information readily fit these characteristics. For the free market to function properly, perfect information about consumer preferences is essential. Without such information the market will fail to properly respond to market signals. This particularly applies to the case of public goods whereby, due to their characteristics, consumers do not volunteer such information. This is due to the *free rider* phenomenon, whereby concealing information about their preference for the public good, consumers attempt to avoid bearing any cost in the financing of that good. Down (1957) has clearly explained, for example, how political information used by the voters is a major source of the free rider problem. His position supports the argument that information in general, and political information in particular, fit into the category of public goods. Such information is the product of mass media.

Thus the more important and specific question is whether information is a public good. While we argued that what the mass media produce can be labeled a commodity, we made a clear distinction between information as a consumer good and information as a producer good. Information is a public good when used as a producer good. For example, information provided by the mass media can be used as an input by the business firms to decide their level of profit maximizing outputs and prices. Mosco (1989, p. 24), when dealing with information as a producer good (resource) identifies four forms that information might take. One of those forms he calls "commons under government leadership" or what is normally called the "publicness" of information. That part of information as a "resource", as elaborated by Oettinger (1980) is what Mosco (1989, p. 23) calls the type of resource that "can be used but not used up."

Information is also a public good when used as a consumer good. For example, educational programs produced and provided by the mass media fall under this category. In Garnham's (1990, p. 160) words "... cultural commodity[20] is not destroyed in process of consumption ... it has been difficult to establish the scarcity on which price is based. Thus cultural goods (and some services, such as broadcasting, for technical reasons) tend toward the conditions of a public good." No matter how we look at information, it is both a private and public good at best.

According to Picard (1989, p. 9) media organizations are there to meet both private and public needs and wants.

Economists are unanimous in accepting the fact that "*externalities generally lead to an inefficient allocation of resources, or market failure, just as public goods*" (Browning and Browning 1983, p. 36). With public goods in general and mass media output in particular, this failure of the market is based on the difficulty in defining the demand for such products. In fact, Granham (1990, p. 161) believes such a task is impossible. In addition, the nature of the mass media industry is such that it may lead to a high level of concentration, mainly due to economies of scale — another reason for the market to fail.[21] This leads Granham (1990, p. 166) to argue that "the public sector too needs to exploit economies of scale . . . ".

If information is a public good, then, as Groves and Ledyard (1987, p. 54) conclude, "in private-ownership economies with public goods, if all agents aggressively follow their own self-interest, decentralized institutions will not lead them to promote the interest of the whole." If public good externality exists, the market will fail to maximize social welfare. Whenever the market fails governments' involvement in the economy is justified. Governments can either become the producer and provider of these goods (information) or regulate their supply to ensure economic efficiency. As Musgrave (1959, p. 44) puts it "the qualitative content of these services, or the wants which they are to satisfy, is such that they must be supplied through public office; even if supplied privately, they require such elaborate supervision that the situation is more or less equivalent to public production."

When media can be used to enrich cultures, the case for public intervention becomes even stronger. Granham (1990, p. 154) provides the following reasons in support of this view: (1) cultures possess inherent values that are subject to much damage by commercial forces; (2) "the need for these values is universal, uncontaminated by questions of class, gender and ethnic origin;" (3) the market does not satisfy this need. All of these indicate that culture supported by the mass media is indeed a public good and governments' involvement is thus justified.

In this context, on the one hand, we need to make a clear distinction between public production and provision of information, and on the other hand, production, provision and management of those activities that leads to the "production" of information by the private sector. Provision does not necessarily require production to be carried out by the same organization. Although it may be possible to "produce" these goods and services (information) in the private sector and leave the task of "provision" to the public sector, at times it may be more "efficient" to allow the government to engage in both production and provision of such goods and services. In large part, this is because, unlike pure private goods, public goods are not readily divisible.

These economic arguments justify the role that governments need to play, possibly in the production, and certainly in the provision of information, through the mass media. The government's involvement is dependent upon the degree to which the market mechanism and economy are developed. The less developed the country and its market system the more the need for government involvement. Mosco (1989, p. 25) argues that one of the most significant tendencies in modern societies is the emphasis on private ownership as opposed to public ownership of economic activities. This is due to the technological advances that make it easier for the market to exclude individuals from the use of goods with social elements. Since technological advancement comes with economic development, as economies grow it becomes more and more possible to shift both the management and production and eventually the provision of information to the private sector. Central and Eastern European countries are not quite there yet.

In the case of these countries, it has been impractical to take the quantum-leap into the market system in general and in the area of mass communication in particular. First, they must allow for the market mechanism to develop fully before they leave all their economic activities to the market. A malfunctioning free market, if left to itself, could cause more harm to these economies than a gradual and well-planned transition. Second, they need to take a hard look at the system of mass communication currently in place. Dismantling the existing system without knowing what is going to replace it would be wrong. Since they do not develop their markets, it would be unrealistic to expect a barely functional market to perform the task of handling the production and provision of information satisfactorily.

While it is true that the central and Eastern European economies collapsed due to the inherent problems of socialism, it does not necessarily follow that free market economies are free of problems. By hastily embracing capitalism, if those problems are ignored, one can expect more economic and social hardship than otherwise. Just as Murrel (1991, p. 59) warns "the institution of capitalism may come in many varieties and cannot be put in place instantaneously" — the institutions of centrally planned economies cannot be set aside without proper "planning". What is most important is that, "economists must look outside the standard models of competition to . . . build a theory of reform" (p. 60). In particular, attention must be focused on what the media do best: the preservation and enrichment of culture. Therefore Williamson's (1958) definition of culture as a realm distinct from economic activities, which mainly deal with material production, becomes relevant. Obviously, as we know it, culture does not have the characteristics of a product that motivate private firms to protect or produce it. Indeed, what cultural activities produce are public goods. Like any other public good it needs to be provided and protected by the central authorities. In other words, it would be difficult, and a mistake, if one relies solely on the market forces to provide the goods and services produced through the mass media. Rotstein (1988, p. 154) points out that "markets deal in commodities — that is, merchandise whose only significant characteristic is its price." He questions if the mass media, due to their relation to culture, can easily fall within the realm of this market. At least regarding culture, therefore, the market is an epi-phenomenon that should not be taken as a proxy for essential purposes and functions of cultural expression. The fallacy is not essentially different from taking defense industries as a proxy for the defense of a country . . ." (p. 155). Despite the overwhelming eagerness in central and Eastern Europe for the establishment of a free market economy, given the nature of the mass media and the inability of the market to deal with issues related to culture, combined with the stage of economic, social and political conditions these countries are currently in, it would be undesirable to assume that the market system can do all the necessary functions to guarantee success.

Rotstein (1988, p. 148), when discussing the role of economics in cultural policies and cultural industries, emphasizes that "markets, in short, are not ubiquitous in the many spheres of society that lie outside the economy." Or as Murrel (1991, p. 73) argues, "reformers need to be sensitive to the notion that there are many visions of the world, each with its own emphasis and assumptions, clarifying and distorting reality. Of course neo-classical economics is one of these visions: but . . . it is not a strong candidate to provide the under pinning for reform." Murrel refers to alternative theories that can be a substitute for the neo-classical approach to social issues — in our case the mass media. He refers to the new informational economics proposed by Stiglitz (1991 p. 73), which suggests a focus on the link between ownership systems and the viability of a different coordination mechanism on the ground that they would end up catering to their sponsors rather than the public interest. Accordingly, what Schramm (1964, p. 259) calls "the cooperative relationship between the organs of government and those responsible for education and other related development" must be pursued vigorously. This cooperative relationship, be it in education or mass media, is the key to the success of central and Eastern European nations. If the task of the government and those of the market are not coordinated properly, the outcome may be absolute chaos.

VI. Information as a Means of Development

One question posed following the recent changes in central and Eastern Europe was the possibility of establishing a western type mass media system to facilitate the process of economic and social transformation and development. With all the changes already underway in there, this process is expected to take a new dimension. Particularly, with the flow of information, in the absence of control, these countries could benefit enormously. As Tehrani (1979, p. 122) explains "The role of communications has been a subject of considerable speculation in development theory. Broadly speaking, three schools of thought seem to have emerged since Adam Smith. First, there are those (including classical and neo-classical economists) who consider communications as an infrastructure in the process of development and therefore view it as a precondition for economic growth. Second, there are those theorists (mostly noneconomists) who view communications to be a critical or integral factor during social change and modernization. Finally, there are those researchers (primarily social psychologists focusing on microsystems and media effects) who consider communications as a residual factor in the process of social change, to be studied on its own and without much prejudice as to its role in the developmental process." No matter which point of view is taken, they all share a common thread; the role of mass media in the process of economic growth.[22]

Hood (1972, p. 7) recognizes and emphasizes the importance of the mass media in the restructuring of Western Europe at the end of the Second World War. In the case of central and Eastern European countries, and others, the media is expected to help bridge the transition from traditional to modern society (see Schramm, 1964, p. 129). In particular, "when we think of information as a non-depletable, strategic resource, arguments about the transition from an industrial society begin to make sense" (Mosco, 1989, p. 24). Thus information, produced and provided by the mass media, can serve as a precondition for developmental change. Mosco (1989, p. 24) emphasizes the importance of information further and states that "what steel and fossil fuels were to transition from an agricultural to an industrial society, information is to the transition from an industrial to a post-industrial, service, or information society."[23] If the mass media can create the type of environment that is receptive to change then its expansion would help economic development and change. In Schramm's (1964, p. 79) words, "when a society begins to modernize, one of the first signs of the development is the lengthening out of communication channels." He later (pp. 131-136) concludes that the "*mass media can create a climate for development . . . and the mass media can help only indirectly to change strongly held attitudes on valued practices . . .* Undoubtedly, the whole movement of national development can be given status through attention by the mass media."

On political and social grounds, the additional information would help the public to participate effectively in the establishment of the goals and objectives of the nation and subsequently evaluate their success. Without the flow of information, the public will be left out of the process and this in turn will translate into autocracy and the dominance of an elite group and thus a passive population. In other words, development goes beyond the border of economics and encompasses different social, political and cultural dimensions as well. In Hancock's (1981, p. 4) words, "by development, therefore, it seems better to argue from a basic notion of reduction in inequalities: of opportunity, of resources, of information access, of capability." At the same time, mass media policy itself is related to many other policies — cultural policies, technology and sciences and even transportation policies. (See Tehrani 1979).

According to Schramm (1964, p. 91), in the 20th century advancements in mass communication technologies have resulted in increased access to information not only by privileged and educated people but by the great masses of people. "Political democracy, economic opportunity, free public education, the Industrial Revolution, and mass communication were all woven together to make a great change in human life and society on several continents." Elsewhere, (pp. 43-44) he adds that the mass media and the increased flow of information provide the kind of climate needed for national development.

Recognizing the importance of the mass media and the role they can play in the modernization process of a country, and the enormous strength and impact that the media can have in educating their population, many governments of developing countries have chosen the mass media as a means of formal and informal public education. This positive outcome is possible, according to Nawaz (1984, p. 44), since the mass media are "often officially owned or controlled" by the government. They use this "to educate and inform their populations and in this way to promote economic and social development." In this context, Schramm (1964, p. 27) agrees with the idea that for a society to go through the process of change, its people themselves must change: "for the task of the mass media of information and the "new media" of education is to speed and ease the long, slow social transformation required for economic development." He later emphasizes the importance of the mass media in educating and upgrading the skills of the labor force for development. Thus, by opening the "door to the wider world of modern technological knowledge" (Schramm, 1964, p. 43), education will significantly help the cause of development. Nawaz (1984) shares these views and believes that the use of the media as an educational instrument will promote efficiency and productivity leading to economic development. This indeed is one of the most important aspects of the use of the mass media.

The emphasis on education through the mass media leads to an important aspect of economic and social change: that of reaching the citizens of the country on an equal basis, be it for education or otherwise. This is similar to the definition by Hancock (1981) cited earlier, which emphasizes equal opportunities in all aspects of life. An important aspect of development relates to not only the provision of equal opportunities but a balanced growth in all regions and sectors of the economy. The failure of the modernization theory, where the establishment of a stable industrial sector was proposed, points to the need to concentrate the development effort through mass communication for education all across the country — both urban and rural areas — to achieve, at least partially, the objective of balanced growth. Given the ability of the mass media to reach remote parts of a country, the contribution of this investment in achieving that objective is obvious. Although the effect of communication on economic development and change is well documented, some thinkers have questioned the direct relationship between them. For example, Stevenson (1988) has questioned the role that the mass media are supposed to play in providing economic development and change, particularly as proposed by Schramm (1964). Stevenson rightly argues that the blind adoption of the western style of communication to less developed countries (LDCs) has not met expectations. This, however, does not refute the hypothesis that mass communication can promote development. Although one can justify Stevenson's (1988 p. 73) claim that the optimism of the 1950s and early 1960s, as far as the effect of the mass communication on economic development is concerned, was overstated, we should note that economic development is a complex and multidimensional process.[24] The failure of LDCs to reach the western standard of living cannot be solely attributed to the failure of the mass media in achieving their goals. Many other factors — including international politics — are responsible for this lack of success, as Stevenson himself correctly points out. Lack of success in some LDCs does not necessarily confirm the inability of the mass media to help bring about social and economic change. If change has not been successfully carried out, due mainly to other factors such as political interference etc., it does not necessarily follow that all those components, including the mass media, that were expected to facilitate change, have failed.

The question, then, is: which one is the cause and which one is the effect, i.e., does economic development lead to more information and effective media or *vice versa*. In Schramm's (1964, p. 41) words, the question of whether better and more developed mass media cause economic development or *vice versa* is a "futile argument." Nawaz (1984) argues that the media have two distinct aspects. One is formal education (direct or a formal role) and the other is the supply of information that will indirectly affect people (indirect or an informal role). The former is more predominant in less developed countries (LDCs) since lacking a highly educated population it would be unrealistic to expect that the informal role can be significant. While I agree with the idea that an unconstrained adoption of western style mass media is not something that central and Eastern European countries should pursue, it does not necessarily follow that a well-designed system of mass media, particularly if used to educate the public, would be ineffective when it comes to economic development. The mass media can *cause* economic development and change particularly through educating people. Once a certain level of development is achieved, the mass media can play its informal role.

Central and Eastern European countries, while pursuing their objectives of modernization and change, can learn from the mistakes of other LDCs. They need to ensure that the mistakes of other LDCs, particularly those related to the political dominance of western powers, do not impede their striving for change. In this process, a properly established system of mass communication without politically motivated control (internal or external) can be a forceful element in the pursuit of development and change. However, the realization of the fact that "... the very concept of development (or, conversely, underdevelopment) is theoretically, multidimensional in character" (Abizadeh and Basilevsky 1986, p. 98) is imperative for these countries. Despite the very important role that the mass media can play in promoting change and development, unless accompanied by other sound and practical economic policies, its effectiveness may be in doubt. Moreover, as Tehrani (1979, pp. 157-158) has argued, "the multidisciplinary nature of the field and the fragmental organization of the media call for an integrated systems approach to its problems of policy and planning." This in turn calls for careful planning by the central and Eastern European countries while attempting to introduce the different elements of market forces in the field of mass media, bearing in mind that "the role of government in all this is best confined to coordination and integration, rather than control and manipulation" (Tehrani, 1979, p. 158).

VII. SUMMARY, GENERALIZATIONS AND CONCLUSIONS

In this paper I argue that information is a product provided by the mass media. This product takes both forms of a consumer and producer (resource) good. Meanwhile, each of these can either have the characteristics of private or public goods. Despite what form information might take, it can be used to generate either positive or negative outcomes. The positive aspect of its use relates to the satisfaction received by individuals and firms when freely using information to facilitate their decision-making. The negative impact, on the other hand, can be due to the deceptive use of the mass media. This may be possible if either the private or public sector controls the media. However, since information can take the form of a public good, government's intervention in the production and provision of information through the mass media is justified. The mass media can play a dominant role in the promotion of development and change. This contribution, particularly through education, is most prominent and accepted.

In light of the foregoing, three sets of policy related issues can be outlined.

1. Overall, given the nature and process of change that is underway in central and Eastern Europe, not everyone is convinced that the adaptation of a pure market oriented system in the field of mass media is the answer. Schiller (1971, p. 39) argues that "the emergence of the market society has permitted a relatively unfettered social condition, but one which has left ordinary working people totally dependent on a wage income derived from an even uncertain unemployment." First, as noted by Murrel (1991, p. 59) "the institutions of capitalism come in many varieties and cannot be put in place instantaneously." Second, central and Eastern European countries, for better or worse, have established their own unique cultural and social institutions. These institutions cannot, and should not, readily be transformed and abandoned before their strength and weaknesses are clearly identified. The movement from a planned socialist economy to a free market system is not continuous. "Rather, it involves an enormous qualitative change in institutions, attitudes, technologies and allocation of human and physical resources" (Wolfson, 1992, p. 42). Third, in the field of mass communication, in particular, cultural issues become predominant. Following Muller (1991, p. 73), reformers must exercise caution and be sensitive to the fact that there are many visions of the world, each with its associated strengths and weaknesses. Abandoning one in favor of the other, before proper analysis of these strength and weaknesses, will be costly indeed.

As Schramm (1964, p. 122) reminds us, if the mass media are used without regards for the complexities of the local culture, their effectiveness will be diminished.

2. If a hasty and direct application of the market system to the mass media is not the answer then governments need to play a role in providing information. However, being aware of the disadvantages of the media operated by the government is important for these countries, particularly if this leads to control. It becomes important for the central and Eastern European countries to discourage the use of information for control. Since there is always a danger that as information technologies became ever more advanced, its control by the public or private sector can become detrimental to social progress. Thus, governments should reduce their control of the media as economic development proceeds.
3. Development of an effective system of mass media requires planning, research and establishment of a proper budgeting for allocating a socially acceptable and efficient level of resources to this sector of the economy. With the type of economic changes happening in central and Eastern Europe, the conclusion may be that they need an immediate and radical change in the mass media to facilitate the desired social and economic changes. However, this transformation may be a difficult task. There exist several bottlenecks to overcome before they undertake a comprehensive restructuring of the mass media. This process requires careful planning and organization by using the existing means and developing them into a system that is adaptable to the realities of their past and perceived political and economic environment. One of the most important aspects of this transformation concerns the degree to which people are involved in decision making. If it is the objective of the central and Eastern European countries to continue to democratize their political and economic system, using the mass media to facilitate people's involvement becomes an important tool for them. For this to happen, there is no need to wait until a technologically sophisticated system of mass communication is in place. If the intentions are pure, which we assume they are, then better use of the existing facilities, while they are developing new ones, could easily lend themselves to the promotion of the dual objectives of social and economic change.

   If the mass media is considered a part of the dynamic of change then, by enabling the public to participate in that process and preparing the public for the acceptance of new values, they allow for new ideas to spread. This can only be done when the mass media, besides other social and economic goods, contribute to the important objective of educating the public.
4. Finally, despite the arrival of globalization, central and Eastern European countries, and for that matter, all of the developing world, should not blindly subject their culture to forces of westernization. Not because western culture and media are inferior, but because, within the context of globalization, for the world

to remain attractive to all, diversity is desirable and should be encouraged. Globalization does not mean and should not lead to uniformity of nations and cultures. The mass media in each country, be it western or eastern, could reflect those diversities and unique features of each culture. Only then will we are able to enrich ourselves by allowing creativity within each culture and contribute to one another by offering alternative choices.

ENDNOTES

1. The term mass media and mass communication are defined in this paper in a very broad sense. They include any means that can provide information. These include the print media, broadcasting, and the Internet. The terms are also used interchangeably to include all media outlets and institutions that can in one way or another produce and provide information to the public. More specifically, and following Hancock (1981, pp. 11-12), we treat "communication as a resource capable of being allocated, consumed and re-distributed like other resources . . . However, the understanding goes beyond that of mass media."
2. This points to the reality that there exists a limited amount of economic theory and analysis useful enough to be applied to the subject matter here. This limitation renders our task even more challenging.
3. For details see Orr (1987).
4. Throughout this paper information will be treated as a commodity. Although it is recognized that the mass media is expected to provide and/or disseminate information, it is equally possible that they may be involved in the "production" and supply of information — the kind of information that does not take the form of news. An example is when the mass media is involved in the "production" and broadcasting of educational programs.
5. Note that the discussions in this paper will step, naturally, beyond the boundaries of economics and into political and social domains. As such, this simple and narrow definition may not readily lend itself to all the issues discussed here. See Picard (1989, p. 7) for more on economic definition of mass media.
6. See Wildman (1982, p. 6) for more detail on this distinction.
7. Orr (1987, pp. 79-80) argues that "until recently, economic analysis has viewed information as not scarce. More recently, in analysis that has acknowledged limitations on information, the process of information gathering has been viewed as a costly integral part of private individual maximization, but information production has continued to be viewed mainly as a by product of

market exchange. These views on information transmission and information processing have made it possible to ignore the media as institutions."

8. This ownership issue becomes important when we later discuss the social and private nature of information as a product. This distinction is different from the use of information for the purpose of control. Control can be exercised whatever the type of ownership assumed.

9. This point is emphasized later to justify the government's role in the provision of information.

10. There is a third set of organizations which provide information. These organizations can be called nonprofit organizations. As for control, they would exert a minimum influence since their target group is usually small and mostly educated with above-average income who can afford making donations in the first place.

11. See Parsons (1990) for details on the power of financial press, for example.

12. Wildman (1982) deals in detail with the nature of consumers' response to advertising by examining those factors that determine such responses under different circumstances.

13. For a very comprehensive and interesting discussion on information as a means of control see Mosco (1989, pp. 29-34) where his emphasis is on how such a control process in society renders "fundamental areas of social life."

14. This is synonymous with what Herman and Chomsky (1988) call "propaganda advertising."

15. See, for example. Babe (1988) for evidence and discussion.

16. For a historical review see Hood (1972, p. 74).

17. It is at times possible that consumption, in the case of some social goods that are not "pure" in nature, become rival. This may be due to congestion.

18. Not only is it inefficient to exclude consumers from the consumption of public goods but it may also at times prove to be technically impossible. The best example of this is national defense.

19. The extreme case is when perfect indivisibility prevails. This would be a "pure" public good. National defense comes to mind again.

20. Note that reference to culture as a subsection of the mass media is well justified in that cultural industries include, among other things, newspapers, book publishing, journal publishing etc. All these are sources of information that we have identified as the output of mass media.

21. See Granham (1990, pp. 162-163) for more details on this.

22. Tehrani (1979) provides an excellent review of literature on the relationship between mass media and economic development.

23. Note that, Mosco (1989), in his analysis, makes a clear distinction between seeing information as a resource and information as defined by system theorists.

24. See Abizadeh and Basilevsky (1986) for a comprehensive discussion on the multidimensional aspect of economic development.

References

Abizadeh, Sohrab and Alexander Basilevsky, (1986), "Socioeconomic Classification of Countries: A Maximum Likelihood Factor Analysis Technique," *Social Science Research*, 15:97-112.

Babe, Robert E., (1988), "Emergence and Development of Canadian Communication: Dispelling the Myths," in Lorimer and Wilson (1988a), pp. 58-79.

Browning, Edgar K. and Jacquelene M. Browning, (1983), *Public Finance and the Price System*, (2nd. ed.), New York: McMillan Publishing Co., Inc.

Cracract, James (ed.) (1988), (2nd ed.), *The Soviet Union Today: An Interpretive Guide*, Chicago: University of Chicago Press.

Downs, A., (1957), *An Economic Theory of Democracy*, New York: Harper and Row.

Granham, Nicholas, (1990), *Capitalism and Communication: Global Culture and Economics of Information*, London: Sage Publications.

Groves, Theodore, Roy Radner, and Stanley Reiter (eds.), (1987), *Information, Incentives, and Economic Mechanisms: Essays in Honor of Leonid Hurwicz*, Basil Blackwell, Oxford.

Groves, Theodore and John O. Ledyard, (1987), "Incentive Compatibility Since 1972," in Groves *el. al.* (eds.) (1987), pp. 48-111.

Hancock, Alan, (1981), *Communication Planning for Development: An Operational Framework*, UNESCO, Monographs on Communication Planning, Paris.

Herman, Edward S. and Noam Chomsky, (1988), *Manufacturing Consent: The Political Economy of the Mass Media*, Pantheon Books, New York.

Hood, Stuart, (1972), *The Mass Media*, London, The MacMillan Press Ltd.

Lorimer, Rowland and Donald Wilson (eds.) (1988a), *Communication Canada: Issues in Broadcasting and New Technologies*, Kagan and Woo Limited, Toronto.

Lorimer, Rowland and Donald Wilson, (1988b), "Threads of Communication Technology in the Fabric of Canadian Life," in Lorimer and Wilson (eds.) (1988a), *Communication Canada: Issues in Broadcasting and New Technologies*, pp. 2-27.

Mosco, Vincent, (1989), *The Pay-Per Society: Computers and Communication in the Information Age*, Garamond Press, Toronto.

Mickiewicz, Ellen, (1988), "The Mass Media," in James Cracract (ed.) (1988), (2nd ed.), *The Soviet Union Today: An Interpretive Guide*, Chicago; The University of Chicago Press, pp. 293-300.

Murrell, Peter, (1991), "Can Neoclassical Economic Underpin the Reform of Centrally Planned Economies? *Journal of Economic Perspectives*, 5:59-76.

Musgrave, Richard, (1959), *The Theory of Public Finance; A Study of Public Economy*, New York: McGraw-Hill Book Company.

Nawaz, Shuja, (1984), "Mass Media in Development: An Overview," *Finance and Development*, 21:44-46.

Nelson, Phillip, (1974), "Advertising as Information," *Journal of Political Economy*, 81:729-748.

Oettinger, Anthony G., (1980), "Information Resources: Knowledge and Power in the 21st Century," *Science*, 209:191-198.

Orr, Daniel, (1987), "Notes on the Mass Media as an Economic Institution," *Public Choice*, 53:79-95.

Picard, Robert G., (1989), *Media Economics: Concepts and Issues*, London: Sage Publications.

Rotstein, Abraham, (1988), "The Use and Misuse of Economics in Cultural Policy," in Lorimer and Wilson (eds.) (1988a), *Communication Canada: Issues in Broadcasting and New Technologies*, pp. 140-156.

Schiller, Herbert I., (1971), "Mind Management: Mass Media in the Advanced Industrial State," *Quarterly Review of Economics and Business*, 11:39-52.

Schramm, Wilbur, (1964), *Mass Media and National Development: The Role of Information in the Developing Countries*, Stanford, Stanford University Press.

Stevenson, Robert, L., (1988), *Communications Development, and the Third World: The Global Politics of Information*, New York: Longman.

Stiglitz, Joseph E., (1991), *Wither Socialism? Perspectives for the Economics of Information*, Cambridge: M.I.T. Press.

Syeymour-Ure, Colin, (1974), *The Political Impact of Mass Media*, Beverly Hills: Sage Publications.

Tehrani, Majid, (1979), "Development Theory and Communication Policy: The Changing Paradigms," in Voigt and Hanneman (eds.) (1979), *Progress in Communication Sciences*, pp. 119-166.

Voigt, Malvin J. and Gerhard J. Hanneman, (eds.) (1979), *Progress in Communication Sciences*, Vol 1, Norwood, N.J.: ABLX Publishing Corporation.

Volgyes, Ivan (1975a) (ed.), *Political Socialization in Eastern Europe: A Comparative Framework*, New York: Praeger Publisher.

Volgyes, Ivan (1975b), "Political Socialization in Eastern Europe: A Conceptual Framework," in Volgyes (1975a), *Political Socialization in Eastern Europe: A Comparative Framework*, pp. 1-37.

Wildman, Steve, (1982), "Economic Consequences of the Informational Characteristics of Mass Media," *American Economist*, 26:5-10.

Williams, R., (1958), *Cultures and Society*, London: Chatto and Windus.

Wolfson, Murray (1992), "Transition From a Command Economy: Rational Expectations and Cold Turkey," *Contemporary Policy Issues*," 10:35-43).

CHAPTER 5

THE INFORMATION SOCIETY MODEL: DOES IT SHED LIGHT ON THE CENTRAL AND EASTERN EUROPEAN TRANSITION?

JOEL NOVEK

I. INTRODUCTION

The information society has been widely viewed as the natural successor to the industrial society in the advanced nations. In an information society the production, transformation and exchange of information displaces the production and exchange of tangible goods as the primary focus of economic activity (Bell, 1981). The notion of an information society has been linked to dramatic advances in computer-communications technology (Hanson, 1982), and to the rise of the mass media as a transformative agent (Carey, 1989), to the globalization of economic relations and the breakup and reformulation of the nation state (Greider, 1997). Some have anticipated the collapse of well-established patterns of mass marketing and mass consumption (Turow, 1997) while others have predicted the demise of traditional state and corporate bureaucracies (Toffler, 1990). A related line of argument (Rifkin, 1995) adapts Marx to the information society by anticipating highly polarized hierarchies divided between the global winners and the increasingly underemployed masses.

It is clear that information-related activities have increased in the advanced nations. Between 1960 and 1980 in the United States such activities grew at an average rate of 8.4% per annum (Hurwitz, 1987). The mass media, advertising, printing and publishing, data processing and electronic communications all expanded enormously. In a path-breaking study for the U.S. Department of Commerce, Porat

(1977) documented the transition to an information economy. He argued that information-based occupations are dominant in the American labor force accounting for about 46% of all occupations. This would include information occupations in industrial and service organizations as well as information industries such as telecommunications, broadcasting, advertising, computers and education. OECD data indicate similar trends in Canada, Western Europe and Japan (OECD, 1986). These tendencies have been accelerated by the explosive growth in the Internet and its transformation from a mainly scientific to a quasi-universal communications medium: the network of networks. The number of computer users with Internet links has been estimated to double every year (Johnston, Johnston and Handa, 1995) and is estimated to equal at least 100 million users worldwide.

While the growth of information activities might not be in dispute, there is considerable debate about their social and political implications. In what ways might the information society perspective shed light on the central and Eastern European transition? I have identified three approaches to the information society perspective. The classification I have employed is not exhaustive but is meant to be suggestive of debates current in the literature. I have labeled the three approaches as "information as freedom", "information as control" and "information as a resource". Each approach represents a different orientation to the social and political impact of information technology. I will now explore the three perspectives in greater detail and assess their utility in furthering our understanding of Eastern Europe's transition to capitalism. I will then discuss some ways in which the East European transition differs markedly from the information society model commonly employed in the advanced democracies.

II. Information as Freedom

This perspective is associated with popular literature on the spread of microcomputers and information technology in general. Notable here has been the work of such writers as Toffler (1980) and Naisbitt (1982). Most important for our purposes, modified versions of this perspective have been taken by a number of influential scholars such as Pool (1983), Cleveland (1985) and Fukayama (1989). From this point of view, information is perceived as the product of technology. In other words, information is what is produced by microcomputers, advanced communications networks, electronic mail, fax machines, video cassettes, cable television and satellite transmission.

The information explosion advances the cause of liberal democracy and freedom throughout the world. It undermines traditional hierarchical and bureaucratic structures such as those described in the writings of Max Weber and Harold Innis (Taylor, 1981). It breaks down the secrecy and monopolies of knowledge on which traditional hierarchies have been based. Information "leaks"; it cannot be easily bottled up or controlled. It is infinitely expandable, diffused, accessible and shareable. Unlike oil or minerals, consumption cannot diminish supply. Scarcity, the usual basis of hierarchical and allocative politics, no longer applies. "Freedom is fostered when means of communication are dispersed, decentralized and easily available, as are printing presses and microcomputers" (Pool, 1983: 5).

As Cleveland observed in 1985: "The new information environment seems bound to undermine the knowledge monopolies which totalitarian governments convert into monopolies of power. In the horoscope of the USSR and the Soviet bloc, a future looms where nobody is in charge" (Cleveland, 1985, p. 193). Or, to quote Fukuyama on the "end of history": "We might summarize the content of the universal homogeneous state as liberal democracy in the political sphere combined with easy access to stereos and VCRs in the economic" (Fukuyama, 1989, p. 8). Whatever our views of the role of information technology in the changes that have taken place in Eastern Europe, these observations cannot simply be ignored as they draw our attention to the precarious state of all claims to authority in an increasingly wired world (Couch, 1996). An interesting example of this occurred in the former Soviet Union, in 1991, when many Muscovites first learned of the attempted coup against Mikhail Gorbachev by watching CNN on cable. In the advanced market economies, the new environment encourages deconcentration, decentralization and demassification. The "Fordist" regime of standardized mass production and mass consumption, under the watchful tutelage of the welfare state, is declining (Piore and Sabel, 1984). In its place is a new system of specialized production geared to the shifting nuances of consumer demand. Just as computerized information systems allow airlines to adjust fares and schedules to changing patterns of demands, so they also allow manufacturers, retailers and advertisers (Turow, 1997) to serve more specialized and segmented markets. Consumers become prosumers. Electronic networks allow for telework (Qvortrup, 1992) meaning more and more service work to be performed at home, supposedly collapsing the separation between work and home which was long seen as a hallmark of the Industrial Revolution.

There is considerable discussion about the decline of the nation state in the information era. National sovereignty means less and less as information and financial networks span the globe. As Valaskakis (1991) suggests, the current stage of globalization involves transborder movements of factors of production such as capital, labor and technology. The world electronic highway de-localizes international production and accelerates the mobility of productive factors. Cleveland (1985) sees the state breaking down at the top with increased pooling of sovereignty in international alliances with Europe as the leading model. It is leaking sideways as multinational corporations cross political frontiers. It is also leaking from the bottom as minorities, special communities and single-issue constituencies take control of their own affairs and seize the information agenda.

The information-as-freedom perspective presupposes the free market ideology which has superseded welfare state Keynesianism as the dominant principle for structuring economic relations. The global information explosion parallels the expansion of the global market economy. Freedom is equated with open access to information in a vast information marketplace. Democracy is equated with citizen choice similar to consumer choice. The role of the mass media is to promote citizen and consumer choice in an information-rich environment. The dominant image is one of individual choice and a high degree of accessibility to information services. State and public sector attempts to control the information marketplace are seen as regressive and counter-productive.

The key issue of social transformation in the information society is one of coping with change -- of taming the information tiger. This is especially the case as the forces unleashed by the information explosion are alleged to threaten all existing hierarchical and vertically-ordered relationships. Order can only be created out of anarchy through the voluntary creation of new, non-hierarchical, horizontal social formations. Taylor (1981) refers to the "electronic grapevine" replacing traditional office hierarchies. Cleveland (1985) refers to a process of "mutual adjustment" based on wide consultation and openness. Pool (1983) suggests a "de-massified" system of electronic media interconnected by convention. All this suggests an electronic social contract in which networks of consensual and egalitarian relationships are created out of the ashes of crumbling hierarchies based on secrecy and scarcity (Toffler, 1990).

Allocative issues are dealt with dismissively in this perspective. In the new information society we are all assumed to be winners with the possible exception of the former elites from traditional hierarchies and knowledge monopolies. Alternatively, success is held to derive from "symbolic" (Angell, 1996) mastery of the new technologies. Critics have charged that excessive focus on the alleged benefits of the information superhighway masks distributional conflicts unfolding in its wake (Rifkin, 1995; Menzies, 1996). Conflicts have arisen over work which has been restructured, downsized, automated or contracted out. Time has also been a bone of contention (Ide and Cordell, 1994). The relentless demands of telephone, fax and e-mail have been used to prolong the working day of many employees. At the same time, large numbers of part-time, temporary or "virtual" employees cannot accumulate enough hours to properly support themselves or their families.

Clearly there are contradictions in the global village. Information can be treated as a free good -- part of a global information commons -- or it can be treated as a commodity -- part of a global information marketplace. If the latter then assumptions of the end of information scarcity -- and of hierarchies built on this scarcity -- must be challenged. We are also looking at simultaneous trends toward deconcentration and the erosion of national sovereignty, on the one hand, and a globalized economy, on the other. If the latter trend is significant, then the growth of multinational corporations and supra-national alliances, riding the world electronic highway, will dwarf the utopian image of a horizontal network of egalitarian information receivers and transmitters. It is this possibility which mega-financier George Soros has recently labeled "the capitalist threat" to the open society (Soros, 1997).

The notion of information as freedom has had great appeal in the east European societies undergoing transition, especially in the heady days leading up to and following the collapse of the Berlin Wall and the Iron Curtain generally. The power of information technology and western communications media to penetrate and ultimately weaken eastern knowledge monopolies by disseminating counterveiling images of a liberal market society was clearly evident. However, many east European societies lack the history and traditions of independent media institutions strong enough to create a truly open market in information. While some nations, notably Poland and Czech Republic have made great strides in liberalizing access to information, in other countries media channels remain tied to the state or branches of the state. Where civil society in the western sense remains underdeveloped, the comparatively weak market and voluntary sectors are unable to create open media channels sufficiently strong to compete with the dominant state ones. For this reason we should be cautious in presuming that the western model of an open, competitive marketplace in information exists in the emerging societies of the east.

III. Information as Control

The polar opposite of the perspective which equates information technology with the spread of liberal democracy is one which sees it as facilitating a deepening of pre-existing tendencies toward control. The analysis of contemporary political economy carried out by most control theorists indicates little potential for using computers and other sophisticated information tools to advance democratic ends. Information supplied under conditions of advanced capitalism does not democratize (Menzies, 1996); instead, wealth and power are concentrated. Tendencies toward decentralization and deconcentration are largely illusory: the decentralization of power is usually thwarted by the economic and political interests of those who have the social power to apply computer and information technology (Mosco, 1989, p. 80).

Control theorists emphasize the use of microelectronic technology by those in positions of influence to strengthen existing patterns of domination. This would include a tendency toward centralized monitoring and control of human behavior in the workplace, in the mass media, in domestic consumption, and in the political arena. Globalized communications networks and powerful electronic highways do not promote liberalism and egalitarianism. Rather, they facilitate new "monopolies of knowledge" (Moshowitz, undated) by powerful transnational corporations that dominate the production and dissemination of information in commodified form. These corporations can use computer-communications networks to organize an international division of labor under centralized command-and-control. "Now the technical means for integrated management of far-flung industrial operations is at hand in the form of computer-communications" (Moshowitz, undated, p. 10). The time/space constraints of such diffuse operations can be overcome.

Reinecke (1984) and Noble (1984) have observed the increasing utilization of information technology to tighten control at the point of production. Sophisticated management information systems replace human labor with machine intelligence and reduce operator discretion in those jobs which remain. Computerized machine tools and robotics have displaced skilled workers from the factory floor from the automotive and heavy engineering industries to printing and publishing. Office work has been simplified and subjected to computerized monitoring and control. The latter has been especially prevalent among airline reservations clerks and telephone operators who have found themselves on the inside of an electronic fishbowl. Hierarchies on the job have not been dissolved; they have been intensified.

Control theorists make similar observations about the control of consumer behavior. Computer networks provide a mass of information for the social management of individuals including a detailed monitoring of consumer choices. As Reinecke observes: "The creations of communications networks increases the potential for surveillance and social control...where people shop, what they buy, how and whether they travel, and whether they stay would be information available instantly to the electronic Big Brother" (Reinecke, 1984, p. 172). Beniger (1986) traces the history of what he calls "The Control Revolution" to industry's need for detailed information and record-keeping of distribution, marketing and mechanizing. Contrary to claims that new information technologies have functioned to increase the availability of information, Beniger argues that many such technologies have in fact been designed to restrict the information flow in the service of large public and private bureaucracies. For example, computer punch-cards and questionnaires are designed to limit the response options of survey subjects and thus make it easier for organizations to process the results.

If information democrats have drawn an image of egalitarian networks or global villages, control theorists have drawn a powerful counter-image of centralized surveillance, of Bentham's Panopticon as outlined in the work of Foucault (1986). Surveillance of the many by the few becomes both metaphor and reality. Control theorists and information democrats are similar in one respect, however. Both link the increasing utilization of technology to the rise of an advanced capitalist economy, though with very different implications. Foucault's "disciplines", which would include surveillance, are necessary characteristics of a sophisticated industrial society. The technological mutations of the apparatus of production, the division of labor, and the elaboration of the disciplinary techniques sustain an ensemble of very close relations. Each makes the other possible and necessary; each provides a model of the other (Foucault, 1986, p. 210).

By taking a critical perspective, control theorists avoid the naive optimism and the failure to give sufficient credence to allocative and distributional questions characteristic of the information democrats. However, control theorists mistake asymmetrical power relations for domination. They create models of domination without paying enough attention to agency, conflict, counterveilling forces or other change mechanisms. Ironically, control theorists present a version of the "end of history" in the form of the global capitalist superstate, backed up by high technology, which is the obverse side of the triumph of liberal democracy. Control theorists miss the sense of possibilities and alternatives which prevails in current public policy debates.

Opportunities have been created to use technology to enhance public access as well as private profit. The environmental movement has strengthened the notion of the global commons in opposition to the global marketplace (Daly and Cobb, 1989). Growing interest in environmental and health issues has led to new uses for information and information technology. Similarly, the women's movement and rising consciousness among native and national minorities in a variety of countries has helped to redefine what we mean by information and, for the matter, knowledge. Finally, the end of the Cold War has weakened the military-industrial complex in the western nations as well as the organization of information channels for national security. It is unclear whether the new focus of international competition along economic lines can call for the same degree of national discipline as did the previous Cold War regime.

In terms of east European realities, the information as control model might have been useful in describing the top-down knowledge monopolies of the recent past but would be far less relevant to the present fluid time of transition. The current period points to a situation of pluralism and diversity in political and social claims representing a sharp break with the rigidities and restraints of Communist party control. Kolarska-Bobinska (1992) describes a situation of anomy in Eastern Europe mediated by greater availability of information than of other socio-economic resources. Information channels, especially those which have been influenced by the west, encourage people to desire a higher standard of living and more political democracy than their present situation permits. This, however, heightens the prevailing sense of dissatisfaction. The old controls have vanished and new forms of control possible with a fully-fledged market society are by no means firmly established.

IV. Information as a Resource

The information-as-a-resource perspective provides a moderate alternative to the democratic enthusiasts and the control theorists. Proponents of this perspective view information as the key resource around which economic and political activity is organized (Castells, 1996). Some theorists, notably Bell (1973; 1981) and Masuda (1981), have viewed the emergence of a post-industrial or information society as representing a historical disjunction, one which is qualitatively different from the industrial society which preceded it. Other such as Oettinger (1980) and Luhmann (1982) see the information analogy as furnishing a useful model with which to analyze complex societies similar to the application of clockwork models in the eighteenth century or natural selection in the nineteenth. "Every society is an information society and every organization is an information organization, just as every organism is an information organism' (Oettinger, 1980, p. 209).

Considerable attention is paid to allocative and distributional issues in the information-as-resource model. Society is viewed as a complex of cross-cutting organizations and socio-cultural divisions. There is neither the individualized anarchy of the information democrats nor the domination of the control theorists. For Daniel Bell (1981), information serves as the "axial principle" around which social life is organized. Social stratification is transformed by the rise of a new professional, managerial and technical class to elite status. New intellectual technologies such as cost/benefit analysis, decision theory and systems analysis become the basis for authoritative and legitimate decision-making. The emphasis on expertise and meritocracy does not obviate the need for political solutions to questions of value, however. If anything, the political arena becomes more highly charged as a variety of interest groups seek technical solutions to questions of value in a time of limited resources.

Since the demands of mobilized interest groups tend to be focused on the political system, the result is government overload as well as information overload. Information resource theorists have championed expertise in the form of an expanded role for scientific, technical and managerial professionals and a greater reliance on the new intellectual decision-making technologies as a solution to the problem of government gridlock. The strategic use of information becomes a key factor in decision-making. Scientific and technical-based information not only forms the basis for decision-making but also legitimates those decisions. As indicated above, a reliance on such expertise does not supplant the political process and hence can only be a partial solution to the problem of government overload and rising social claims.

Whereas information democrats and control theorists base their analysis on the centrality of the capitalist free market, information resource theorists tend to downplay its significance. What the information resource theorists tend to overlook is that privatization and deregulation have also been utilized as strategies to relieve the pressure on governments. Market allocation can replace political allocation of values. The continuing preference for free market applications also challenges claims to ascendancy of a new professional and technical class and of new intellectual technologies as the basis for allocative decisions. Market-based principles of allocation and stratification remain central to any analysis..

Information resource theorists have tended to give insufficient attention to the implications of a global economy and global information network. The polity of the nation-state has been presumed to be the basis by which allocative decisions are made. However, this can no longer be assumed. The nation state is weakening at the top, bottom and center. Decisions are increasingly being taken at the transnational or supra-national level. Ethnic nationalism and regionalism are also eroding national authority. No discussion of the information society or even the information resource can take place in isolation from this reality. This is especially the case in Eastern Europe where many governments lack the legitimacy to deal effectively with rising ethnic and regional conflicts and where ethnic nationalism can complicate the transition to democracy.

V. Discussion

The notion of an information society holds interest for an explanation of the east European transition because open access to information serves as a common element in the development of economic markets and political democracy. Theoretical perspectives on the east European transition to capitalism and democracy have been divided into structural and process arguments (O'Neil, 1996; Kopstein, 1996). Structural arguments are related to modernization theory and place emphasis on the macro-level conditions necessary for the evolution of democracy out of formerly authoritarian political regimes. Such factors as technological development, industrialization, urbanization, education and per capita income are viewed as important correlates of modernization (Chirot, 1986). Process arguments, on the other hand, are related to mobilization theory and are focused on the historical circumstances and events by which actual authoritarian regimes are subject to dissolution and reformulation in a democratic format. The key players in the transition are political elites and their strategies and outcomes rather than broadly based socio-economic variables. Structural arguments tend to be deterministic and evolutionary (Bova, 1991) whereas process arguments tend to be dynamic and contingent.

Perspectives based on the information society model generally fall into the structural category. In this perspective, technological, economic and social transformations of the type associated with modernization theory play a major role in bringing about the dissolution of the former Communist regimes and the transition to the western ideal of a market economy with a democratic polity. Daniel Bell (1981), in his classic work on post-industrialism, has outlined the variables most representative of the emergence of the information society mode of organization. Technologically, there is a shift from energy and machinery-based systems to information, communications and data-transmission-based systems. This includes computers, micro-electronics, software and networks. Economically, there is a relative decline in the importance of agriculture and of goods production as engines of growth and employment; advanced business services such as trade, finance and insurance and public services such as health, education and research enjoy a surge of growth. Occupationally, there is a shift from engineering and semi-skilled workers to a more differentiated and upgraded labor force with growth in scientific, technical, professional and managerial categories. Finally, information, knowledge and intellectual technology replace energy and machine technology as the key economic resources.

It is doubtful if any of these trends were evident, let alone dominant, in Eastern Europe during the period leading up to and including the time of transition. In the fundamentals of information technology--computers, micro-electronics, software and networks--the basic building blocks of the information society, the former Soviet Union and its east European allies found themselves far behind the West during the 1980s with the gap widening rather than narrowing. This was noted by Adirim (1991) in his essay on the development and dissemination of computer technology in Russia. He points out that Russia has suffered a deficit both in the development and production of computers and in their application across the broad spectrum of the Russian economy. Furthermore, this comparative backwardness has become more pronounced towards the end of the past decade. Dyker (1997; 1996) makes a similar point for the transition economies of Eastern Europe, arguing that technological failures played a central role in their descent into stagnation and then decline. Their most striking failure was in relation to micro-electronic technology.

As a result (of the information technology gap), the socialist countries of Eastern Europe missed out on a complete generation of new generic technologies, notably flexible production systems, digital communications technology, etc. "These failures, common to the most developed and least developed CMEA countries played a direct role in the collapse of the Soviet-type economic system and its clones" (Dyker, 1997, p. 446).

While such assertions may beg the question of the precise connection, if any, between technological failures and regime transitions, their major point is well taken. An information society model cannot be used to explain current transitions--except as some sort of vague blueprint for the future--unless the basic infrastructure and building block technologies of its implementation are in place. This is far from the case at present in Eastern Europe where the implementation of computerization continues to lag behind the west even though the pace of technology transfer far exceeds what was possible under the previous Communist governments.

Similarly, data on economic sectors, occupational shifts and quality of life indicators show that the east European societies lagged far behind the west in the development of patterns of social organization consistent with the information society model. The kinds of sectoral shifting we take for granted in the West-- out of primary and secondary processing and into professional, technical, and informational activities-- were not a significant factor in the east European transition. Data from the former Soviet Union indicate that agriculture accounted for 31% of the Soviet GNP in 1950 declining to 14% in 1980 while the relative share of manufacturing almost doubled from 20% to 37% in the same period (Lane, 1985, p. 54). The combined share of agriculture and manufacturing in the Soviet economy actually increased from 45% to 51% between 1950 and 1980 which suggests little likelihood of any shift into advanced services and informational modes of economic activity.

Occupational data indicate a similar pattern. Manual workers and collective farmers represented 81.6% of the Soviet labor force in 1959 falling gradually to 74.9% in 1979 and 74.1% in 1983 (Lane, 1985, p. 189). This is far from the occupational structures common in the west where clerical, service, technical and information workers predominate.

The backwardness of Soviet and east European technology, management and industrial organization impeded the movement of technical and human capital out of agriculture and industry and into emerging service and informational activities. Bialer (1986) has noted that Soviet labor productivity growth fell from over 3% per annum during the 1960s to a situation of stagnant or negative productivity growth in the period 1980-84. At the same time, capital productivity was negative leading to significant declines in total factor productivity by the early 1980's (Bialer, 1986, p. 60). This meant that the Soviets, and by implication east Europeans in general, would have had to devote considerable more labor, capital and natural resources than their western counterparts to produce the equivalent agricultural and industrial commodities. The economic transition to an information society, facilitated by higher productivity in established industrial and agricultural sectors, was effectively blocked.

Quality of life indicators also demonstrate the comparative backwardness of Eastern Europe. The United Nations Development Programme (1995; 1996) established the human development index, a comprehensive ranking of human development based on measures of life-expectancy, education and GDP per capita drawn from 1992 data. It examined such indicators as life expectancy, infant mortality, population-per-doctor, primary, secondary and post-secondary enrollment ratios and newspapers and televisions per 100 people. The transition countries of Eastern Europe find themselves, without exception, ranked at the bottom of the list of industrial nations (United Nations Development Programme, 1995, p. 18). Czech Republic, Slovakia, Belarus and Estonia are ranked the highest of the transition group, listed as 38th, 40th, 42nd and 43rd, respectively, among industrial nations just behind Malta and Portugal. A middle group consisting of Hungary, Poland, Russia and Ukraine is ranked 50th, 51st, 52nd and 54th, respectively. At the bottom are such countries as Armenia, Georgia and Romania, ranked below at least fifty developing nations in Africa, Asia and Latin America.

Advanced capabilities in education, health care and the social services, at the core of the information society model, remain a distant dream in much of Eastern Europe which has had to confront decline and loss of capability in many areas of social service delivery. Between 1980 and 1993, the human development index for the nations of Eastern Europe and the former Soviet Union fell by 7%, the only region of the world to experience a decline in that period (United Nations Development Programme, 1996, p.15). This decline mirrors a number of staggering social and economic problems such as sharply negative rates of economic growth, falling life expectancy and an upsurge in criminality, unemployment and ethnic fragmentation.

However, the major reason why the information society model does not easily lend itself to an explanation of the east European transition is that it is based on developments in advanced capitalism and market institutions which have few counterparts in the former East bloc nations. According to Castells (1996), the information society represents a new departure in the evolution of capitalism. Information becomes the key strategic resource applied to knowledge generation and information processing which is crucial for stimulating innovation and sustaining economic activity. Critical markers in the emergence of informational capitalism include: globalized markets in finance, products, services, technology and information itself; flexible forms of enterprise allowing for rapid adaptation to changing technological and market conditions; and network enterprises allowing for flexible linkages among firms and units of firms. Advances in information technology permit the development of interactive, computer based flexible processes of management, production and distribution (Castells, 1996, p. 170). The entrepreneurial spirit is pervasive as enterprises are formed, merged, spun off, linked, networked and dissolved.

This new mode of informational capitalism assumes an established infrastructure of private property, markets and a business-minded middle class with the aptitude, resources and influence to be the driving force behind capitalist institutions. This would include a strong market sector along with a state sector whose mission is largely to provide support for business activity. The strong market sector, then, becomes the launching pad for the development of informational capitalism. In the classical version of modernization theory (Moore, 1966; Lindblom, 1977), a rising middle class of entrepreneurs and merchants is behind the growth of markets and private property and seeks to limit the power of government to intrude on its wealth and economic opportunity. The new bourgeoisie is responsible not only for economic development but also for political freedom as its demand for limits on governmental power evolves into modern forms of political democracy. An open market in information services and the infrastructure which makes this possible provide the link between free markets and democratic politics.

The problem with this theory is that in most of Eastern Europe, the nascent bourgeois classes were too weak and uninfluential to carry out their designated role of leading the transition to economic marketization and political democracy. Bova (1991), writing about Poland and Russia, observes: "While, as previously noted, Communist regimes have lacked the ability and desire to eliminate all private economic activity... they have managed to preempt the emergence of any potential political challenge from a rising capitalist elite by effectively monopolizing control of the commanding heights of their industrial economies. Whether a substitute stratum (the managerial class? intellectuals? foreign governments and capital?) can emerge to fill the historical role of the merchant and entrepreneurial classes remains to be seen" (Bova, 1991, p. 134).

More recent writings have taken up this question and examined alternative social groups who could substitute for the bourgeoisie in bringing about the transition to market society. David Lane (1996) has drawn the parallel between contemporary Russia and nineteenth century Germany and Japan. In the latter two nations, the indigenous mercantile classes were too weak to lead the transition to industrial capitalism, and so this function was carried out by elements of the landowning and aristocratic strata of the *ancient regime*. Lane argues that in Russia subgroups from within the current political leadership are attempting to bring about the transition to marketized social relations based on models imported from the west: "Hence, like the move to capitalism in Germany and Japan; Russia under Eltsin has had to pursue a revolution from above" (Lane, 1996, p. 545).

Others have argued in favor of a somewhat different version of this thesis, suggesting that the transition to capitalism is being directed less by current political elites but rather by a group composed largely of the former Communist nomenklatura leadership. Brym's (1996) observations on Russia and Rosenberg's (1993) on Poland suggest continuity of power at the elite level. Brym asserts that criminal elements, as well as the former nomenklatura, are playing a leading role.

In the mid-1980's, when private enterprise was legalized after a nearly 60 year hiatus and some of the controls that have previously hampered business activity were removed, two groups were organized and wealthy enough to seize most of the new economic opportunities in the USSR. One was the Communist Party of the Soviet Union and some of its affiliated party and state bodies such as the Komsomol and the KGB. The other was the criminal underworld. The history of Russia in the past decade is the story of how these two groups and their capital pools managed to grow, intertwine and take over most of the economy.(Brym, 1996, p. 396)

There are several points that should be made here. One is that it is important to distinguish those who are directing the transition to a market economy from those who arc merely benefiting (Lane, 1996). Secondly, there are important differences among transition economies in their progression along the road toward economic liberalization. Based on 1995 data, only in Czech Republic and Eastern Germany is as much as two-thirds GDP generated in the private sector (Kaser, 1997, p. 465). In another ten states--including Hungary, Slovakia, Poland, the Baltic States and Russia--the balance between public and private sectors stands at 50%. Since state institutions remain paramount in most eastern countries while market institutions are less developed, it is not surprising that those who controlled access to state resources in the former command economy, as well as those who control them in the new transition economy, are able to stake out a favorable position for themselves. To the extent that the market remains subservient to the state, the ascendancy of the political class in the market is reinforced. The communications field in which most of the media channels are either state-controlled or dependent on state support is one which is especially prone to influence by those with political connections. New technologies, new forms of business enterprise and capital markets have afforded the most dynamic segments of various political elites with the opportunity to profit from the social vacuum and expand their position ahead of other groups.

While we in the west should be concerned about these developments and their possible negative implications for democracy, we should not be surprised. A considerable amount of the economic history written about non-English speaking nations has documented the significant role played by political or aristocratic elites from agrarian regimes in bringing about the transition to industrial capitalism in the late nineteenth and early twentieth centuries. We have already referred to the "revolutions from above" in Germany and Japan where industrialization was promoted as an essential means toward the goal of military and state power rather than the Anglo-American goal of a liberal market society (Fallows, 1993). A revolution from above, on the nineteenth century German and Japanese model, raises the specter of top down control and limits on the free flow of information necessary for both open markets and political democracy. Political elites are able to occupy leading positions in Eastern Europe's transition to capitalism since state authority over the market remains strong while indigenous entrepreneurial classes are too weak to contest the former's leadership. The tight linkages between political and market power look less like the open society championed by Fukuyama (1989) and Soros (1997), among others, though by no means like the authoritiarian regimes of Germany and Japan earlier this century .

VI. Conclusions

Three perspectives on the growing role of information in advanced industrial societies have been reviewed and analyzed. All contain useful insights. None can be held to be exhaustive of the subject. The question that needs to be addressed is how useful is the information analogy or information model in providing an explanation of Eastern Europe's so far imperfect transition to market capitalism and political democracy. The question is complicated by the fact that the technological, occupational, economic and social factors associated with the development of an information society are still very much less evident in the east than they are in the west. For this reason, concepts developed in the west to describe the transition to information-based forms of activities should only be applied with caution to the east.

REFERENCES

Adirim, I., (1991), "Current Development and Dissemination of Computer Technology in the Soviet Economy", *Soviet Studies*; 43 (4): 651-667.

Angell, I., (1996), "Winners and Losers in the Information Age", *Culture and Society*, November/December, 81-85.

Bell, D., (1981), ``The Social Framework of the Information Society" in *The Microelectronics Revolution,* Tom Forrester, ed., MIT Press: Cambridge MA.

Beniger, J., (1986), *The Control Revolution,* Harvard University Press: Cambridge MA

Bialer, S., (1986), *The Soviet Paradox*, Knopf: New York.

Bova, R., (1991), "Political Dynamics of the Post Communist Transition", *World Politics*, 44: 113-138.

Brym, R., (1996), "The Third Rome and the End of History: Notes on Russia's Second Communist Revolution" *Canadian Journal of Sociology and Anthropology,* 33 (4): 391-406.

Carey, J., (1989), *Communication as Culture,* Unwin: Boston.

Castells, M., (1996), *The Information Age: The Rise of the Network Society,* Blackwell: Oxford.

Chirot, D. (1986), *Social Change in the Modern Era*, Harcourt, Brace Jovanovich: San Diego.

Cleveland, H., (1985), "The Twilight of Hierarchy: Speculation on the Global Information Society", *Public Administration Review*, 45, 1: 185-195.

Daly, H. and J. Cobb, (1989), *For the Common Good.* Beacon Press: Boston.

Dyker, D., (1997), "Learning the Game--Technological Factors of Economic Transformation." *Europe -Asia Studies,* 49(3):445-461.

Dyker, D., (1996), "The Computer and Software Industries in the East European Economies: A Bridgehead to the Global Economy?" *Europe-Asia Studies,* 48(6): 915-930.

Fallows, J., (1993), "How the World Works" *Atlantic Monthly,* 272 (6): 60-87.

Foucault, M., (1986), "Panopticism" in *The Foucault Reader*, P. Rabinow, ed., Pantheon Books: New York.

Fukuyama, F., (1989), "The End of History?", *The National Interest,* 16:3-18.

Greider, W., (1997), *One World Ready or Not,* Simon and Schuster: New York..

Hanson, D., (1982). *The New Alchemists.* Avon Books: New York

Hurwitz, R., (1987), "Patterns of Media Use in Developed and Developing Countries". In *World Pulp and Paper Supply and Demand.* Rome: FAO. Ide, T.R. and A.C., (1994), "The New Tools". In *Shifting Time,* A. Yalnizyan, T. R. Ide and A. Cordell, eds., Between the Lines: Toronto.

Johnston, D., D. Johnston and S. Handa, (1995), *Getting Canada On Line.* Stoddart: Toronto.

Kaser, M., (1997), "Securing the Market System After Transition." *Europe-Asia Studies*, 49 (3): 463-467.

Kolarska-Bobinska, L., (1992), "The Changing Face of Civil Society in Eastern Europe" in *Social Policy in a Changing Europe,* Z.Ferg and J. Kohlberg, eds., Westview Press: Boulder Colorado.

Kopstein, J. (1996), "Chipping Away at the State: Workers' Resistance and the Demise of East Germany". *World Politics*, 48: 391-423.

Lane, D., (1996), "The Transformation of Russia: The Role of the Political Elite." *Europe-Asia Studies,* 48(4): 535-549.

Lane, D., (1985), *Soviet Economy and Society*, New York University Press: New York.

Lindblom, C., (1977), *Politics and Markets*, Basic Books: New York.

Luhman, N., (1982), *The Differentiation of Society,* Columbia University Press: New York..

Masuda, Y., (1981), *The Information Society as Post Industrial Society,* World Future Society: Bethesda, MD.

Menzies, H., (1996), *Whose Brave New World?*, Between the Lines: Toronto.

Moore, B., (1966), *Social Origins of Dictatorship and Democracy,* Beacon Press: Boston.

Mosco, V., (1989), *The Pay-Per Society,* Garamond Press: Toronto.

Moshowitz, A., "Information Technology and the Division of Power". Working Paper #3, *Studies in Communication and Information Technology.* Montreal and Kingston: McGill and Queen's University Press, undated.

Naisbitt, J., (1982), *Megatrends,* Warner: New York.

Noble, D., (1984), *Forces of Production*, Knopf: New York.

OECD., (1986), *Trends in the Information Economy*, OECD: Paris.

O'Neil, P., (1996), "Revolution From Within: Institutional Analysis, Transitions From Authoritarianism and the Case of Hungary." *World Politics*, 48: 579-603.

Piore, M. and C. Sabel, (1984), *The Second Industrial Divide,* Basic Books: New York.

Pool, I. de Sola., (1983), *Technologies of Freedom,* Belknap Press: Cambridge MA.

Porat, M., (1977), *The Information Economy,* U.S. Department of Commerce: Washington.

Qvortrup, L., (1992), "Telework: Visions, Definitions, Realities, Barriers". In *Cities and New Technologies*, OECD: Paris.

Rinecke, I., (1984), *Electronic Illusions*, Penguin Books: New York and Toronto.

Rifkin, J., (1995), *The End of Work,* Putnam: New York.

Rosenberg, T., (1993), "Meet the New Boss: Same as the Old Boss" *Harpers Magazine*, (May): 47-53.

Soros, G., (1997), "The Capitalist Threat", *Atlantic Monthly,* 279 (2): 45-58.

Taylor, J., (1981), "The Office of the Future: Weber and Innis Revisited" *In Search,* 8: 2-13.

Toffler, A., (1980), *The Third Wave,* William Morrow: New York.

Toffler, A., (1990), *Powershift*, Bantam Books: New York.

Turow, J., (1997), *Breaking Up America,* University of Chicago Press: Chicago.

United Nations Development Programme, (1995/1996), *Human Development Report,* Oxford University Press: New York. Valaskakis, K., (1991), "What Exactly is Globalization and What is its Relationship with Information Technology?" in *Canada's Information Revolution,* Conklin, D. and L. Deschenes, eds., Institute for Research on Public Policy: Halifax.

Part Two: Country Cases

CHAPTER 6

THE CZECH EXPERIENCE OF THE INITIATION OF EDUCATIONAL CHANGE SINCE 1989: IS A NORTH AMERICAN MODEL APPLICABLE?*

ANNABELLE MAYS, ELEOUSSA POLYZOI AND SHEENA GARDNER

I. INTRODUCTION

The starting point for this investigation was provided by Průcha (1992) who identifies several major social, political and educational changes which occurred in Czech Republic since the Velvet Revolution of 1989: (a) the political independence of education (change from a totalitarian regime to no political governance in education); (b) the change from Marxist doctrine to philosophical and ideological pluralism in education; (c) the introduction of school alternatives through privatization; (d) the decentralization of education; (e) the change from political criteria, e.g., party membership for educational access, to criteria related to achievement and ability; (f) the change from Russian to English as a first foreign language; and (g) the curricular reformation. These areas formed the framework and background for our initial thinking about events in Czech Republic. Průcha's paper, however, while informative about the broad nature of political, social and educational changes that had occurred, does not address the process of change as events unfolded. Fullan, on the other hand, focuses both on the "what" and the "how" of educational change (Fullan, 1991).

One of the tenets central to Fullan's understanding of educational change is that "change is a process, not an event" (1991, p. 49). Most researchers, he notes, acknowledge three broad phases to the process: initiation, implementation, and continuation. Phase one, initiation, "consists of the process that leads up to and includes a decision to adopt or proceed with a change." The implementation phase, two to three years in length, involves the "first experience of attempting to put an idea or reform into practice." Continuation "refers to whether the change gets built in as an ongoing part of the system or disappears by way of a decision to discard or through attrition" (1991, pp. 47-48). The present study focused its data-collection primarily upon the events and process immediately following the Velvet Revolution. It is for this reason that the discussion will confine itself almost exclusively to an examination of the initiation phase of educational transformation in Czech Republic.

Our aim is to examine the initiation phase of the process of transformation of education in Czech Republic since the Velvet Revolution of 1989 within the framework of the educational change and reform literature, particularly the work of Fullan. This examination will shed some light on the utility of a model informed primarily by North American cases of change at the school or district level within a relatively stable political system, for understanding the events in a Central European setting where change occurred rapidly under conditions of sociopolitical revolution. A revised model is proposed-one that better accounts for the Initiation Phase of educational change in Czech Republic and arguably in other post-Soviet countries.

II. Method

A three-member research team visited Czech Republic in May, 1995. Lengthy interviews were conducted with 22 key individuals, including senior members of the Ministry of Education, educators from British and American organizations, teacher educators, university researchers, and members of advocacy and school reform organizations. Interviewees were selected for their role within the educational system and its transformation. The research team also visited one state and two private schools where they spoke with teachers, school administrators, parents and students.

The variety of participants interviewed was deliberately in accordance with Fullan's concept of "shared meaning of change". Fullan proceeds from a phenomenological basis to explain the social reality of change, to explain why change works as it does. Central to his concept of educational change is the problem of meaning and he argues it is important to understand both the small picture, "the subjective meaning or lack of meaning for individuals at all levels of the educational system" and the larger picture, "the sociopolitical process" (1991, p. 4).

The data collection was enriched considerably when a number of the interviewees contributed important primary documents related to the process of educational transformation. These documents described selected innovative programs, provided statistical data on various aspects of the educational system, and described legislative changes that have been introduced in Czech Republic since 1989.

The authors recognize that the study was based on a restricted period of time and a limited number of interviewees. It is also based on the researchers' perspective and interpretation of events and literature. The sample was broadly-based, but, by necessity, limited geographically to Prague. Despite these limitations, the researchers collected a wealth of information and interviewed many informed, key individuals in the short time available.

Analyses of the data took the form of examining the transcriptions of the taped interviews as well as the extensive notes and documents acquired by the research team. The data were organized and analyzed in order to develop a description of the Czech experiences as a "case" of educational transformation and to assess the extent to which there has been transformation in a number of areas. The data were then matched against models and elements of educational change, identified by Fullan, in order to understand the transformation as a "change" process. A revised model for the initiation of change was developed that better accounts for the Czech experience.

III. Fullan's Model of the Initiation of Educational Change

Fullan notes that there is an infinite range of variables involved in determining whether a change program gets initiated. In his discussion, he concentrates on the factors associated with "planned or action-oriented change" (1991, p. 50) (See Figure 1). He identifies the following eight sources, taken from the literature, which affect initiation: (a) external change agents; (b) new policy--funds (federal/state/local); (c) advocacy from central administration; (d) problem-solving and bureaucratic orientations; (e) community pressure/support/apathy; (f) existence and quality of innovations; (g) access to information; and (h) teacher advocacy. Fullan suggests that change may be initiated from any combination of these sources (1991, p. 61), implying there is no obvious order to these factors. The following case study addresses the utility of each of these factors for understanding particularly the initiation phase of educational transformation in Czech Republic.

IV. The Context

A. Education in Czech Republic before 1989

The Czech Republic is a country with a long tradition of national pride and a history of educational excellence coupled with a predisposition to educational reform. In 1918 Czech independence was achieved with the creation of the First Czechoslovak Republic (1918-1939). During this period the educational system was internationally recognized, the product of decades of scholarly writings (e.g., Comenius, Jan Hus), reform-oriented perspectives and solutions to educational

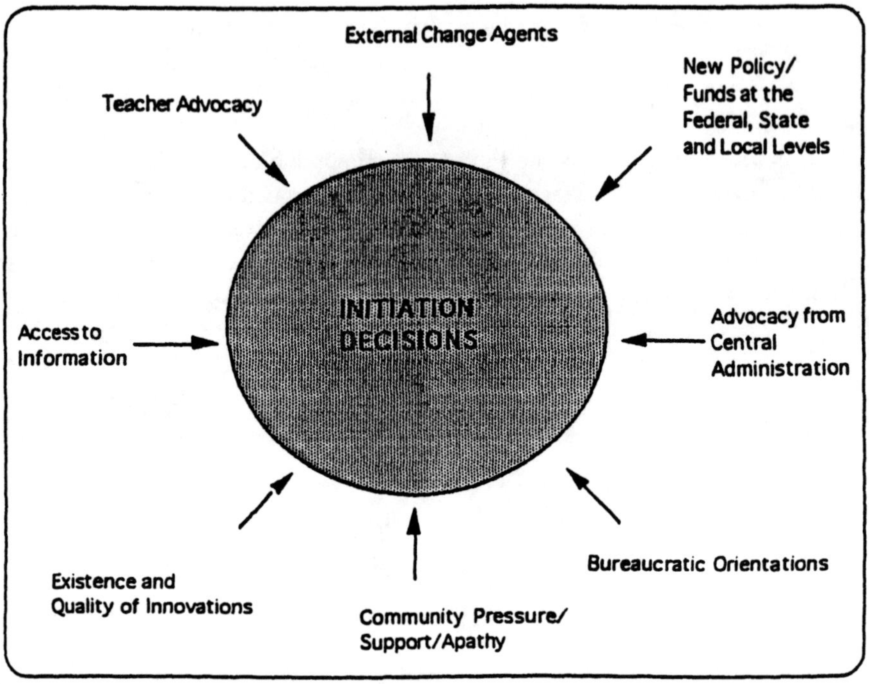

Figure 1: Factors Associated with the Initiation of Change
Source: Fullan, M. (1991). The New Meaning of Educational Change. Toronto: OISE Press, p. 50.

problems, all grounded in a distinguished educational tradition and an exposure to the influences of both European and North American thought (Rydl, 1994, p. 258).

The First Republic came to an end with the events that led up to World War II, and following a period of political difficulty, a constitutional coup d'état resulted in the country entering a long period of Communist rule (1948-1989). The educational system became overlaid with the beliefs of a foreign ideology, Marxist-Leninism, which promoted conformity at the expense of individual development. The application of this doctrine affected the educational system in other ways as well. The educational system became uniform, the curriculum was infused with the

Marxist-Leninist ideology, access to higher education was politically based, and professional isolation was the experience of most educators at all levels of the system (Ministry of Education, Youth and Sports of Czech Republic, 1994; Rydl, 1995). Parents, fearful of spoiling their children's educational and hence occupational chances, generally, neither openly challenged nor participated in the formal educational process. What many did do, however, within the secrecy of their homes, was to pass along to their children the cultural values and historical perspective of the days of the First Republic (Pilátová, 1995). This practice increased following the Prague Spring of 1968, after the Soviet invasion, which served to disillusion many who had been prepared to give Communism a chance.

B. The Velvet Revolution In November, 1989

1989 was a year of tremendous unrest and change as the phenomenon of *glasnost* brought political change to central and Eastern Europe. By November 1989, the popular movement for democracy had overturned the Communist government in Czechoslovakia and the Velvet Revolution was well underway. The first post-'89 government was almost exclusively made up of the leaders of the dissident opposition: writers, economists, political scientists, and lawyers. The Velvet Revolution changed the political, economic and social direction of Czechoslovakia. The country experienced a radical political shift "which replaced the totalitarian regime with a democratic and pluralistic social system", followed in short order by "some fundamental changes in the political and economic sphere" (Průcha, 1992, p. 38). Essentially, the major changes were the following: (a) the constitution of Czechoslovakia was modified expunging the influence of the party and the spirit of Marxist-Leninism from its position of power and control in all spheres of Czech society; (b) a pluralistic parliamentary system was restored and; (c) major changes to the economic system, moving from a centrally-planned economy based strictly on state ownership to a free-market economy highlighting privatization of state-run enterprises, free price setting and competition, and foreign capital investments were introduced (Průcha, 1992).

These political and economic changes resulted from a major shift in the societal values which emerged from the opportunity provided by the withdrawal of Soviet influence. This value shift, however, was experienced in other societal institutions as well. In November 1989 the educational system was still characterized by policies reflecting the values of the Marxist-Leninist ideology and a totalitarian approach which largely negated individual rights and differences and institutionalized the concept of "planning" at all levels of the society. The events of late 1989 set the scene for a major contradiction within the educational system. Educational changes in the form of new legislation were thus initiated to bring greater coherence between societal values expressed in the new political and economic legislation and those reflected in the structure of the educational system. As Amsterdamski and Rhodes (1993, p. 399) so aptly put it, while there is "a widespread and well-founded suspicion of 'master-plans' in the region, there is perhaps a stronger distaste for incoherence" (cited in Farnes, 1996, p. 10).

V. Analysis of the Czech Experience Using Fullan's Model

At least three features of the Czech case set it apart from typical cases of educational change depicted by Fullan. First, the initiation of a process to achieve educational change in Czech Republic occurred virtually overnight with the enactment of significant legislation; second, it was largely conducted in the absence of any established plan for initiating a desired vision or goal; and third, this process occurred both at the national level and at the level of the school. Fullan presumes that the purpose of educational change is "to help schools accomplish their goals more effectively by replacing some structures, programs and/or practices with better ones" (1991, p. 15). While this need not necessarily be construed as meaning that educational change begins at the local school level as opposed to the national level, or that it begins at the level of the individual institution rather than the society at large, the statement does typify much of Fullan's discussion. Conversely, that educational change occurs at the national level need not entail that the ultimate purpose is not change at the classroom, school or district level. The immediate goals and perspectives are, however, different. The following description of Fullan's eight factors as they apply in the Czech case reveals where the differences lie.

A. External Change Agents

In the case of the Czech experience perhaps the most logical place to begin in order to understand the process of change is with some understanding of the external change agents. In the case of Czech Republic, educational change was not simply an innovation or project being introduced at some local level. Fullan classifies external change agents as regional, state or national roles, external to the district (p. 56). In this sense, an examination of the external change agents as a factor affecting initiation in the Czech experience is potentially problematic since the unit of analysis for educational transformation in Czech Republic is at the national level, at least for the original impetus for change. One must look therefore outside Czech Republic for external change agents.

At the state level, several groups of external change agents can be identified. One could perhaps build the argument that an external agent, *glasnost*, enabled the emergence of internal change agents in the form of legislators to initiate change. Moreover, what *glasnost* had begun, the Velvet Revolution accelerated so that increased contact with the rest of the world brought many external change agents.

First, there was an influx of westerners and an increase in the activities of western organizations (Litalouš, 1995). For example, funding for educational projects and human resources was provided by PHARE (European Union Program for 11 Central and Eastern European countries), the Soros Foundation, the British Council, the American Information Agency, MENT (Man, Education and New Technologies), Education for Democracy and the Peace Corps (Griffiths, 1995; Perclová, 1995). Secondly, there were increased opportunities for contact with Western European countries through teacher and student exchanges, conferences and professional development opportunities in other countries. These held the potential for change or transformation at the classroom level (Rydl, 1995). There was also increased access and attention to scholarly literature from around the world by university and other scholars who had the potential to work for change through teaching, participation in reform and advocacy groups, and the development of reform proposals (Spilková, 1995).

Although the external change agents were noted, documented, and acknowledged by many interviewees in Czech Republic, it is interesting that a significant group of interviewees did not perceive them as shaping the nature of the changes that occurred. This view that change had come from internal sources emerged in relation to both legislative changes from the top as well as changes initiated by individual teachers and parents, at the grass roots level. The relative influence of external versus internal change agents led to two different views of the future of education in Czech Republic, as expressed in terms of the proposals submitted to the Ministry.

B. New Policy Funds

Fullan acknowledges the important role that the various levels of government can take in initiating major educational change through legislative action. New policies, he notes, "especially if accompanied by funds, stimulate and sometimes require initiation of change at the local level" (1991, p. 58). It has already been noted that subsequent to the Velvet Revolution new political and economic legislation was quickly enacted which set the stage for major changes in the Czech educational system. In some cases educational change was mandated by the legislation while other legislation enabled change to occur as a consequence. The major policy changes include the following.

1. The teaching of Marxist doctrine in primary, secondary and university school curricula was abolished, inadvertently creating a vacuum of suitable instructional materials for teachers to use in history, social science and civic studies (Průcha, 1995). According to some, a new ideology of democracy and tolerance has not yet taken its place (NEMES, 1995).

2. The Proposal for the Innovation of Act No. 29, 1984, in the System of Basic and Secondary Schools, 1990 allowed for the creation of private and religious schools to be funded by the state. It has been suggested that these private schools serve as a catalyst for change in the state schools (Rydl, 1995; Průcha & Walterová, 1992). Although private schools have been in existence for five years, no data currently exist on how they function or how effective they are.

3. The Act of the Czech National Council on the State Administration of Education and School-Based Management introduced decentralization in the school system. Decision-making had been centralized in the hands of the Ministry but the new act gave more responsibility to teachers, principals, and local authorities (Průcha & Walterová, 1992).

4. The Act on Higher Education and other legislation accorded autonomy and political independence to institutions of higher education (Průcha & Walterová, 1992).

5. The teaching of Russian as a foreign language was no longer obligatory. English became the first foreign language of choice among students (Průcha, 1992).

6. In 1990 a new system of funding for schools was also introduced. Funding was shifted from a needs-based approach to normative funding where "money followed the student." Students were free to select the school they attended and as a result schools became very competitive. The system of normative funding has indirectly prompted schools to begin developing alternative curricula and unique programs to attract more students.

These policy changes constitute "change from the top" but what was noticeably absent was an encompassing vision which informed and linked these legislative initiatives (Kalouš, 1995). At the same time, however, a concurrent trend was evident at the grass roots level. The newly elected government in June, 1990, recognizing that it had no expertise in educational reform solicited public participation in the development of proposals for transforming the educational system. These submissions were to serve as a basis for discussion in Parliament and for the creation of subsequent legislation. Between 1990 and 1992, some 70 proposals were submitted by institutions, organizations, and individuals.

The proposals essentially fell into two camps. Groups such as the Ministry of Education, and the Faculty of Pedagogy, Charles University argued for maintaining the form and structure of state schools (Rydl, 1995; Průcha & Walterová, 1992). Reform groups argued for the introduction of autonomous schools, a child-centered curriculum, the humanization of education, a focus on development of critical skills and problem-solving, and diversification of curricular options. The three reform groups whose proposals were most influential were NEMES (Independent Interdisciplinary Group for the Reform of Education and School), an independent, interdisciplinary group with several hundred members including teachers, psychologists, sociologists and economists (NEMES, 1995); IDEA (Independent and Diverse Educational Alternatives), which presented a vision of a "democratic, pluralistic and open educational system" with "effective legislative and economic tools for both the transition period and the final stage" (Botlík, 1994); and PAU (Engaged/Involved Teachers Association), a group of approximately 300 teachers. These community reform groups, which typically spontaneously formed in the first year or two following the revolution, have inspired an emerging vision through their program initiatives which have not always been embraced by the Ministry of Education.

C. Advocacy from Central Administration

Fullan states that "initiation of change never occurs without an advocate, and one of the most powerful is the chief district administrator" (1991, p. 54). Within the context of the Velvet Revolution it would be difficult to attribute advocacy to a single role. One could argue, however, that change was advocated for at all levels of society. According to Kalouš (1995), the fall of Communist rule was like "opening a prison." There was immediate national consensus that change was desirable, indeed expected, after 40 years of totalitarian rule. There was no consensus, however, regarding the direction in which the change should go. One view was to allow the free market to decide the direction of educational change while another suggested a slower, more cautious approach, allowing time for the development of a vision (Kalouš, 1995). These views parallel the philosophical differences between then Prime Minister Klaus, an economist, and President Havel, a humanist and playwright. What can be said, however, is that there were advocates who not only introduced educational change at the highest level of government but who also actively moved to bring about some change, in accordance with Fullan's view of the importance of senior people in the initiation of change.

D. Bureaucratic and Problem-Solving Orientations

This particular factor, as it is described by Fullan, speaks particularly to the orientation that units such as school districts bring to adoption decisions, that is, decisions to introduce an innovation or change. Decision-makers may be either bureaucratic (opportunistic), using the opportunity to gain extra financial and human resources or as a symbolic act of appearing to respond to a given situation, or problem-solvers, using the opportunity to solve a problem. Fullan notes that bureaucratically speaking, "the political and symbolic value of initiation of change for schools is often of greater significance than the educational merit and time and cost necessary for implementation follow-through" (1991, p. 61). Further, he argues for the importance of the symbolic value of decisions. "Such decisions may be necessary for political survival, may be needed first steps that set the preconditions for real change in practice, or may represent the only change possible in certain situations" (1991, p. 61).

There are those in Czech Republic who take a very cynical view of the role of the government in initiating legislative changes, arguing that only what was needed to survive politically was done; that the government adopted, in the absence of any vision, a band-aid approach to educational change. Conversely, there are those who see the government and its bureaucrats as having facilitated change through the vehicle of legislative and policy changes. There is probably some truth in both views and what cannot be disputed is that decisions were taken that initiated educational change.

E. Community Pressure Groups

Fullan acknowledges that the role of the community in the initiation process "may be in the form of exerting pressure for a solution to a problem, opposing a potential innovation or adoption, or, doing nothing" (1991, p. 56). In the case of Czech Republic, the community, in the form of the general populace, joined in the call for legislative reform immediately following the events of November, 1989. As has already been noted, when the Ministry of Education requested proposals on the direction the new educational system should take, 65-70 proposals were submitted. Those from NEMES, PAU and IDEA were taken most seriously. Community input was also sought in the form of proposals for experimental projects. Of the several hundred initiatives proposed, 25 were accepted. The new legislation establishing school-based management sought to encourage parent involvement in education through participation on the newly created school boards, but many of these boards were characterized by apathy rather than pressure for change. It was feared by some that the existence of these boards might discourage change in the classrooms in that parents would be more concerned with their children passing entrance exams to the next level of schooling than encouraging change in the classroom which might be perceived as threatening that very possibility. Thus, the situation in Czech Republic reveals community responses that varied from group to group and from the local to the broader societal level.

F. Existence and Quality of Innovations/Access to Information

Interviewees identified three sources of information about innovations relevant to the Czech experience: the collective memory of the educational innovations of the First Republic (1918-1938); the current influence of innovations from North America and Europe; and the more specific programmatic innovations or proposals by local community groups (NEMES, PAU, and IDEA).

Fullan (1992) suggests that individuals' immediate history with change is an important consideration; however, the Czech experience suggests that we must also take into account the national consciousness. The pre-war school reform in Czech Republic was influenced by German pedagogy, French educational psychology, and North American progressive education (Rydl, 1994, p. 258). In 1930, Czechoslovakia was one of the European leaders in school reform. However, this unique social movement was interrupted by World War II, revived for three years following the war, and then destroyed again by the Communist regime in 1948. Following the Velvet Revolution in 1989, new reform schools reviving those of the early 20th century began to reappear (e.g., Waldorf, Rudolf Steiner, Montessori, and Society of Friends of Jan Hus schools). These innovations, however, were rather isolated (Rydl, 1995).

Prior to 1989, innovations emanating from the west were introduced (e.g., new math in the 1970s ((NEMES, 1995); communicative English language teaching in the 1980s (Řepka, 1986)), but innovations visibly connected to the west that were perceived as threatening the political ideology were summarily suppressed. After 1989, cooperative links between Czech state schools and other European and North American schools began to proliferate through teacher exchanges, student travel abroad, and increased access to western and European literature. Such information served to influence, often in a fragmented manner, an emergent vision supported by the more reform-minded teachers (NEMES, 1995). A number of the interviewees, including faculty at Charles University, members of the community reform groups, and government officials at the Ministry of Education, had all traveled abroad and incorporated ideas from the foreign educational literature into their teaching, development of educational policy, or formulation of experimental school proposals such as the "Live School" developed by Cindr, Cindr, Hausenblas and Hávlínová (1995). Thus there are indeed quality innovations in Czech Republic that draw on both a former tradition and contemporary ideas from around the world.

G. Teacher Advocacy

While Fullan observes that teachers as a group, particularly at the school level, have less opportunity than other educators to come into contact with new ideas and less time and energy to follow through on them, he also notes that on a more global level, "national teacher unions have lately become strong advocates of reforms" (1991, p. 55). Certainly, these observations capture the Czech situation. As noted earlier, teachers and other professional educators have combined forces to create reform groups such as NEMES, PAU and IDEA. These groups have been instrumental in creating a grass roots movement promoting a more liberalized, child-centered philosophy of education.

The majority of teachers in the Czech school system, however, are not involved in these grass roots movements. It was estimated that approximately 20% of the teachers support school reform and approximately 40% would be interested in learning about different ways of teaching, but many feel isolated, frustrated and stressed. Primary school teachers who have studied pedagogy tend to be more change-oriented than the secondary school teachers whose training is more specialized and discipline oriented. Although primary teachers are beginning to communicate with secondary teachers, many realize that they do not have a common language (NEMES, 1995). Many competent teachers have unfortunately begun to leave their positions for industry because the challenge of educational transformation is too overwhelming (Rydl, 1995) and the conditions, status and salaries are not competitive.

VI. Additional Factors Arising from the Czech Case

The examination of the Czech case of educational change suggests a number of additional factors which could be incorporated into Fullan's model of the initiation phase of the change process.

A. Window of Opportunity

Rapid political change in the form of *glasnost* and the Velvet Revolution created a window of opportunity for Czech Republic, the "opening of the prison doors", or the "critical time period" for the changes which occurred very quickly in the two years following November 1989. After 40 years of Communist indoctrination, there was an expectation and desire for change to take place speedily. Between 1990-91, educational initiatives were easily introduced and options were flexible. The need for "off with the old", to destroy or rebel against the previous system led to several changes, not all of which might have happened if more planning had taken place or if people had thought more objectively about the consequences. In fact, the concept of "planning", particularly "master planning" (Farnes, 1996) was firmly associated with the Communist regime and it, along with other values and "ways of doing things," was rejected after the Velvet Revolution.

However, the Czech experience as it is unfolding strongly suggests that the opportunity presented by the Velvet Revolution is time-bound and that increasingly change will be more difficult. According to Rydl (1995) many individuals, organizations, and institutions no longer work cooperatively. Many are tired or "burned out" after expending great energy on initial change. Each has their own vested interest, based on different philosophical orientations that have become more entrenched with time. "It is becoming increasingly difficult to agree on the basic direction that education should take ... We have lost that critical time period when we were open to change." (Rydl, 1995). Implicit within Rydl's statements is acknowledgement of the importance of the "window of opportunity" for the introduction of change, the acknowledgement that opportunity can be "lost."

B. Predisposition to Change

A second factor identified from this case and seen to be important to the initiation of change is the predisposition to change. In the Czech case, this predisposition results from past collective and individual experience. Czech Republic has a long and valued tradition of educational reform and innovation. As a result there exists among the educational community a predisposition to change stemming from a collective memory of a pluralistic, innovative educational system typified by the turn-of-the-century Steiner and Waldorf schools. In addition to this scholarly educational tradition, there had been some advanced preparation for change (Kaufman, 1966, p. 638) in the form of changes to the math and English curricula, amongst others. Further, there had been expanded access to non-Soviet ideas with increased *glasnost* which planted seeds of change. Also inherent in the Czech disposition is a desire for consistency, so there was a great need to resolve the value contradictions that arose between the new hopes for humanitarianism, liberty and democracy and the existing education system which enshrined uniformity and Marxist-Leninist ideology.

On an individual level, the personal experience of people at all levels of the system was also a significant aspect of the predisposition to change. That the totalitarian education system had to be changed was agreed upon, but it was those who had experienced or observed its harmful effects personally who often were the driving forces in the initiation of change. These individuals were propelled by the conviction that the old system was guilty of "damaging children for life" and contained many features that had to be eradicated (Hudcová and Nováčková, 1993).

The researchers heard accounts of personal experiences from administrators, educators, and parents of children who for different reasons, disability or giftedness, did not conform to the "norm", failing therefore to thrive under the rigid structure of the Communist system. These were the individuals who established private schools for their own children or who advocated for the rights of such children to appropriate education and toward this end promoted organizations such as the "Blue Key School" (Černá, 1995). These parents and educators knew, from personal experience, that the old system was particularly harmful to some children, but did not necessarily have a vision of what might be put in its place. Their drive, determination and absolute faith in their humanitarian instincts were powerful factors affecting the initiation of change.

It may be that under conditions of planned change, the predisposition to change is assumed, particularly in those parts of the North American educational scene where innovation and change are almost a constant at the school level. However, under conditions of rapid change, characterized by a "window of opportunity", the predisposition to "seize the moment" is critical to the initiation of change.

VI. CONCLUSIONS

In answer to the question posed in the title of this paper, a North American model of educational change can be usefully applied to the Czech experience. However, Fullan's model of the factors that affect the initiation of change does not account for some aspects of the Czech case that were perceived to be very significant in initiating change. These include the notion of a window of opportunity and the predisposition to change.

The next step is to examine the implementation phase of the Czech experience within the parameters of Fullan's discussion of educational change. Educational change has been initiated. The next question is to what extent has change been implemented and sustained? To what extent has the educational system of Czech Republic been transformed? One might hypothesize at this point that features such as a window of opportunity and "off with the old" bring about change that is structural, administrative, quickly effected and implemented to satisfy general public demands in the way that was alluded to earlier. On the other hand, features such as predisposition to change, resulting from personal experience and advanced preparation might set the stage well for real change in conceptions and role behavior (Fullan, 1991, p. 38) or transformation (NEMES, 1995) of the way people conceive education and apply the new societal values and principles in the classroom.

The transformation of a whole educational system does not happen overnight. "It is possible to change 'on the surface' by endorsing certain goals, using specific materials, and even imitating the behaviour without specifically understanding the principles and rationale of the change...It is possible to value and even be articulate about the goals of the change without understanding their implications for practice" (Fullan, 1991, p. 40).

Teachers who have been trained to deliver a highly structured curriculum from the front of the classroom with the objective of producing pupils who do well in exams are unlikely to be able to change their teaching without retraining, no matter how much they wish to do so. Such transformation of the system is a long term process and requires planning. An examination of the implementation phase should also reveal whether the suspicion of the "master plan", a legacy of the Soviet era, will diminish as the desire for a coherent system, an inherent national characteristic, increases. The revised model should be applied to the cases of other central and Eastern European (CEE) countries as well as other non-European countries that have undergone large-scale societal change through political unrest or peaceful democratization. Such examinations would identify the similarities and differences among the cases, both for the process of initiation and for the subsequent implementation of change. The Czech case, in some respects, has much in common with that of Hungary, Lithuania, and Poland. For example, Marxist-Leninist ideology was removed from the curricula and the teaching of Russian was no longer compulsory in the three countries (Kaufman, 1996, p. 639; Servaite, 1996; Novak-Fabrykowski & Sosnowski, 1995; Tran, 1995).

The initiation of change differed in at least two of the cases, however. Reform had begun earlier in some areas in Hungary (Kaufman, 1996, p. 638; Farnes, 1996, p. 6) where access to the west had been more readily available, and power had been transferred from the central administration to the individual schools before the revolutionary changes of 1989 (Kaufman, 1996, p. 638). Hungary was also ahead of other CEE countries in a number of areas, such as distance education (Farnes, 1996, p. 2, 12). Lithuania, on the other hand, was inadvertently inhibited in its progress by some post-1990 reforms (Farnes, 1996, p. 7). What is particularly interesting about the Lithuanian case is that educational reform was inhibited for at least one other reason. The withdrawal of the Soviet influence created the same window of opportunity for reform but the withdrawal of Soviet power was more protracted, and violent, thereby changing the nature of the window of opportunity.

In Czech Republic, the initiation of educational change occurred very rapidly; it was conducted in the absence of any established plan or vision; and the process occurred both at the national level and at the level of the school. The inconsistency between the legacy of the centralized Communist educational system with its administrative rigidity, and the emerging democratic structure following the events of 1989, made change inevitable. However, while it was clear that the people desired change, the form and direction of that change were not well defined.

The current exploration has not only extended our understanding of the initiation of change in Czech Republic since the Velvet Revolution but also has expanded our theoretical understanding of the factors related to the process of change itself, as addressed in the literature. The current study suggests the need for a modification of Fullan's model to account more fully for the initiation of change in cases of rapid socio-political upheaval, such as that which occurred in Czech Republic in the aftermath of the Velvet Revolution of 1989.

* This study was funded by the Social Sciences and Humanities Research Council, Aid to Small Universities Program (Thematic Focus: Social Transition and Transformation in Central and Eastern European). The authors would like to express their gratitude to the participants who generously shared their experiences and insights on the Czech education system, to research assistants Sarah Heselgrave and Marie Pilátová, as well as to the interpreters and translators, Marie Pilátová, Anna Pilátová, and Patricia Havličkôvá.

This paper is reprinted with permission from Mays, A., Polyzoi, E., & Gardner, S. (1996). The Czech Experience of the Initiation of Educational Change Since 1989:

Is a North American Model Applicable? *Canadian and International Education*, Vol, 26, No. 1

References

Botlík, O., (1994), Recent developments of the Czech educational system. In H. Avenarius (Ed.), Restructuring education and educational administration after the breakdown of socialism: proceedings of the VIIth European Intervisitation Programme from 11th to 17th October 1993 in Berlin (pp. 222-225). European Forum on Educational Administration. Frankfurt am Main: Deutsches Institut fur Internationale Padagogische Forschung.

Černá, M., (1995), Interview on educational transformation in Czech Republic with authors, Prague. Unpublished raw data, May.

Cindr, J., P. Cindr, O. Hausenblas, & M. Havlínová, (1995), Live school: a proposal for basic building blocks of educational programs in elementary schools (1-9). School for Children Foundation: Prague.

Farnes, N., (1996,), New structures to reform higher education in Central and Eastern Europe - the role of distance education. Paper presented at the Symposium on Educational Transitions in Former Socialist States, AERA Annual Conference, New York, April.

Fullan, M., (1991), The new meaning of educational change. (Rev. ed. with S. Stiegelbauer) Toronto: OISE Press.

Griffiths, M., (1995), Interview on educational transformation in Czech Republic with authors, Prague. Unpublished raw data, May.

Hudcová, H. & J. Nováčková, (1993), Principles for the implementation of freedom of education in the Czech school. Prague: NEMES, August.

Kalouš, J., (1995), Interview on educational transformation in Czech Republic with authors, Prague. Unpublished raw data, May.

Kaufman, C. C., (1996), Roles, regulations, and relearning: Teaching in a transitional society. Phi Delta Kappan, 637-40.

Ministry of Education, Youth and Sports of Czech Republic, (1994,), Quality and accountability: The programme of development of the education system in Czech Republic. Prague: Ministry of Education, Youth and Sports of Czech Republic, October.

NEMES, (1995), Interview of members of NEMES on educational transformation in Czech Republic with authors, Prague. Unpublished raw data, May.

Nowak-Fabrykowski, K. & A. Sosnowski, (1995), "Education in Transition: Changes in the Polish School System", *Canadian and International Education*, 24(2), 55-64.

Perclová, R., (1995), Interview on educational transformation in Czech Republic with authors, Prague. Unpublished raw data, May.

Pilátová, M., (1995), The endless history of the kingdom of Bohemia. Unpublished manuscript, The University of Winnipeg.

Průcha, J., (1992), "Transformation of education in Czech Republic: Urgent requirements for educational research", Paper presented at the symposium Strukturwandel Deutscher Bildungwirklichkeit, Humboldt-Universitat, Berlin, December.

Průcha, J., (1995), Interview on educational transformation in Czech Republic with authors, Prague. Unpublished raw data, May.

Průcha, J. & E. Walterová, (1992), *Education in a changing society: Czechoslovakia*, Prague:

Průcha & Walterová. Řepka, R., (1986), "The process of ELT reform in Czechoslovakian schools", *ELT Journal*, 40(3), 221-5.

Rydl, K., (1994), "National traditions of democratic education as an important source for the current restructuring in education in Czech Republic", in H. Avenarius (Ed.), Restructuring education and educational administration after the breakdown of socialism: proceedings of the VIIth European Intervisitation Programme from 11th to 17th October 1993 in Berlin, 222-225. European Forum on Educational Administration. Frankfurt am Main: Deutsches Institut fur Internationale Padagogische Forschung.

Rydl, K., (1995), Interview on educational transformation in Czech Republic with authors, Prague. Unpublished raw data, May.

Servaite, L., (1996), Cultural and educational change in Lithuania since 1990. Paper presented at The University of Winnipeg, April.

Spilková, V., (1995), Interview on educational transformation in Czech Republic with authors, Prague. Unpublished raw data, May.

Tran, D.T., (1995), "Education in Poland: A system in transition", *Canadian and International Education,* 24(2) 65-84.

CHAPTER 7

THE STATUS OF WOMEN'S EMPLOYMENT IN POLAND

WILLADEE WEHMEYER

I. INTRODUCTION

Since the early 1950s women in the planned economies of Central Europe (CE) have experienced higher labor force participation rates than their counterparts in the market economies of the west. Their ability to work outside the home was supported by the push for the rapid expansion of industry, the availability of child-care facilities, access to legal abortion, and liberal parental benefits. With the adoption of market-based models, CE countries have either reduced or eliminated many of the state-supported mechanisms that enhanced the ability of women to participate in the labor force. Additionally, these countries have experienced extended periods of recession with high levels of unemployment for both men and women. While women in Poland have thus far continued to enjoy relatively high rates of employment, some authors have suggested that their position in the labor market has deteriorated. Moreover, some believe that women are increasingly subjected to "blatant discrimination" in employment and fear that such discrimination, if left unchecked, will end with the marginalization of Polish working women.[1]

As the process of economic transformation continues, it is appropriate to investigate the changing role of women in the labor force and to assess whether the patterns of employment will more closely resemble those of more mature market economies. Indeed as one observer of women's employment in Poland has argued, "...to neglect the gender implications of transition is short-sighted and ultimately inefficient in terms of the success of the economic reform process itself." (Einhorn,

1993, p.132). The purpose of this paper is to review the status of women's employment in Poland. Section II provides the background for the analysis by summarizing the general economic changes that have taken place in the CE countries in general and in Poland in particular since the adoption of economic reforms in 1990. Section III addresses the pre- and post-1990 labor market and women's employment therein. Section IV examines political and economic factors that influenced women's participation in the pre-1990 labor force and identifies key environmental opportunities and threats that are likely to prove important in the future.

II. Economic Performance in Poland, 1990-1996

From the outset, policy makers in the CE countries along with foreign and domestic economists generally agreed that the creation of efficient markets would take a number of years to accomplish. Nonetheless, it was believed that at least some of the benefits associated with a market system, especially the elimination of shortages, improved access to goods and services, and liberalization of business activities, would materialize relatively quickly. Although specific dates typically were not set, it was assumed that economic growth would resume after a relatively short adjustment period of perhaps one to two years.[2] Unfortunately, the reality of market reform proved harsher than policy-makers and economists initially anticipated. All of the transition economies were hit by deep recession, high rates of unemployment, and rapidly rising prices. Moreover, those asked to bear the bulk of the burden of transition (in loss of jobs, deteriorating purchasing power, and reduced social services) quickly accused reformist governments of incompetence, wrongdoing, and corruption. Yet, many successes have been claimed: democratic and pluralistic political systems were established; central planning and state controls dismantled; prices liberalized; national currencies made convertible; consumers and producers freed to make their own economic decisions; inflation reduced; and, endemic shortages eliminated. Many problems remain, including privatization of large state-owned enterprises, financial sector reform, and reduction of unemployment and inflation, and rebuilding an appropriate infrastructure.

While Poland has been deemed a "success" among the transitional economies, it has not escaped the general trends described above.[3] The so-called Round Table agreement of February 1989 marked the beginning of Poland's drive to liberate its political structure from Communist control. The accord legalized Solidarity, established rights of free speech and association, and provided for democratic elections to state bodies. In the June 1989 elections, voters soundly rejected the Communist Party by electing Solidarity-backed candidates to the majority of the open seats in the National Assembly and to ninety-nine out of one hundred seats in the Senate.[4] In December 1989, the Solidarity-led government's economic reform package was enacted. Dubbed the "big bang," the Economic Transformation

Program (ETP) included lifting most price controls, sharp cuts in producer and consumer subsidies, immediate liberalization of imports, free convertibility of the zloty at a fixed nominal rate, wage indexation below the rate of inflation, and a restrictive credit policy. The removal of restrictions on private business and the elimination of state monopolies complemented these measures.[5]

The International Monetary Fund (IMF) and the World Bank (WB) provided support for the ETP. The IMF assisted the economic team in drafting the stabilization component of the reform program and the WB assisted in the design of the structural and institutional reforms. In addition to technical support, financial support was made available to back up the zloty: the IMF approved a one-year standby arrangement for SDR 545 million in March 1990 and the leading industrial nations provided a contingent fund of $1 billion. The WB formulated a country assistance program of loans that amounted to $3.7 billion to be approved between 1990 and 1993.[6]

The first two years of economic reform in Poland were characterized by deep recession, high rates of unemployment, and inflation. In 1990, Gross Domestic Product (GDP) fell by almost 20% and the downward spiral continued in 1991 with another 7% loss. The negative trend in GDP was reversed in 1992 with a gain of 2.6%. Since that date GDP has continued upward with gains of 3.8%, 5.2%, 7.0%, and 6.0% in 1993, 1994, 1995, and 1996 respectively. The rate of unemployment reached a high of 16.4% in 1993, then declined to 16.0% in 1994 and to 14.9% in 1995. Similarly, inflation, measured by the CPI, has shown continuous decline since 1990.

The Polish economy has continued to thrive with GDP registering another gain of over 6.1 percent in 1997. The rate of unemployment has dropped to 10.7 percent in the same year while the rate of inflation was 13.5. Much of the economic development observed in recent years can be associated with increased investment and consumption. For example, Leszek Zienkowski of the Warsaw Statistical and Economic Research Institute recently estimated that real fixed investment grew by 22% in 1996 while household spending advanced in real terms by 11%. Moreover, World Bank economist Adam B. Czyjewski estimated that the rate of increase in exports was 7-8% in 1996 and that direct foreign investment amounted to some $4 billion.[7]

Despite the obvious and continued success of Poland's economic reforms, the politicians who initiated the reform package did not escape criticism and out-right rejection. In the September 1993 elections the largest number of seats in the Parliament went to a coalition of former Communists led by Aleksander Kwasniewski of the Democratic Left Alliance.[8] With the elections of 1995, the nation's presidency, executive branch, and parliament were once again controlled by what has been described as "the faction that ruled by totalitarianism for 45 years" (Sikorski, 1996, p.15). While the full impact of such political realignment is not obvious, the pace of institutional reform declined after 1995. Currently, the nation's economic structure is characterized by two types of enterprises: large, formerly or currently state-owned enterprises that are distinguished by management structures that concentrate on politics rather than strengthening their competitive position; and by small private enterprises struggling to survive. The absence of middle ground may prove hazardous to both a viable market-system and to democracy (Szomburg, 1997).

III. The Labor Force and Women's Employment

A. Women and Employment, Pre-Transition

In order to assess the status of women's employment during the years preceding the transition it is appropriate to examine rates of economic activity (RsEA), terms of employment (full-time/part-time), and the incidence of job segregation by sex, earnings, and rates of unemployment. As reported in Table 1, RsEA for women in Poland were somewhat higher than those of women in other countries of central and Western Europe. However, Polish women's RsEA were far less than the rates reported in Eastern Europe. This disparity might be reasonably expected because the Eastern European countries listed were members of the Soviet Union where women were encouraged much earlier to enter the paid labor force.

Table 2 disaggregates the data concerning the economically active population in Poland on the basis of sex and age for the census years 1978 and 1988. The economic impact of the inefficiencies in the command economy is evident from the observed decreases in RsEA for both men and women between 1978 and 1988. However, while RsEA for men decreased in every age cohort, it is important to note that women between the ages of 35 and 49 increased their participation during this period. It is also notable that while RsEA for women aged 50 and over decreased, the percent decline for women was not as large as that observed for men in the same age groups. However, at the other end of the age spectrum (ages 20 -34), women suffered larger declines than did men.

The data in Table 2 also illustrates the fact that women in Poland, unlike their counterparts in Western Europe and the United States, maintained high rates of labor force participation throughout their child-bearing years. In the United States, for example, RsEA for women aged 20 through 44 were 51.6%, 68.6%, and 73.9% in 1971, 1982, 1993 respectively (Fullerton Jr., 1995, p. 33). Activity rates were also high among Polish women of retirement age (ages 60 and over), reflecting in part the tendency of women in rural communities to run their own farms beyond the normal retirement age.[9]

Table 1: Economically active (EA) female population, selected countries and years (%)

Country	Year	(1) EA as a proportion of female population aged 15 and over	(2) EA as a proportion of total female population
Central Europe:			
Czechoslovakia	1991	*	45.6
Hungary	1990	46.3	37.4
Poland	1988	57.0	43.3
Romania	1991	54.9	42.6
Eastern Europe:			
Belarus	1989	61.3	48.3
Estonia	1989	64.6	51.3
Latvia	1989	64.1	51.5
Lithuania	1989	61.6	48.6
Russian Federation	1989	61.0	47.9
Ukraine	1989	*	46.4
Western Europe:			
Austria	1990	43.0	36.6
France	1989	44.5	36.5
Germany	1990	39.2	33.0
Greece	1988	35.2	28.7
Italy	1990	*	30.3
Portugal	1990	48.1	39.7
Spain	1991	*	27.0
Turkey	1990	35.9	24.3

*Not available

Source: *Yearbook of Labor Statistics (1992),* 52nd issue, (Geneva: International Labor Office, 1992)

Table 2: Poland, economically active population by age and sex

Age	1978	1988	Change
Females:			
20-24	68.4	64.0	-4.4
25-29	75.1	70.0	-5.1
30-34	79.5	76.7	-2.8
35-39	81.9	83.0	+1.1
40-44	82.7	85.5	+2.8
45-49	78.5	81.2	+2.7
50-54	71.6	71.1	-0.5
55-59	57.9	50.6	-7.3
60-64	37.4	34.3	-3.1
65-69	27.8	26.8	-1.0
Total	58.7	57.0	-1.7
Males:			
20-24	82.7	79.0	-3.7
25-29	96.2	94.3	- 1.9
30-34	97.1	96.1	-1.0
35-39	96.2	95.6	-0.6
40-44	94.8	94.1	-0.7
45-49	92.1	89.6	-2.5
50-54	87.1	82.4	-4.7
55-59	81.5	72.0	-9.5
60-64	62.4	53.6	-8.8
65-69	43.0	40.4	-2.6
Total	76.6	74.3	-2.3

Sources: Data for 1978 cited by Marek Gbra, Irena Kotowska, Tomasz Panek, and Jaroslav Podgorski, "Poland: labor market trends and policies," in *Structural Change in Central and Eastern Europe: Labor Market and Social Policy Implications,* Georg Fischer and Guy Standing, eds., (Paris: OECD, 1993), p. 140. Data for 1988: *Demographic Yearbook (1994),* Forty-sixth issue (New York: United Nations, 1996).

With respect to the terms of employment, it is likely that women's employment in the pre-transition economy was on a full-time basis. In Poland, as in all of the CE countries, both labor codes and social security regulations included provisions that allowed for shorter hours and/or more flexible time schedules for mothers. However, such regulations were of little practical relevance because employers were reluctant to use them and in 1987, for example, the overall proportion of part-timers in the labor force was a mere 6% (Hübner, et al., 1993, p. 226).

While both high RsEA and high levels of full-time employment may be regarded as positive indicators of women's status in the labor force, job segregation on the basis of sex is generally viewed as a negative indicator. In pre-transition Poland, women were represented in only a small number of sectors, including light industry, health, law, administration and clerical. Moreover, they tended to be in middle ranking and low-skilled jobs. In 1988, for example, women held only 4.5% of management positions (Einhorn 1993, p.125). Perhaps more important, while wage equality legislation existed, gender-based segregation of employment coupled with bonus plans that handsomely rewarded employment in heavy industry guaranteed a substantial differential between men and women workers (Góra, et al., 1993, p. 262). There are numerous ways to compare earnings, including by broad occupation categories, by sectors of the economy, and by education, but regardless of the method of comparison chosen, as the data in Tables 3-4 indicate, working women in pre-transition Poland earned substantially less than their male counterparts.

Table 3: Poland: Females' average monthly compensation as a percent of males' average monthly compensation by education (1988)

Education Level	%
Elementary	74.0
Lower technical	71.7
Secondary	79.2
Technical	77.5
University	81.4

Source: Monica Fong and Gillian Paul, "Women's Economic Status in the Restructuring of Eastern Europe," p. 228.

Table 4: Poland: Females' average monthly compensation as a percent of males' average monthly compensation by sector (1988)

Sector	%	Sector	%
Construction	82.0	Transport	83.6
Mining	56.2	Education	81.4
Agriculture	87.3	Health Services	79.8
Science/Research	80.2	Culture/Arts	89.7
Trade	83.4	Finance/Insurance	91.8

Source: Fong and Paul, p. 229.

Table 5: Poland: Earnings differentials by occupation and sex, Poland 1980 (male professional earnings 100)

Sex	Occupation	Earnings	Gap(M-F)
Male	Professional	100	
Female	Professional	79	21
Male	Administrative and clerical	86	
Female	Administrative and clerical	65	21
Male	Skilled workers	82	
Female	Skilled workers	57	25
Male	Unskilled workers	77	
Female	Unskilled workers	57	20

Source: G. Kertesi and G. Kövái: *Real wages in Eastern Europe,* (Budapest, 1986, mimeographed) cited by Hübner, et. al., "Women's employment in central and Eastern Europe: Status and prospects," p. 225.

Unemployment was not officially recognized in Poland in the pre-transition period.[10] It is, therefore, somewhat risky to speculate about the magnitude of unemployment and the relationship between unemployment rates for men and women. Nevertheless, some analysts have done so and have reported that in 1985 there were three times as many women as men unemployed and that three times as many jobs were available for men as for women.[11] To the extent that these estimates are an accurate reflection of the pre-transition labor force, women were vulnerable to joblessness more often than men.

In sum it can be said that women's employment in pre-transition Poland was characterized by high rates of economic activity and that in sharp contrast to many countries in the west, their employment was almost certainly on a full-time basis even during the child-bearing years. Moreover, women in Poland tended to be segregated in the job market, to earn lower wages than their male counterparts, and probably were exposed to joblessness more often than men.

B. Women and Employment, Post-1990

A notable characteristic of the Polish labor market since the ETP was enacted in January 1990 is its failure to reach full-employment. While GDP moved to steady growth in 1992, employment continued to contract until 1993 when the overall rate reached 16.4%. Since then the overall rate of unemployment has continued to fall. While the burden of joblessness should not necessarily adversely affect women's employment more than men's, as noted earlier some authors maintain that women's position in the labor force has deteriorated. In order to appraise the accuracy of such claims it is instructive to examine comparative RsEA, unemployment rates, wages, and part-time versus full-time employment patterns in the post-1990 period.

Rates of economic activity by sex and age for 1988, 1992, and 1994 are shown in Table 6.[12] Changes in women's RsEA between 1988 and 1992 indicate a mixed response during the initial phase of the transition. Women between the ages of 15 and 44 appear to have come into the paid labor force while older women, aged 45+, appear to have left. A similar response is seen for men, except that the reduction in economic activity began with the 35-44 age cohort instead of the 45-54 age cohort. In comparison to their male counterparts, the overall reduction in economic activity observed for women was smaller, 2.8% compared to 4.3%. By 1994, one year after the overall unemployment rate reached its peak, men continued to decrease their economic activity with declines observed in all age cohorts. A net decrease in economic activity was also observed for women; however, two of the five age cohorts listed, 25-34 and 45-54, showed increases. Overall, the 3% decrease in economic activity for men and 2% decrease for women, indicate that while the basic measures of economic activity showed improvement beginning in 1992, both women and men felt the effects of transition in 1994.

Table 6: Poland, economically active population by sex and age (%)

Age	1988	1992	Change (>88-=92)	1994	Change (>92-=94)
Females:					
15-24	39.3	41.7	+2.4	38.5	-3.2
25-34	73.6	75.6	+2.0	76.1	+0.5
35-44	84.1	85.9	+1.8	84.6	-1.3
45-54	75.9	71.6	-4.3	72.3	+0.7
55+	30.3	18.6	-11.7	15.9	-2.7
Total	**57.0**	**54.2**	**-2.8**	**52.2**	**-2.0**
Males:					
15-24	49.1	50.6	+1.5	46.2	-4.4
25-34	95.3	95.4	+0.1	95.1	-0.3
35-44	94.9	93.6	-1.3	92.2	-1.4
45-54	85.9	81.7	-4.2	80.6	-1.1
55+	49.8	33.5	-16.3	30.2	-3.3
Total	74.3	70.0	-4.3	67.0	-3.0

Source: *Yearbook of Labor Statistics (1991-1995),* 52nd – 54th issues (Geneva: International Labor Office, 1991-1995).

Turning to unemployment rates for men and women between 1992 and 1994 (Table 7), perhaps the most striking statistics are the extremely high rates of unemployment in the 15-24 age cohort, which indicate that young workers bore the brunt of job loss.[13] It is also significant that rates of unemployment for women in the various age categories, with few exceptions, exceeded those reported for men. Over all age cohorts, women's rate of unemployment was approximately 4 percent higher than their male counterparts in all three years. In absolute numbers of unemployed persons, women were clearly in the majority, in spite of the fact that on average over the three-year period, the number of economically active women was 1,364,000 less than the number of economically active men. The only age cohort that showed a decrease in reported rate of unemployment was women aged 45-54. However, even in this case, the absolute numbers of unemployed women increased between 1992 and 1994.[14] It is clear that women have shouldered the burden of joblessness in greater proportion than men.

Table 7: Poland, unemployment rates by age and sex (%)
(Numbers unemployed appear in italics, (in 000s))

Age	1992	1993	1994	Change (92-94)
Females:				
15-24	43.8 *(461.3)*	50.4 *(524.3)*	50.3 *(521.7)*	+6.5 *(60.4)*
25-34	19.9 *(418.1)*	22.9 *(455.1)*	23.0 *(436.3)*	+3.1 *(18.2)*
35-444	7.5 *(336.0)*	14.2 *(382.8)*	14.2 *(382.1)*	+6.7 *(46.1)*
45-54	12.4 *(111.2)*	9.2 *(132.0)*	9.3 *(143.8)*	- 3.1 *(32.6)*
55+	1.4 *(12.0*	1.6 *(13.0)*	1.5 *(11.2)*	+0.1 *(0.9)*
Total	**16.3 *(1338.7)***	**18.8 *(1507.3)***	**18.9 *(1495.1)***	
Males:				
15-24	31.8 *(406.4)*	37.6 *(470.7)*	40.4 *(495.8)*	+8.6 *(89.4)*
25-34	12.0 *(328.0)*	14.8 *(369.6)*	14.2 *(341.1)*	+2.2 *(13.1)*
35-44	9.8 *(284.3)*	11.8 *(346.3)*	11.5 *(336.2)*	+1.7 *(51.9)*
45-54	8.1 *(120.4)*	9.7 *(152.2)*	9.7 *(158.6)*	+1.6 *(38.2)*
55+	2.9 *(31.4)*	3.9 *(43.5)*	4.6 *(46.9)*	+1.7 *(15.5)*
Total	**12.3 *(1170.5)***	**14.8 *(1382.3)***	**15.0 *(1378.6)***	

Source: *Yearbook of Labor Statistics (1993-1995),* 52nd – 54th issue, (Geneva: International Labor Office, 1993-1995).

While relative rates of unemployment are important in terms of appraising women's status in the labor force, it is also enlightening to examine the categories of employment. Table 8 shows the distribution of economically active men and women among six occupational categories in 1988 and 1994.

Over the six year period, the largest losses for both men and women is in the occupational category of "Professional, technical, and related." However, the percentage of economically active women employed in occupations in this category has declined by 23.88% whereas for men the decrease has amounted to 8.77%. While for women the next largest loss is in the occupational category, "Agriculture/animal husbandry, forestry, fishermen, and hunters" (8.02%), for men it is in the area of "Production and related" (7.64%). Gains of 10.14% and 11.32% have been made by women in the occupations of "Administrative and managerial" and "Sales and service". For men, the largest gains are found in "Sales and service" and "Clerical and related" which showed increases of 6.77% and 6.13% respectively. The reshuffling of workers among the occupations listed is indicative of the privatization process. However, the sizable losses by women, particularly in the professions may prove difficult to make up in the near future.

Table 8: Poland, economically active population by sex and occupation (000s)

	Male		Female	
Occupation	1988	1994	1988	1994
Professional/ technical and related	1,528	653	2,328	344
Administrative managerial	94	471	17	912
Clerical and related	245	623	818	1,168
Sales workers/ service workers	162	688	820	1,859
Agriculture/ animal husbandry/ forestry/ fisherman and hunters	2,202	2,165	1,569	
Production and related		4.751	2,081	1,757

Source: Yearbook of Labor Statistics (1991 and 1995).

With respect to less than full-time employment, it has been reported by Gregory, et. al., that the proportion of women in the 25-49 age cohort who worked part-time increased from 6.2% in 1992 to 7.1% in 1994. Gregory et al. (1996), and others, have suggested that women in the post-transition economy have been forced into part-time employment. However, part-time work for men in the same age cohort increased from 4.3% to 4.9% over the same time period. Clearly the 14.5% gain in the proportion of women working part-time compared to the 14% increase in the proportion of men working part-time does not provide sufficient evidence to conclude that part-time work in Poland is becoming feminized. Nevertheless, it should be noted that the available data covers only three years which makes it impossible to determine the nature, if any, of the trend in part-time employment.

In terms of equality of earnings, women's position remained clearly inferior to that of men in the post-transition period. Comparing the relative earnings of men and women, it has been reported that between 1993 and 1994, the average Polish woman's monthly salary was only 65.9% of her male counterpart's. In the same period, the figure in Hungary was 78.7% and in Bulgaria it was 76.7%. Only in the Russian Federation did women earn a smaller percentage: 58.7% of male average income. Disregarding differences between men and women, such as work in businesses that traditionally offer different pay scales, women in Poland still earned on average only 73.9% as much as men. Worse yet, when total monthly incomes from all sources are considered, Polish women's earnings were only 56.4% of men's (Domanski, 1995, p. 362).

In sum it can be said that while women continued their high rates of economic activity in the Polish labor force during the post-transition period, they have suffered serious losses in terms of unemployment and their average earnings as compared to men have deteriorated. The economy appears to have created some opportunities for part-time employment and women have increased their employment in such positions. However, it is not clear whether women have chosen to take advantage of such opportunities or if they have been forced to accept part-time employment. In light of the short period of time for which reliable data is available, the lack of evidence with regard to the transition's impact on this aspect of women's employment is not surprising.

IV. Determinants of Women's Status in Employment

A. Pre-transition Era

Women's employment emerged from the Communist era marked by paradox. On the one hand, a large proportion of women were economically active and many had succeeded in entering some traditionally male-dominated professions, and occupations, and sectors of the economy. On the other hand, women found themselves barred from employment in a number of industries and, in the jobs that were open to them, they were most often found in subordinate positions earning low wages. The factors that were influential in shaping women's status in the labor force during the initial stages of the Communist era include severe shortages of labor resulting from the decimation of the population during the War, the push for rapid industrialization, and prevailing ideology. Over the course of the ensuing four decades of Communist control, particularly since the mid-1970s, the impetus for the expansion of women's labor force participation was boosted by price shocks that made it difficult for families to meet their basic needs without the wages of at least two workers. While these factors pulled women into the paid labor force, a series of factors and events over the forty years of Communist control, including insufficient and/or unaffordable household services, lack of control over fertility, limited educational opportunities, and protective labor legislation, served to limit their ability to participate on an equal footing with men.

During the initial stages of the development of Communism in Poland, women as well as men were encouraged to embrace the notion that the citizen's responsibility was to work while the state's responsibility was to provide a broad range of social services. Participation in this arrangement promised women liberation from their subordinate role in the family, a promise that sprang from early Marxist texts. Engels, for example, in his essay *On the Origin of the Family, Private Property and the State* (1884) declared: "The emancipation of women becomes possible only when women are enabled to take part in production on a large social scale, and when domestic duties require their attention only to a minor degree."[16] Such sentiments combined with the short supply of labor following World War II and the drive to recast Poland as an industrial giant, provided policy makers with a unique opportunity to address the issue of women's equality. Unfortunately, this opportunity was not seized. Women were encouraged to take jobs outside the home, but men were not encouraged to take up their share of household responsibilities. Instead of finding themselves liberated by the new order, women discovered themselves subordinated in both their familial and economic roles.[17]

The only response offered by policy makers to the "double burden of responsibility" was the socialization of housework. While this was a theoretically feasible solution, a number of serious obstacles made it unworkable. First, all domestic responsibilities could not be delegated. Someone had to be in charge of day-to-day operations: purchasing goods, supervising the provision of services, and taking care of the emergencies. Such duties remained largely in the hands of women. Secondly, to the extent that domestic duties could be socialized, someone still had to do the work. As might be expected, men were no more anxious than women to take jobs in the low-paid service sector of the post-war Polish economy. Therefore, to the extent that socialized domestic services were made available, women, who had fewer employment opportunities than men, continued to do the work. Thirdly, and most important, the socialization of housework required capital investment in the service sector on a grand scale, an investment that the state was unwilling and/or unable to make.

Lack of adequate provision for child-care is but one example of the state's failure to supply household-related services. Maria Ciechocinska has reported that the number of spaces available in nurseries (suitable for children aged 0-3) was never equal to demand and that the situation grew decidedly worse over time (Ciechocinska, 1993, p. 316). According to Ciechocinska, in the 1980s the number of factory-run nurseries decreased by 25%, the number of spaces available dropped by 33% and the number of children enrolled decreased by 50%. Ciechocinska also found similar downward trends in the number of kindergarten spaces (suitable for children aged 3-6) available and in children's and youth's recreation and out-of-school activities. She concluded that the decline in provisions for child-care was not the result of demographic phenomena, but rather the state's withdrawal of subsidies made such facilities and programs unaffordable for many working mothers.

In the post-war period, the difficulty of combining paid employment with full responsibility for the home was exacerbated by lack of reliable methods of birth control. Women's access to information and services related to birth control was severely limited by religious tradition and by the reluctance of political leaders to embrace measures that would reduce fertility in the face of labor shortages. In this environment, the issue of abortion took on enormous significance. Abortion was formally banned in Poland in 1932 and while discussion of the issue reopened after the War, the ban was not lifted until 1956. Even then, a woman's right to choose was not recognized. Instead, only a liberal interpretation of the clause that permitted abortion "...if the pregnant woman had 'difficult living conditions'", made it possible for the procedure to be secured. However, one (perhaps unintended) effect of the feminization of the medical profession was physicians' willingness to base their appraisal of "difficult living conditions" on the woman's own assessment. Precise estimates of the total number of abortions performed vary. However, it has been estimated that in the 1980s approximately 130,000 to 140,000 (that is, 13.2 per 1000 women aged 15-49 and 18.2 per 100 live births) registered abortions were performed per year and that unregistered abortions amounted to some 55,000 to 85,000 per year (Fuszara, 1993, p. 292). The large number of procedures performed corroborates the claim that abortion was the major form of contraception in pre-transition Poland (Hauser et al., 1993, p. 260).

The unresolved conflict between women's productive and reproductive roles was further aggravated by the state's development of a segmented educational system which emphasized vocational and technical training for boys and general education for girls. In the 1950s, three types of secondary schools were established: *lower vocational* schools aimed at preparing students for skilled and semi-skilled jobs (primarily in heavy industry, mining, and construction); *lyceum,* 4-year schools offering traditional college preparatory academic training; and, *tecknikum,* 5-year programs emphasizing scientific and technical subjects. Both the lyceum and *tecknikum* conferred diplomas and the right to sit for entrance examinations for higher education. Additionally, the recipient of a *tecknikum* diploma could immediately obtain a highly-paid technical job in one of the sectors of the economy.

Throughout the 1950s, secondary education developed rapidly in Poland and by the early 1960s, 60% of girls and 68% of boys were entering some kind of secondary school. Male and female students were not, however, evenly distributed among the three types of secondary schools. From the outset, girls more often than boys chose *lyceum* training and by the 1960s, 28% of girls were attending the *lyceum* as their first choice of secondary school while only 8-9% of boys were doing so. By the mid-1970s *lyceums* were 70% female (Bialecki and Heyns, 1993, p. 114). Since the function of the *lyceum* was (and is) college preparation, those who earned *lyceum* diplomas were encouraged, if not obliged, to go on to the university. Thus, the expansion of the numbers of women in *lyceum* can be credited with increasing the numbers of women in the university and eventually to the feminization of white-collar work.

While some jobs, like office and administrative, might have become feminized as they did in the west regardless of the education system, women's access to higher education in Poland allowed them to move into a wide variety of professional and service occupations. Feminization occurred in medical and specialized legal fields with well established requirements for special credentials and training, and virtually all of the health and social service occupations were feminized before the 1980s. The same process operated in the humanities and social sciences--the feminization of diverse occupations such as sociologist, psychologist, editor, journalist, and accountant, was at least in part the legacy of education policies put in place in the 1960s and 1970s. However, while women's freedom to pursue higher education might have conferred employment advantages in western economies, in Poland technical and vocational training was more highly prized than university training. Therefore, as shown earlier, not only were average earnings of university women less than their male counterparts, women's earnings were on average less than those earned by men in all types of work.

Poland's labor laws reinforced women's limited access to the highest paid jobs in the economy. According to ethnographer Ewa Hauser, with the liberalization in Communist doctrine after 1956 the state's policies toward women began to lose their egalitarian content. As a consequence, at the end of the Communist period, women were subject to a series of laws that placed them in a restricted and unequal position. The Labor Code barred women from ninety specific jobs in eighteen branches of industry. These restrictions (still in effect today) were viewed by many as "pro-woman" because they were thought to protect women from physical harm in the workplace (Hauser et al., 1993, pp. 259-60). However, as was found in the United States and other western economies, protective labor legislation that applies to women alone can be and often is used to limit freedom of choice and to perpetuate traditional role division by sex.

B. Post-Transition

Despite their relatively low standing in the labor market women continued to experience high levels of economic activity in the post-transition period. Polls aimed at determining women's work motivation conducted by the Central Statistical Office

(GUS) in 1983, 1987, 1991, and 1994 have consistently revealed that their primary reason for working is their family's or their own financial situation. For example, 34% of the respondents in a 1994 poll said that they work because "their husbands' income is not enough to maintain the family." Another 25.2% cited "financial independence" as their prime motivation, while 23% wanted to "improve their families' living standards." Eighteen percent of the respondents stated that "every adult should work" and 18.6% were "eager to meet new people." (Ostrowska, 1995). While motivations vary from the financial to the ideological to the social, it can be inferred from these survey results that women are likely to remain attached to the nation's labor force. In the 1990s, as earlier, women who work outside the home face a number of environmental threats that tend to retard their ability to compete successfully in the new labor markets. At the same time, the new market environment promises to open doors that were previously closed to these workers.

The restructuring of the Polish economy has involved large-scale displacement of the workforce through the elimination of over-staffing, the closure of non-competitive firms, structural change, and de-beaucratization. Evidence of the extent of excess labor supply can be inferred from the relationship between employment and productivity in the post-1990 period and from the rapid development of the grey market (the informal sector).

Table 9 shows that between 1992 and 1995, GDP and productivity increased by 19.4% and 23.3% respectively, while employment fell by 3.8%, indicating a downward trend in the labor intensiveness of growth as measured by the employment absorption coefficient.[18] Thus, averaging over the entire period, each 1% increase in GDP was associated with a 0.2% decrease in employment. Preliminary studies conducted by Warsaw's Employment and Welfare Institute attribute the increase in joblessness to ongoing reduction in disguised unemployment, which they estimate involves some 800,000 to 1,200,000 workers.

Table 9: Poland: GDP, Employment, and Productivity, 1992-1995 (1990 = 100)

Year	GDP Index	Employment Index	Productivity Index	Absorption Coefficient
1992	102.6	97.2	105.5	-1.08
1993	106.5	95.6	111.4	-0.45
1994	112.0	96.6	115.9	+0.21
1995	119.4	96.8	123.3	+0.03
1992-95	119.4	96.8	123.3	-0.20

Source: *Poland International Economic Report 1995/96*, (Warsaw: World Economy Research Institute, 1996) , p. 66.

In addition to the high levels of disguised unemployment, the Polish labor market is characterized by a significant quantity of unregistered employment in the so-called grey market. In 1995, the Central Statistical Office (GUS) estimated that as many as 2,034,000 were employed in Poland's grey market. Its existence explains why in spite of a negative employment absorption rate over the 1991 - 1995, official unemployment rates have come down.

In spite of its abundant labor supply, Poland currently lacks the necessary experience and expertise in areas of accountancy, finance, insurance, and counseling to meet the growing demands for such services and this may have positive consequences for women workers. Women have a long tradition in Poland's service sector. In 1989, women were 84.5% of all employees in finance/insurance; 81.4% in health services; 76.5% in education; 69.7% in trade; and, 64.4% in public administration (Hübner, et al., 1993, p. 223). As a result of privatization these jobs as well as jobs in other fields including personnel management, manpower planning, and marketing have begun to gain prestige. Women, who possess the requisite training, skills, and experience, are positioned to take advantage of this new market opportunity.

However, it is to be expected that as restructuring continues, there will be a realignment in men's employment: that is, decreased prestige and earnings associated with the industrial sector coupled with increased prestige and earnings associated with the service sector is likely to draw men from the former to the latter. Such adjustments can, in turn, be expected to increase the competitiveness of the labor market in the service sector. In fact, as demonstrated in Table 8, such realignments have already begun. Whether future generations of women will be able to compete with men for these jobs very much depends on their ability and willingness to compete for the available slots in the nation's institutions of higher learning.

In contrast to the Communist era's emphasis on egalitarianism, passiveness, and entitlement, Poland's new focus on the market stresses individual initiative. Indeed, growth in the numbers of small and medium-sized businesses as well as in the numbers of self-employed persons suggests that entrepreneurial activity is becoming an important aspect of the Polish economy. Important for this analysis is the evidence with respect to women's participation in the growing and dynamic phenomenon of entrepreneurship.

Economist Ewa Lisowska of the Warsaw School of Economics, who recently completed an inquiry into entrepreneurial activity in Poland, has reported that the proportion of women entrepreneurs is growing. Out of the total female workforce, the percentage of self-employed women grew from 3.7% in 1989 to 7.5% in 1991 to 22% in 1995. Moreover, the percentage of women business proprietors among total population of entrepreneurs grew from 27% in 1989 to 33% in 1991 to 39% in 1993 (Lisowska, 1996, p. 4). While the numbers of women business owners is still small in absolute terms and relative to men, women's increased willingness to take on the risks associated with business ownership suggests their adaptation to changing market conditions.[19]

Results from Lisowska's research indicate that women who started their own businesses were educated, older (aged 40+), and married with one or two grown children. Survey respondents also tended to have had many years of professional experience typically in state enterprises. Among the women entrepreneurs, the highest proportion were economists (22%) and technicians (20%), followed by women with higher education in the humanities (15%) and engineers (15%). Women without a formal occupation but who had finished secondary school made up 11% of women business owners in the survey (Lisowska, 1996, p. 3). Given the characteristics of women entrepreneurs identified by Lisowska, it seems likely that at least some women in the age cohort experiencing the highest rates of unemployment are responding by opening their own businesses. Additional evidence related to the changing status of employment is shown in Table 10.

Table 10: Poland, economically active by status of employment and sex (%)

	Male		Female	
Status of Employment	1988	1994	1988	1994
Employers and own- Account workers[20]	19.1	22.4	8.3	17.1
Employees	75.0	62.2	73.3	63.5
Unpaid family workers[21]	4.6	4.0	17.9	5.8
Members of Producer Cooperative	1.3		0.5	
Not classifiable by status[22]		11.4		13.6
Total	100.0	100.0	100.0	100.0

Source: Yearbook of Labor Statistics (1991 and 1995)

The data in Table 10 indicate that while 9.8% of women have moved out of the status "employee", 8.8% have moved into the ranks of "employer or own-account worker." It is likely that many of these women are the highly educated professionals, doctors, sociologists, economists, and so on, who have lost their jobs in the socialized sectors of the economy. The decrease in percentage of women in the "unpaid family worker" category can be construed favorably, if and only if they have moved into jobs that yield higher real income--this, of course, cannot be determined from this data. The 13.6% of women who are "not classifiable by status" is somewhat disturbing. On the one hand, part of the observed increase is probably due to new entrants. In 1994, for example, approximately 5% of economically active women were new entrants to the labor force.[23] On the other hand, it is almost certainly true that some of "not classifiable by status" are in the grey market. The realignment by status of employment for men appears more straightforward. That is, the reduction in percentage of men "employees" is almost completely accounted for by gains in the category of "employers and own-account workers" and "not classifiable by status." While the percentage of men in the former category was some 5.3% greater than that observed for women, the percent gain made over the past six years is approximately 5.5% less than the gain made by women. In terms of the latter, again it appears likely that some part of the increase observed is due to new entrants (3% of economically active men were new entrants in 1994), the remainder are very likely in grey market production.

Poland's transition to a market-based economy has created many new opportunities for working women. However, their success in taking advantage of these opportunities depends not only on their education, training, and prior experience, but also on attitudes and opinions regarding the appropriate role for women and men in household production. While the evidence is limited, results of a 1993 opinion survey suggest that a majority of women (55%) prefer a marriage in which both spouses allotted approximately same amounts of time to work, and both gave equal attention to home and family. Only 28% of the polled women expressed a preference for the traditional family model wherein only the husband was engaged in paid-employment while the wife attended to domestic matters. The mixed model, in which both marriage partners work outside the home, but only the wife performs household chores, was preferred by only 14% of the women polled (Lisowska, 1997, pp. 32-34).

In spite of the preferences expressed, results from the same poll show an entirely different picture of the division of labor within the households surveyed. As indicated in Table 12, men typically did not contribute to the household duties that traditionally have been identified as falling in the domain of women's work. Any such contribution is usually confined to shopping.

Although more labor-saving household goods and services are available in the Polish economy, very few families can afford them. For example, studies have shown that barely 19% make use of any type of eating-out facility (restaurants, cafeterias at school or work, etc.). Similarly few can afford laundry services or domestic help of any kind.

Table 11: Participation in household duties in families of women who work outside the home (%)

Household Chore	Person Performing Chore		
	Woman	Man	Both
Preparing meals	67	3	14
Washing dishes	53	4	13
House cleaning	46	2	17
Washing	78	1	4
Ironing	75	0	4
Everyday shopping	49	10	18

Source: Results of poll conducted by the Public Opinion Polling Center cited in *The Situation of Women in Poland,* p. 33.

Likewise child-care poses a problem for the majority of working parents. The number of nurseries and kindergartens has decreased dramatically since the early 1980s. Several explanations have been offered for this trend. First, beginning in 1980, women were entitled to three years of maternity leave and many have chosen to exercise that option. Secondly, reductions in state subsidies for child-care coupled with rising prices throughout the 1980s and 1990s have made nurseries and kindergartens unaffordable. In 1995, for example, the cost of sending one child to a state kindergarten represented as much as 30-45% of the earnings of a young woman with higher education. Finally, many mothers were unhappy with the standard of care in state-supported facilities. While we can observe the negative trend in the numbers of children enrolled in nurseries and kindergartens between 1980 and 1993 in Table 12, we can only speculate on the negative impact that the lack of quality day-care options has on women's ability to participate successfully in the workforce. However, it is unlikely that women who carry a double burden of responsibility without the benefit of affordable domestic services and child-care will be able to compete on an equal footing with men in Poland's labor markets.

As discussed earlier, an important determinant of women's participation in the labor market is their ability to control fertility. In this area, there appears to be little change since the transition. A representative 1991 study of fertility in Poland revealed that 80% of mothers did not use any contraceptive measures before having their first two children. More recently, a 1993 nationwide survey disclosed that 63% of married couples who already have children do not use any contraceptive measures (Lisowska, 1996, pp. 34 and 47-48). In this setting, legal abortion continues to be an important means for controlling fertility.

Table 12: Numbers of children of a given age per 1000 children in nurseries and kindergartens

	Nurseries-	Kindergartens-	
Year	Children up to 3 years of age	Children aged 3-5	Children aged 3-6
1980	52	329	488
1990	42	295	471
1993	23		

Source: Central Statistical Office (GUS) 1994.

However, there have been efforts to rewrite the 1956 law governing the termination of pregnancy. While these efforts have thus far failed, there is evidence to suggest that many physicians, clinics and hospitals are refusing to perform the procedure. Doctors in Katowice province's 42 obstetrics and gynecology wards have opted not to perform abortions and doctors in a number of other provinces have followed suit (Bakowska, 1997). Such refusals attest to the success of the reportedly 100 local and national pro-life organizations in Poland. While pro-life organizations may have been successful in reducing the number of abortions that take place in state-supported clinics and hospitals, their success in persuading women not to have the procedure is unclear. For example, Andrej Zbonikowski, director of the Health Ministry' s Health Policy Department, has reported that some doctors who refuse to perform abortions in hospitals are performing them in their private offices. Whatever the outcome of the abortion debate, it is certainly true that the inability to time and/or limit the number of pregnancies continues to be an important determinant in women's ability to compete successfully in the nation's labor force.

V. Concluding Remarks

In sum it must be acknowledged that too little time has passed to definitively conclude that women's status in the post-transition Polish economy is either superior or inferior to her status prior to the transition. While the structural changes that have taken place since 1990 have adversely affected women and men alike, available evidence suggests that women have been subject to higher rates of joblessness than men. On the other hand, the demands of the market-based economy seem to more closely correspond to the skills and experience possessed by women than was the case in the pre-transition economy. Moreover, the evidence suggests that some women have been successful in opening and operating their own businesses. Recent evidence also suggests that the majority of working women continue to be responsible for much of the production that takes place in the home and this, in turn, limits their pursuit of meaningful and highly-paid work outside the home. Unfortunately, the products and services that could lighten the load of domestic responsibilities remain largely unavailable or unaffordable for the majority of working women.

ENDNOTES

1. The Situation of Women in Poland: The Report of NGO's Committee-Beijing 1995 Warsaw: Polish Committee of NGSs, March 1995, p.21.
2. See, United Nations, (August 1996), pp. 3-4. Belka , et.al., (1996, p. 22) suggest that the period of adjustment in Poland was expected to be accomplished by the end of 1990.
3. Among all the CEE countries in transition, the Visegnid Group (Czech Republic, Hungary, Poland, Slovak Republic, and Slovenia) were the most economically developed prior to 1990 and for this reason were expected to suffer less severe economic consequences than other CEE countries. While Poland was the first to show positive GDP and Industrial Production growth (1993), all of the VG countries showed positive growth in these areas by 1994.
4. See, Radek Sikorski, (1996, pp. 15-22).
5. See, World Bank, (1995, p. 1).
6. See, World Bank (1993, p. 2). Also see, Ryszard Wilczynski, (1994, pp. 36-50).
7. See *Warsaw Voice*, (January 26, 1997 and January 5, 1997).Prior to December
8. 1989, Krasniewski was the Minister of Youth Affairs. In the elections of 1995, Kwasniewski defeated Walesa and gained the Presidency.
9. Under Article 26, Clause 1, item 1 of the Retirement Pension of Employees and Their Families Law (14 December 1982), a woman employee was qualified for a retirement pension at the age of 60 whereas a man was not eligible until age 65. Additionally, a woman was eligible for a pension after 20 years of employment while the eligibility requirement for a man was 25 years.
10. The concept of unemployment was officially recognized with the passage of the Employment Act of December 12, 1989 (amended July 1990).
11. See, Hauser, et al., (1993, p. 262).
12. 1994 is the latest date for which reliable data, categorized by sex and age, is available.
13. The official definition of an unemployed person (Employment Act of December 12, 1989) is: "A person able and ready to start a job, who does not have a job, who is registered with the appropriate regional labor office, and is not drawing an old-age pension; is not the owner or co-owner of a farm; does not run his/her own business; and is not covered by social security for any other reason.
14. The rate of unemployment decreased in this age cohort as a result of a sufficiently large increase in the numbers of economically active.
15. See, Gregory et al., (1996, p. 17).
16. See, Friedrich Engels, "The Origin of the Family, Private Property and the State

(1884)", cited by Hilda Scott, (1976, p. 35).

17. It is not surprising that men were not encouraged to share domestic responsibilities. Many of the early socialist writers viewed housework in a negative light. Lenin, for example, referred to household work as "domestic slavery [that] crushes, strangles, stultifies and degrades." Such sentiments could hardly be viewed as a ringing endorsement of the joys of household production. See, V.I. Lenin, (1975, p. 484).
18. The employment absorption coefficient is calculated by dividing the percentage increase in employment by the percentage increase in GDP.
19. In 1995, 257,000 women were self-employed and of these 148,00 were employers. (Lisowska, 1996, p. 5).
20. Employer: a person who operates his/her own enterprise, or engages independently in a profession or trade, and hires one or more employees. Own-account worker: a person who operates his or her own enterprise, or engages independently in a profession or trade, and hires no employees.
21. Unpaid family work: usually a person who works without pay in an economic enterprise operated by a related person living in the same household.
22. Persons not classifiable by status: experienced workers whose status is unknown or inadequately described and unemployed persons not previously employed (new entrants).
23. See, Yearbook of Labor Statistics, (1995, p. 451) for details.

References

Bakowska, M., (1997), "Doctors Just Say No." *Warsaw Voice,* February 2, No 5 (432)

Belka,M., A. Krajewska, S. Krajewski, and A. Santos, (1993), "Country Overview Study: Poland" *Eastern European Economics.*

Bialecki, I. and B. Heyns, (1993), "Educational Attainment, the Status of Women, and the Private School Movement in Poland." In *Democratic Reform and the Position of Women in Transitional Economies,* ed. Valentine M. Moghadam. Oxford: Clarendon Press.

Ciechocinska, M., (1993), "Gender Aspects of Dismantling the Command Economy in Eastern Europe: The Case of Poland" In *Democratic Reform and the Position of Women in Transitional Economies,* ed. Valentine M. Moghadam. Oxford: Clarendon Press.

Domanski, H., (1995), "Attitudes Harden Toward 'Women's Work," *Warsaw Voice,* October 1, No. 40 (362).

Einhorn, B., (1993), *Cinderella Goes to Market: Citizenship, Gender and Women's Movements in East Central Europe.* London: Verso.

Fong, M. and G. Paul, (1993), "Women's Economic Status in the Restructuring of Eastern Europe." In *Democratic Reform and the Position of Women in Transitional Economies,* ed. V.M. Moghadam, Oxford: Clarendon Press.

Fullerton, Jr., H.N., (1995), "The 2005 labor force: growing, but slowly." *Monthly Labor Review.*

Fuszara, M. (1993), "Abortion and the Formation of the Public Sphere in Poland" In *Gender Politics and Post Communism,* eds. Nanette Funk and Magda Mueller. New York: Routledge.

Góra, M., I. Kotowska, T. Panek, and J. Podgorski, (1993), "Poland: labor market trends and policies." In *Structural Change in Central and Eastern Europe: Labor Market and Social Policy Implications,* eds. Georg Fischer and Guy Standing. Paris: OECD.

Gregory, A., M. Ingham, and H. Ingham, (1996), "Women's employment in transition: the case of Poland." Paper presented at the Women, work and transformation seminar, University of Bath, 12-13 January.

Hauser, E., B. Heyns, and J. Mansbridge, (1993), "Feminism in the Interstices of Politics and Culture: Poland in Transition." In *Gender Politics and Post-Communism,* eds. Nanette Funk and Magda Mueller. London: Routledge.

Hübner, S., F. Maiek, and H. Rudolph, (1993), "Women's employment in central and Eastern Europe: Status and prospects" In *Structural Change in Central and Eastern Europe: Labor Market and Social Policy Implications,* eds. Georg Fischer and Guy Standing, Paris: OECD.

International Labor Office, (1992-95), *Yearbook of Labor Statistics.* Geneva: International Labor Office.

Klejn, Z., (1997), " A Dilemma Wrapped in a Conundrum." *Warsaw Voice,* January 5, No 1 (428).

Lenin, V. I., (1975), "On the Heroism of Workers in the Rear." Quoted in Robert C. Tucker, ed., *The Lenin Anthology*, New York: Norton.

Lisowska, E. (1996), *"Situation of Women Entrepreneurs in Poland-Barriers to a Wider Participation by Women in Private Sector Growth."* Paper presented at Enterprise in Countries Undergoing Transformation-The Role of Women in Private Sector Development conference, Warsaw School of Economics, 30-31 May.

Ostrowska, Kystyna. (1995), "Women Bear Brunt of Transformations." *Warsaw Voice,* October 1, No. 40 (362).

Polish Committee of NGOs. (1995), *The Situation of Women in Poland.' The Report of NGO's Committee-Beijing 1995.* Warsaw: Polish Committee of NGOs, March.

Scott, H., (1976), *Women and Socialism: Experiences from Eastern Europe.* London: Allison and Busby.

Sikorski, R., (1996), "How We Lost Poland: Heroes Do Not Make Good Politicians." *Foreign Affairs,* September/October.

Szomburg, J., (1997), "Toward a Polish Vision of Capitalism." *Warsaw Voice,* February 2, No. 5 (432).

United Nations, (1996), *Demographic Yearbook (1994).* New York: United Nations.

United Nations. (1996), *Sustainable Development and International Economic Cooperation: Integration of the Economies in Transition into the World Economy.* New York: United Nations, 13 August.

Warsaw Voice. (1997), "Inflation Higher Than Government Targets." Warsaw: *Warsaw Voice,* January 5, No.1 (428).

Warsaw Voice (1997), "Counting a Year's Worth of Beans." Warsaw: *Warsaw Voice*, January 5, No.1 (428).

Wilczynski, R., (1994), "The Role of International Financial Institutions in Poland's Transition to a Market Economy." *Eastern European Economics,* September/October.

World Bank, (1995), "Structural Adjustment Lending to Poland: A Window of Opportunity" *OED Précis.* New York: World Bank, July.

World Economy Research Institute, (1996), *Poland: International Economic Report 1995/96.* Warsaw: Warsaw School of Economics.

CHAPTER 8

THE EMERGING MARKET ECONOMY IN SLOVAK REPUBLIC*

KAREN S. VORST

I. INTRODUCTION

Slovakia, or Slovak Republic, is one of the two successor countries of the former Czechoslovakia. On January 1, 1993, it was established as an independent, sovereign state after nearly fifty years of Communist rule. Today, Slovak Republic continues along the road to a market economy, grappling with some very basic economic issues, such as privatization of state-owned businesses, capital formation and the development of its financial system.

This paper discusses the current state of economic affairs in Slovak Republic. A background of the country's economy and its relative performance in recent years are given in Section II Section III contains a discussion of the sources of funds available for investment and expansion in Slovakia and a brief description of the banking system. The main activities of the central bank, the National Bank of Slovakia, and its efforts to steer the economy forward are discussed in Section IV. A summary and conclusions are in Section V.

II. RECENT MACROECONOMIC PERFORMANCE

Slovak Republic today is in the midst of a significant economic transformation from a Communist economy to a market system. It is a relatively small country with a population of approximately 5.2 million people. Its capital is Bratislava on the Danube River in southwestern Slovakia near the Austrian border. Slovakia is a country rich in history and one that has potential for economic growth and development.

When Slovakia became an independent state, policymakers were expecting a period of adjustment in the short run. During its first full year of independence, 1993, Slovak Republic experienced a recession, which was really a continuation of its economic problems in the 1990s. The GDP fell by 3.7% in 1993, compared to a 7% decline in 1992, and a decrease of 23.7% for the 1990-1993 period (*Annual Report*, National Bank of Slovakia (NBS), 1993, p. 24). Growth in GDP since 1993, however, has been positive, increasing by 6.9% in 1996. While progress has been made, it should be noted that GDP in constant prices in 1996 was still lower (by SK 50 billion) than constant GDP in 1989 (*Annual Report*, NBS, 1996, pp. 115, 119).

The Slovak economy consists mainly of heavy industry, construction, agriculture and services. One of the main problems in the economy is with heavy industry, the production in which was about 40% of the output of the mechanical engineering sector in recent years (*Annual Report*, NBS, 1993, p. 23). Much of it was still geared toward arms production. With the breakup of the Soviet Union and the development of Slovakia and other east European countries, the demand for arms has decreased significantly and so has this industry's output.

Industries such as refined oil products, coke, nuclear fuel, wood and paper products recorded a decrease in value added of 0.5% in 1996 and contributed a smaller share to GDP, down to 26.2% in 1996 from 28.6% in 1995. Industrial production overall recorded a relatively small gain of 2.6% in 1996, compared to 1995's 8.3% and 1994's 4.8%. Growth of 22.1% was achieved, however, in the manufacture of vehicles, wagons and ships (*Annual Report*, NBS, 1996, p. 22).

The services component of the overall GDP continued to expand in 1996, comprising 54.8% of the GDP. The main service areas include transportation, telecommunications, and banking and insurance services. As domestic demand increased in 1996, there was development in new service areas, such as real estate, computer engineering, sports and cultural activities.

While construction experienced growth in 1996 amounting to 4.4% over 1995, agriculture recorded a 4.4% decrease in the volume of grain harvested. Agriculture is not an area in which significant growth can take place, in part due to the soil and topographical attributes of Slovakia[1] and to the need for updated machinery and technology. The agricultural sector was adversely affected in 1996 by a negative trade balance, by the relatively low competitive nature of Slovak Republic agricultural products and by a lower-than-EU-average farm subsidy to Slovak farmers. However, agriculture received some support from a special financing program by the National Bank of Slovakia (*Annual Report*, NBS, 1996, pp. 21-25).

The rate of inflation in consumer prices in 1996 was 5.8%, with a projection for 1997 of 6.1%. After experiencing a high of 61.2% inflation in 1991, the single-digit rates of the past few years have been a great improvement for the economy. Contributing to the fall in the inflation rate were (1) significant decreases in food prices, (2) gradual price deregulation, (3) lower producer prices, and (4) decreased pressure on the National Bank of Slovakia to monetize the government's debt, given developments in the banking sector and capital markets (*Annual Report*, NBS, 1996, pp.17-18).

The unemployment rate in 1996 was 12.4%, down from a peak of 14.8% in 1994. Projections for 1997 show a rate of 13.1 (Komínková and Mučková, 1998, p. 192). The increase in economic growth is surely one reason for this decrease. However, there was an increased number of Slovak workers commuting to Czech Republic on a daily basis to work in the construction industry and in areas around Moravia near the border. Slovak economists believe that the unemployment rate will continue to fall slowly but that it will take at least another two years of robust economic growth to see the rate drop below 10%.

Average monthly nominal wages in industries with 25 or more employees increased by 15.2% in 1995 over 1994, while construction monthly wages were up 14.9%, transportation monthly wages increased by 17.9% and those in trade industries increased by 13.2%. Overall, the average monthly wage per employee was Sk 7,195 (~$216) in 1995, an increase of 14.1% in nominal terms from 1994 (a 4.4% increase in real terms). Real wage growth, however, exceeded the growth in labor productivity by about 0.2%, which could have a negative impact on the relative competitiveness of industrial products produced in Slovakia in the future and could cause inflation (Vanous, 1995, pp. 20-21).

Foreign trade is an essential and significant part of the growth of the Slovak economy. In 1996, the balance on current account showed a deficit of Sk 59.5 billion, or 10.1% of GDP, while the trade deficit itself was Sk 64.5 billion. This result is significant compared to the moderate surplus in the trade account of Sk 717 million in 1995. Contributing to the trade deficit were (1) the decline in the growth rates of EU and other trading partners, (2) the slowdown in the export of raw materials and semi-products, (3) increases in imports of 28.5% over 1995 and (4) lower surpluses in the service sector (*Annual Report*, NBS, 1995, pp. 20-21; 1996, pp. 29-30).

Overall, the Slovak economy in 1996 witnessed a mixture of trends. While the inflation rate continued downward and economic growth was a respectable 6.9%, problems continued in the labor market with unemployment still above 12% and in the foreign sector with the balance of trade deterioration. Relative to other emerging economies, Slovakia's economic performance is moderate,[2] though problem areas remain. One of the major problems remains the country's ability to finance investment and growth, an issue discussed in the next section.

III. Sources of Funds

As an economy in transition, Slovak Republic has experienced its share of turmoil and uncertainty. While economic growth in 1996 was comparable to other Central European transition economies, one of the constraints on growth in Slovak Republic is the lack of a fully-functioning capital market, a market that today is still developing. In this section, we discuss the sources of investment funds in Slovak Republic and the difficulties the government and the private sector face in obtaining appropriate funds for growth.

Development within Slovak Republic has been relatively slow. Much of its industry is in need of updating and funds have been relatively scarce in order to finance the new technology. While the funding sources in Slovak Republic are similar to those in most other economies, there is a considerable difference in the way in which the government, commercial banks and the private sector operate.

A. Government as a Source of Funds

The government is saddled with a huge amount of debt (Sk 27 billion in 1996; *Annual Report*, NBS, 1996, p. 40), in part left over from the government of the former Czechoslovakia. Therefore, direct subsidies to industry from the government would simply add to its debt and generally would be out of line with the transitioning process. Tax rates are already very high (45% for individuals and businesses and 55% for banks), though tax revenues are generally low because of low income levels. While the government has generated some funds through the sale of some of its assets via its privatization program, these funds cannot be counted upon to make a significant contribution to deficit reduction year after year. Furthermore, the government initially was reluctant to speed up privatization, fearing massive unemployment that would create more turmoil for the economy and more government debt.[3]

The debt and/or deficit could be monetized. In fact, the central bank, the National Bank of Slovakia (NBS), had been required to buy all of the government debt within one year of its issue. When the debt is first issued, it may be sold to anyone. However, the secondary market for Slovak government securities is not well developed and, therefore, the NBS becomes involved in purchasing the debt. This action in the past has restrained the NBS from achieving its goal of low inflation through a lower rate of growth of the money supply. However, this restraint was lessened recently by the growing interest of commercial banks in holding government debt. For the year 1996, the percentage of government debt held by the NBS was 21.8%, down significantly from 53.9% in 1995 (*Annual Report*, NBS, 1995, p. 36; 1996, pp. 40-41).

B. Commercial Bank Sources

As an alternative to state financing and in line with privatization efforts, the government of Slovak Republic encouraged the development of private commercial banks, both domestic banks and foreign bank branches. At the end of 1996, there were 24 banking institutions operating more than 1843 organizational units within Slovak Republic. There were 5 branches of foreign banks and 12 representative offices of foreign banks operating a total of 50 units in Slovak Republic (*Annual Report*, NBS, 1995, pp. 73-74; 1996, p. 81). One of the most recent foreign branches to open in Bratislava was Citibank in November 1995 with its agenda "to prepare Slovakia for foreign investment" (*Slovak Economic Sheet*, December, 1995).

While current commercial banks generally are set up both to take in deposits and make loans, the banking system continues to be dominated by a few large banks, the holdovers from the old system. The Investment Development Bank and the VUB General Credit Bank are state-run financial institutions that dominate the credit side of the market. Total credit extended by public financial institutions at the end of 1995 was about 70% of the total (*Slovak Economic Sheet*, November, 1996). Funds would come directly from the government and/or from the state-run Slovak Savings Bank which only took in deposits and continued to dominate the market for deposits. As the transitional process continues and more private commercial banks get in a position to participate in private financing, it is expected that the state's influence in the credit allocation process will diminish.

In 1996, the average short-term bank deposit rate was 8.8%, compared to 11.2% in 1995 and that for time deposits were 9.1% in 1996, compared to 12.2% in 1995. While savings rates are relatively high, ranging from 10% to 15% of income, the volume of savings is fairly low because wages and income in Slovak Republic are relatively low. With relatively high rates paid on savings, banks must charge a higher rate on loans. The average short-term bank loan rate in 1996 was 12.4%, down from 14.3% in 1995 (*Annual Report*, NBS, 1995, pp. 130, 135; 1996, pp.135-137). Thus, short-term bank loans for new technology were relatively expensive, unless they could be subsidized by the government as they have been in the past; however, such subsidization generally was not forthcoming.

The term structure of interest rates was shaped as an inverted U. For example, in December 1996, the overall short-term average monthly lending rate was 11.95%, the medium-term rate was 12.99% and the long-term rate was 9.33%. This pattern held for all sectors, except the household-lending sector that had an average of 13.9% on short-term loans, 12.6% on medium-term and 3.8% on long-term. This structure is most likely to encourage long-term loans. Deposit rates followed the same inverted-U structure, effectively encouraging shorter-term savings. Average time deposit rates were below the average lending rates by about 2.5%, allowing banks this margin for profit (*Annual Report*, NBS, 1996, pp. 135-137).

A complication for bank profitability and the further extension of credit was the fact that "...the amount of outstanding debt which probably will not be paid back to Slovak banks has almost equaled the annual revenue of the Slovak national budget...state-owned banks make 75% of all loans in Slovakia; however, their portfolios include almost 90% of the bad debt." (*Slovak Economic Sheet*, December, 1995). Many of these bad bank loans were the inherited product of soft budget constraints of state-controlled banks before 1989 and the lack of sufficient loan expertise in the transition period. These bad loans are a burden on a bank's capital position and may cause liquidity problems when loans are delayed or not repaid. In the short run, banks have become increasingly cautious in extending new loans, opting instead to take the less risky road of purchasing government bonds.

The National Bank of Slovakia took a major step in 1995 to improve the operations of banks. In March 1995, the NBS approved regulations that called for the evaluation of certain bank assets and liabilities according to the risk incurred. Banks now must make provisions to cover their risks. Capital adequacy ratios were set at 8% in 1994, to be achieved by the end of 1996. All but four commercial banks met these minima at that time. Net credit exposure limits also were enforced. These regulations improve the integrity of the banking system and allow for more uniform evaluation of a bank's capital position and credit risk exposure. With an improved capital position and a re-education of bank loan officers that could foster a better collection record on future loans, the banking system in the future will be better able to participate in private financing (*Annual Report*, NBS, 1995, p. 76; 1996, pp. 83-85).

C. PRIVATE SECTOR AND FOREIGN SOURCES

Besides the government and banks as sources of funds, the private sector has become increasingly involved in financing its own projects. The government has relaxed many of the restrictions on private ownership and the number of new businesses has been increasing. As of August 1995, there were approximately 42,000 profitable private firms (95.2% of all private firms) in Slovak Republic, less than two full years into the country's movement toward a market economy (*Slovak Economic Sheet*, December, 1996). Two exchange systems were established to assist in the generation of private funds and in the trading of issues: the Bratislava Option Exchange (BOE), trading in futures, options and other terms; and the Bratislava Securities Exchange, (BSE), trading securities and shares of over 500 companies. In 1996, the value of shares traded on the BSE was Sk 114.1 billion, an increase of 184% from 1995 (*Annual Report*, NBS, 1996, p. 65).

To assist in private funding, investment companies were encouraged to set up investment funds. Initially, over 160 investment funds were established and were able to amass approximately Sk 58 billion (~$2 billion) during the first phase of privatization. Investment funds were an important part of the initial privatization program in Czechoslovakia. These companies were able to purchase up to 20 percent of the stocks of an individual firm, an amount sufficient enough to allow investment funds to participate in management decisions of the firms and provide some oversight for operations. The largest industry-related investment fund in Slovak Republic in 1995 held "...shares in 148 trade, production, and financial companies..." (Hake, 1997, p. 5).

However, investment fund activities in Slovak Republic were significantly reduced in 1995. Two of the largest independent investment funds, The First Slovak Investment Privatization Company (PSIPS) and The First Slovak Investment Company (PSIP) had their licenses revoked in the spring of 1995 under circumstances that probably were politically motivated. PSIPS had been one of the most active funds heading four trust companies and three separate "...investment funds which accounted for approximately half of the trades on the stock exchange" (Hake, 1997, p. 8). Other investment funds with political connections received favorable treatment and continued to grow, resulting in increased concentration of shareholdings. However, even these investment companies would see a slowdown of growth opportunities with the implementation of new privatization rules in 1994 that favored direct sales of state property by the National Assets Fund (NAF) and bypassed investment companies. Finally, in 1995, these companies were entirely excluded from the bond privatization program and were encouraged through a compensation plan by the NAF to give up their licenses altogether. By the middle of 1996, 90 of the existing 166 investment companies had voluntarily given up their licenses (Hake, 1997, p. 13). Such action greatly reduced the ability of investment companies to continue to play an active role in the capital markets.

Complicating the development of the capital market was the decision in late 1995 by the Ministry of Finance to deny the license renewal of the Bratislava Option Exchange (BOE). This ruling essentially took away the BOE's ability to act as an organizer of option and term trades in securities. The decision to cancel the "...activities of an organizer of a capital market without its breaking the law is unprecedented in the world," (*Slovak Economic Sheet*, December, 1995) and is being appealed.

Slovak Republic, like other countries, is increasingly aware of the importance of its participation in the international financial community. It is striving to update and/or revise its banking system so that it can operate on a worldwide basis. Sixteen of the 24 commercial banks are authorized to conduct foreign exchange transactions in order to facilitate international trade and commerce. As of December 1996, foreign ownership in domestic banks was 39.6% of total bank capital, up from 13.5% in 1993. The two countries with the biggest shares of Slovak bank capital were Czech Republic and Austria, while Germany, the U.S. and the Netherlands also contributed significant capital to Slovak banks (*Annual Report*, 1995, p. 73; 1996, p. 81). At the end of 1996, five banks were 100% foreign owned, nine banks had more than 10% of capital coming from foreign sources, and 3 banks had less than 10% foreign capital.

Though the government would prefer that domestic investors provide the necessary capital support for industries, the need for foreign investors' help cannot be denied in Slovak Republic, or for that matter, in many of the transition economies. The attraction of foreign investors depends heavily upon the government's desire to allow such capital investment and upon the willingness of the government to put into place and enforce regulations that protect such investments. For Slovak Republic, foreign investors at times have had a 'wait-and-see' outlook with regard to the Slovak government's attitude toward foreign participation in the privatization process and with regard to policy changes that could affect industry growth and the return on capital. Despite these reservations, the volume of foreign investment in Slovak Republic changed from Sk 16.5 billion in 1994 to Sk 21.9 billion in 1995, before decreasing to Sk 7.8 billion in 1996 and rising again to ~Sk 36 billion in 1997. However, relative to other Central European emerging economies, Slovakia's foreign direct investment was small.[4] The largest numbers of investors in Slovakia were from Germany, Austria, Czech Republic, Britain, France and the United States

IV. The National Bank of Slovakia (NBS) and Monetary Policy

On the day that Slovakia became an independent state, January 1, 1993, the National Bank of Slovakia also was established. The NBS "is the successor bank of the former State Bank of Czecho-Slovakia, which was the central bank of the CSFR (Czech and Slovak Federal Republic)" (*National Bank of Slovakia*, 1994, p. 1). The NBS performs duties that are characteristic of most central banks. For example, the NBS (1) formulates and implements monetary policy in order to stabilize the economy, (2) regulates and supervises the banking system, and (3) acts as the bank of the government. Additionally, the NBS is responsible for maintaining the convertibility of the Slovak crown internally so as to promote business and individual international transactions. Externally, it maintains the exchange rate and can operate effectively in international money and capital markets.

The NBS attempts to control the money supply via its control over the monetary base. Standard tools, such as open market operations, the discount rate and reserve requirements are used to achieve its monetary goals. In addition, the NBS uses refinancing of credits to commercial banks and the imposition of credit limits on commercial banks to control the money supply.

Table 1: Monetary Statistics, 1993-1996

	1993	1994	1995	1996
Money Supply, M1				
Q1	- 14.7	- 7.5	- 7.0	- 3.1
Q2	2.2	1.4	1.7	6.9
Q3	- 1.0	4.0	5.5	4.4
Q4	15.3	10.6	14.2	13.1
Year-to-Year %	7.4	18.9	20.5	17.2
Money Supply, M2				
Q1	- 3.0	- 2.7	- 1.0	1.2
Q2	1.9	2.2	2.2	4.0
Q3	0.6	2.7	3.2	2.3
Q4	12.0	10.2	11.2	10.6
Year-to-Year %	18.5	21.0	21.2	16.5

Source: Annual Report, National Bank of Slovakia, 1993, p. 87; 1994, p. 87; 1995, p. 107; 1996; p. 127.

Money supply fluctuations from 1993 through 1996 are shown in Table 1. The quarter-to-quarter variation in M1 and M2 are relatively small for the second and third quarters of each year. Curiously, the first quarter of each year for both M1 and M2 shows a negative growth rate, which is more than made up for throughout the year, culminating in double digit growth rates in the last quarter of each year. The average annual increase in M1 and in M2 for each of these years was significant; with the exception of the 7.4% increase in M1 in 1993, all of the other growth rates were close to 20%. These numbers, together with the excess liquidity in the banking system may help to explain why the goal of lower inflation was difficult to achieve in the early years. These significant yearly money growth rates, however, are inconsistent with the general achievement made with regard to inflation, especially given the fact that the NBS on occasion has had to monetize part of the government debt.

In addition to the money supply, the NBS monitors credit extended to the public and to the private sectors and it tracks interest rates. The NBS sets limits on credit extension from banks but also extends credit itself to banks. Banks may borrow from the NBS at the discount rate, which started 1995 at 12%, fell to 9.75% by the end of the year and was 8.8% throughout 1996 (*Annual Report*, NBS, 1996, p 137). The term on discount loans is 6-9 months, relatively long by U.S. standards. There is usually a requirement of collateral on these loans. In addition, the NBS may extend credit to banks through a system of refinancing, which basically involves a kind of repurchase agreement arranged by the NBS. The bank may use its portfolio of government securities as collateral on these loans. It is expected that the bank would complete the repurchase agreement before the end of each month. This arrangement of credit helps banks with inter-month liquidity problems.

The NBS is also responsible for maintaining stability in the exchange rate and regulating commercial bank activities in the foreign exchange market. It does not permit the free movement of the Slovak crown in and out of the country but strives to maintain sufficient amounts of convertible currencies since Slovak Republic is significantly dependent upon foreign trade.

The information from Slovak publications lists the NBS as an independent central bank with an autonomous monetary policy. The "independence" of a central bank is not a new concept in Slovak ideology. In the prior Czechoslovak system, there was some evidence since 1970 of "...slow but steadily increasing emancipation of the macroeconomic (or "truly monetary") dimension of monetary policy broadly defined" (Klaus, 1990, p. 63). The Czechoslovak central bank for the past two decades had been moving away from following every government directive toward applying 'efficiency' criteria to credit extension. "In some periods the [central] bank conducted a more restrictive policy in which it was possible for regional offices of the bank to refuse to grant credits to inefficient enterprises..." (Klaus, 1990, p. 63). However, like the independent U.S. Federal Reserve, the NBS does come under some influence from the government. Its three top officials, Governor and two Vice-Governors, are appointed by Slovak Republic President. The other six board members are recommended by the President and appointed by the government. This arrangement is one that can generate some governmental influence on NBS activities.

Additionally, the NBS Act that set up the central bank mandated that the bank "...support the economic policy of Slovak Republic," but that it fulfill its tasks "...independently of instruction given by the President" (*National Bank of Slovakia Act*, 1992, p. 6). However, due to a lack of sufficient development in the money and capital markets, the government is not able to finance its deficit/debt completely in the private sector. For example, "as early as March [1993], the size of the budget deficit and the increased volume of Treasury bills on the market exceeded the absorption capabilities of commercial banks" (*Annual Report*, NBS, 1993, p. 55). Therefore, the NBS had little choice but to participate in government deficit financing. In fact, the balance sheet of the NBS as of December 31, 1996, carried not only the recent government deficit of Sk 25.6 billion, but also included deficits from previous years for a total of Sk 28.6 billion, up from 1995's total of Sk 25.7 billion, but down from the 1994 total of Sk 46.4 billion.[5] The total government debt held by the NBS decreased significantly due to the increased ability of commercial banks to hold government securities. While this development has worked to increase the independence of the NBS, the NBS cannot be totally independent until the private financial markets are developed sufficiently in order to handle the government debt without significant aid from the NBS.

V. Summary and Conclusions

Slovak Republic is one of many countries of Europe in transition from a centrally-planned economy to a market system and it is making progress. The year, 1996, saw some improvement over previous years, with economic growth picking up and inflation continuing to moderate. Unemployment, however, continued at a double-digit pace, the government budget deficit was recorded at 4.4% of GDP (up from 1.6% in 1995) and the balance of trade was in deficit (down from a slight surplus in 1995) (*Annual Report*, NBS, 1996, pp. 116, 120).

In order to continue its progress, the Slovak economy has several systemic problems that need the attention of the government.[6] Foremost among these is the development of a fully-functioning capital market. The stock exchanges and trading centers are still underdeveloped, though volume has been increasing. Privatization efforts generally have not been completely satisfactory either in the generation of new capital or with regard to equity effects throughout the system. Foreign capital should be encouraged as an alternative capital source. Further development in these areas can move the system forward somewhat but much remains to be done in order to ensure the development of a capital market that can efficiently allocate resources.

An important element in the development of a capital market is the efficient operation of commercial banks. Banks should continue to evolve as important depositories of savings by households and businesses and thereby become a significant source of funds. However, before they can operate effectively, they must have sufficient capital and must move beyond the shadow of non-performing loans that has limited bank growth. Banks must have their own capital at stake and must learn how to allocate credit according to sound economic principles.

Development and reform come with substantial costs in terms of resources and time. Transition economies must find a way to balance future payoffs with current costs. Slovak Republic progress, though costly, has been deliberate. As the needed reforms are implemented and markets are developed further, increased economic benefits should be forthcoming.

Endnotes

*The author would like to thank Mr. Peter Dovčiak of the Slovak National Bank Slovakia and Dr. Willadee Wehmeyer for their helpful comments.

1. There are a series of mountain ranges that cover most of the middle and eastern sections of Slovakia. The fertile soil of the lowlands around the Danube River has been developed for agriculture, though heavy marsh areas cover some of this

region as well.

2. See Chapter 2 in this volume for a comparison of economic growth rates, inflation rates and unemployment rates of Slovak Republic, Poland, Hungary and Czech Republic.
3. However, the government's program to privatize industry continued, amid arguments that the procedure was faulty, showed favoritism, and was generally unfair. After participating in a first wave of coupon privatization, the government canceled the so-called second wave of coupon privatization significantly slowing the process in 1995. The National Property Fund, the government agency in charge of privatization, implemented a program to replace coupon privatization in 1996. The NPF began to issue bonds to Slovak citizens that in turn could be used to buy stock in companies that were to be privatized. Despite these efforts and a pledge in October, 1995, by the Slovak Premier, Vladimir Meciar, that privatization would be completed in eight months (*Slovak Economic Sheet*, October, 1995), the government in September, 1996, appeared to be at a deadlock concerning the methods of future privatization and even whether or not to continue the process (*Slovak Economic Sheet*, September, 1996).
4. Numbers for foreign direct investment ranked Poland first in 1997 with USD 20.6 billion; Hungary ranked second with USD 17 billion; Russia ranked third with USD 9.3 billion and Sloven Republic attracted USD 1.9 billion (*Slovak Economic Sheet*, March, 1998, 5; *Annual Report*, NBS, 1993, p. 16; 1995, p. 19; 1996, pp. 32-33).
5. This latter amount includes Slovak Republic deficit before separation of the Czech-Slovak Republic and a portion allocated to Slovak Republic after the breakup (*Annual Report*, NBS, 1995, pp. 74, 79; 1996, p. 100).
6. Economists have written policy prescriptions regarding the necessary economic reforms in the newly-formed market economies of Eastern Europe. See Hunter (1993) and Brainard (1991), for example.

REFERENCES

Brainard, L.J., (1991), "Reform in Eastern Europe: Creating a Capital Market", Federal Reserve Bank of Kansas City *Economic Review*; January/February, 49-58.

Hake, E.R., (1997), "The Rise and Fall of Investment Companies in Slovakia," forthcoming in the *Journal of Comparative Economics*, pre-published manuscript.

Hunter, W.C.(1993), "Banking Reform and the Transition to a Market Economy in Bulgaria: Problems and Prospects." Federal Reserve Bank of Atlanta *Economic Review*, 78, January/ February,15-22.

International Economic Report on Poland, 1995/96, (1996),World Economy Research Institute, Warsaw, Poland: Warsaw School of Economics.

Klaus, V. (1990), "Monetary Policy in Czechoslovakia in the 1970s and 1980s and the Nature and Problems of the Current Economic Reform." *Communist Economics*, 2; 61-71.

National Bank of Slovakia, Annual Report, 1993, 1994, 1995, 1996.

National Bank of Slovakia, (1994), government pamphlet, Bratislava, Slovakia.

National Bank of Slovakia Act, (1992), The National Council of Slovak Republic, Bratislava, Slovakia, November 18.

Slovak Economic Sheet. 5, November, 1995; 6, December, 1995; and 7, January, 1996.

Slovakia Today, (1994), government pamphlet, Bratislava, Slovakia, January.

Vanous, J., editor, (1995), "Slovak Economic Monitor," *PlanEcon Report*, **11**, 34-35: 1-43, November 10.

CHAPTER 9

ERNEST GELLNER, CIVIL SOCIETY AND FREEDOM OF THE PRESS IN CZECH REPUBLIC

ALLEN MILLS

"You see, Dubenka, what a lot of trouble we have with our history, it's a constantly postponed beginning, and a simultaneous ending."
Bohumil Hrabal

I. CIVIL SOCIETY AS A CONCEPT

A powerful ideal haunted Eastern Europe in the 1980s. It was that of civil society. The concept has a long ancestry. Hobbes used it in the 17th century; and it was a central idea of the thinkers of the Scottish Enlightenment in the 18th century and, later, of Hegel and Marx. For Marx civil society was a bourgeois illusion masking what were exploitative relations of economic production and, as regards the state, political subjection. With more than a little cunning of history, the idea of civil society returned in the 1960s and again, emphatically in the 1980s, as a critique of societies that were authoritarian in state structure, centralist and socialist in economics and ostensibly Marxist in purpose. That is, the concept was now employed to uphold such liberal values as liberty, pluralism and the market.

Evidently, the idea of civil society is long of history and varied and contradictory in meaning. The term was part of the conceptual repertoire of socialist reformers in the Prague Spring of 1968. Two of them, Michal Lakatoš and Zdeněk Mlynář employed it to emphasize the importance of a quasi-liberal, political pluralism: "Mlynář saw the fundamental general duty of Czechoslovak socialism as 'preserving from among the driving forces of the European capitalist era (and in many respects even the European pre-capitalist era, such as the ancient legacy and, in the sense of values, especially Christianity) the requisite independence of the individual human being while abolishing private property'"(Kusin, 1971a, p. 100). And, "Lakatoš saw 'civic society' as the outcome of modern social activity and initiative in post-feudal Europe... (D)emocratic principles were firmly embedded in it. Without democracy, every regime, including socialism, in fact reverted to pre-civic structures of society. Democracy was presented as government on behalf of society whereas it should be understood as a government which depended on civic society...(However) what Lakatoš termed 'civic society' was really infrastructure, i.e., the non-governmental institutions and political parties associated in the National Front" (Kusin, 1971a, p.116).

These two were not the only authors of the innovative ideas of that fateful spring. There were others: Vladímír Klokočka, Ivan Sviták, Pavel Kohout and Ota Šik, for example. Also part of the group was Václav Havel, then a dissident playwright and, in the 1970s, a *samizdat* pamphleteer and prisoner of conscience. His writings at that time conveyed the modern sense of a civil society though without actually using the term. Influenced by ideas from Heidegger and Husserl and other existentialists and phenomenologists, Havel talked of the foundational importance of a *Lebenswelt* or natural world, pre-rational and pre-suppositionless. In this world are found the truths about the essential nature of life: its mystery, variety, openness and uniqueness. The *Lebenswelt*, correlatively, discloses a foundational ethics of individuality, freedom, compassion, honesty, sincerity and honour.[1] Havel's essay, "The Power of the Powerless" (1978) captured well the social implications of these ideas and came close to uttering the phrase "civil society": "What is this independent life of society? The spectrum of its expressions and activities is naturally very wide. It includes everything from self-education and thinking about the world, through free creative activity, and its communication to others, to the most varied free, civic attitudes, including instances of independent social self-organization. In short, it is an area in which living within the truth becomes articulate and materializes in a visible way" (Havel, 1991, p. 177).

By January 1994, now President of a newly separate Czech Republic, Havel spoke explicitly of his ideal of a "civil society." Of course, he disagreed with others over the meaning of the term, notably with his post-revolutionary nemesis, Václav Klaus. For Havel the concept flowed naturally into voluntarist, decentralist and avowedly political channels. The principles of such a society, he said, must continue to surge through the economy but they should also be extended into the "political" realm. By this he meant not so much the state but the non-economic, *public* life of society; its associations and cultural life; its participatory schemes of self-help: "The central rationality of the state- be it ever so enlightened- cannot continue to take the place of the pluralistic richness of ideas, the knowledge, the experience, and the inventiveness of individuals and the great variety of associations they naturally create" (Havel, 1997, p. 145). It is the participating citizen, he continued, that makes a civil society function. Government should be devolved; the non-profit sector encouraged; and there is a necessity to deepen the sense of civic solidarity: "If our daring economic reforms are not accompanied by the purposeful development of all aspects of civil society, our life will soon become one-dimensional and arid, limited to a race for profits, accompanied by an apathy toward public affairs and a dependence on the state to do everything for us" (Havel 1997, p. 147).

II. The Czech Lands and Civil Society

By reasonable standards, and when they have been allowed to be in the 20th century, the Czech Lands can lay claim to being a civil society in the liberal democratic sense and that is how I will use the terms in what follows. The emergence of such a society anywhere will never be an overnight, sudden crystallization of the individualistic, the libertarian and the pluralistic. A civil society takes time to emerge; and there is a sense in which its very existence defies the "laws" of history. As Ernest Gellner wryly observes; at most times human beings have been governed and awed by a mixture of coercion and superstition (Gellner, 1994a, p. 31).

Conventional wisdom has it that the modern account of freedom entered a new, progressive stage in the 16th century with the Protestant Reformation and other contemporaneous events: the revolution in science and technology and the emergence of capitalism and industrialism. The Czech Lands too played some part in these matters. Although Jan Hus was not alone in his pre-Lutheran Protestantism, he was with John Wyclif the most significant of the proto-Reformers. Burned at the stake for heresy in1415, he helped bring Protestantism to lord and peasant in Bohemia in the 16th and 17th centuries. Religious non-conformity and aristocratic independence offended the dynastic and religious ambitions of the Habsburg monarchy. Hussite dissent was defeated in 1620 at the Battle of the White Mountain, and its supporters crushed. The offending gentry lost their estates and non-conforming peasants were expropriated, displaced and slaughtered. A new feudal, patrimonial and Counter-Reformation order was established. German became the language of economic rule and political pretension and Roman Catholicism the re-established religious hegemony. Czech-speaking peasants in Bohemia in the 17th and 18th centuries were among the most impoverished in Europe (Anderson, 1974, pp. 312-22; Seton-Watson, 1943, pp. 131-2).

Improvement of sorts came in the late 18th century. Maria Theresa (1717-80), consort to Francis I, and Joseph II (r. 1765-90), her son, embraced secular reforms based on contemporary Enlightenment ideas. The Jesuits were evicted from their lands in 1773; and in 1781 an Edict of Toleration was declared and serfdom abolished. The following year, monastic lands in the Czech Lands were dissolved. The French Revolution and Napoleon's military adventures put a crimp in the reformist resolve of even enlightened absolutist monarchs and many of the Josephine reforms were abandoned or compromised. But change was underway. In Bohemia and Moravia in the 19th century there occurred the Czech national revival. Young Czechs, instead of entering the priesthood, became teachers and journalists and agitated for nationalism. The Czech school system was expanded; in 1861 *Národni listy*, the first, large, Czech political daily newspaper, was founded; education was made compulsory in the Austrian lands in 1868; and in 1881 a Czech-speaking part of Charles University was established..

In its earliest stages, nationalism in 19th century Europe advanced in step with liberalism, and its individualist values and belief in representative government. Nationalism was often about the freedom and equality of nations against strong central states. Such a world view could easily include a defense of individualism and personal rights. The Habsburgs had little appreciation for nationalist strivings though their record on other aspects of liberalism was not altogether lacking especially towards the end of the century. Where their policies were clearly deficient was in the area of *democratic* political rights. Vienna did establish a half-heartedly representative Reichsrat in 1867 but the Old Czech nationalist leaders, Palacký and Rieger abstained from participating in it. Property qualifications limited the franchise though this was altered after 1896 and especially after 1907 when universal manhood suffrage was conceded. By then, German-Czech rivalries had brought Austrian politics to a nasty pitch. Industrialism was also changing Czech society. Bohemia was the industrial heartland of the Austrian half of the Dual Monarchy in the thirty years before the First World. At the same time popular education had made Czechs all but universally literate. When the War broke out the Czech Lands experienced contradictory loyalties: the Emperor demanded total loyalty and military support but Czechs felt confined within the Habsburg system and in any event they were being asked to go to war against their fellow Slavs in Russia.

The First Czechoslovak Republic, constituted in 1918 at the hands of Masaryk, Beneš, Kramíař and Štefánik, was in many respects a paragon of *liberal* nationalism. Part of President Woodrow Wilson's scheme of national self-determination, Czechoslovakia nonetheless was a multi-ethnic state. The new nation embraced from the beginning universal *adult* suffrage and employed the relatively novel electoral system of proportional representation which allowed for extensive minority representation; industrial capitalism was remarkably successful there in the 1920s but like other countries Czechoslovakia suffered the ravages of the Depression. The new state avoided both church-domination and anti-clericalism; and its politics steered clear of the authoritarianism of such neighbors as Poland and Hungary; the new nation was remarkably advanced technologically and culturally.

This is, perhaps, a mildly favorable account of the First Republic. It says nothing about the Czech tendency to be overly centralist in their dealings with the Slovaks and the Sudeten Germans; it overlooks the political fragmentation of the inter-war party system; and it omits mention of the submissive posture of the ruling elites in the face of Nazi aggression after 1938. That said, the balance of evidence still requires the conclusion that the First Republic was a civil society of a liberal democratic sort. The Czech Lands were especially diverse in population: there was a significant Protestant minority and also a secular one, those in the census 'without a church connection'; and the inter-war Jewish community was especially dynamic and influential. These diversities induced important cross-cutting affiliations and they blunted polarizations: "If Czechoslovakia could be described as politically an ideal half-way house between the extremes of the Right and the Left, it was partly because the Catholic Church was strong enough to prevent the complete triumph of the latter, but not sufficiently strong to establish a conservative ascendancy" (Seton-Watson, 1943, p.332). Diversity led, admittedly, to multi-party political fragmentation but the *Pětka* system, lubricated with suitable amounts of civic deference and stable bases of party support, brought a centrist, pragmatic, moderate, consociational quality to politics and reinforced liberal democratic values. A vibrant economy, at least before 1930, offset a modestly interventionist state. There was a healthy public opinion and a variegated political party press. As late as 1940 there were some fifty-five dailies published in the Czech Lands (Táborský, 1961, p. 560).

It is, then, reasonable to conclude that in Bohemia and Moravia there existed a culture emerging out of the 15th century which by the 20th century bore the attributes of a "civil society": that is, a culture that was rational, individualist, broadly tolerant and resistant to the traditional authority of Church and aristocracy. Enduring and resilient, mainly due to geo-political contingencies this culture nevertheless has rarely been allowed political expression except during the all too brief period of the First Republic.

Whatever elements of civil society existed under the First Republic were, of course, obliterated after the Nazi occupation in 1938/9 and the Communist coup in February 1948. Multi-partyism ceased and, rapidly, in the 1950s the economy was socialized. Publishing was converted into a state monopoly and non-Communist newspapers banned. A multifarious press before 1940 was reduced to seventeen dailies in the Czech Lands, with each newspaper being published by a Communist organization (Táborský, 1961, p. 560). The two radio networks, *Československo* and *Praha*, were owned by the state as was the Czech television system after its founding in 1953. Intellectual and journalistic activity was channeled through a number of official unions: the Union of Journalists, the Writers' Union and the Film Makers' Union.

So was imposed what Antonín Liehm called an "official pyramid", a state-controlled hierarchy, with government, party apparatus and bureaucracy at the top and a variety of "transmission belts" of unions and state-sanctioned bodies underneath, all leading to the domination of public opinion and the control of information (Kusin, 1971b, pp. 73-8). Resistance began in 1953, after censorship was definitively introduced. Czechoslovakia became a fully fledged Stalinist regime, just as its eponymous hero was about to expire. After Khrushchev's speech to the

20th Congress of the Communist Party of the Soviet Union in March 1956, some Soviet satellites sanctioned criticism of Stalinism but not in Czechoslovakia where Party First Secretary Antonín Novotný ruled with an iron hand. Stalinism militated against many of the cultural values of the Czechs, especially the liberal, skeptical and critical characteristics of their tradition. Intellectuals had historically seen themselves as surrogates for an absent indigenous, non-German aristocracy: "Of all the social groups, the creative intelligentsia- in the humanities, science, and technology- probably felt the worst under Novotný. Restrictions of freedom of action and thought went against the grain of the essentially European-oriented Czech intellectual...Scientists and scholars took over the job which a nobility would have played in other circumstances. The intellectual became the aristocrat of spirit, endowed with the three basic traits of his nation: nationalism, democratism and an inclination to heresy" (Kusin, 1971a, pp. 135-6).

Liehm, who played such a large role in the dissident activity of the Writers' Union during the Prague Spring, also favored the view that the Czech intellectual was a substitute for an absent native aristocracy. Liehm had grown up between the Wars and was disdainful of the First Republic because of its pacifist complicity in the Munich agreement and the Nazi occupation. After 1945 he regarded himself as an idealistic socialist whose task was to liberate Czechoslovak culture from the heavy hand of both state and market. Yet he saw some continuity between the Writers' Union and the First Republic: "This publishing organization became the sole heir of the first republic. And though there was little resemblance to pre-war publishing in terms of content, the outer form and the emphasis upon the intelligentsia were sufficiently reminiscent of pre-Munich books and magazines for the new publishers to inherit a considerable segment of the old readership" (Kusin, 1971b, pp. 72-3).

Communism came to Czechoslovakia late. By 1948, the Russian Revolution was already thirty years old; and Czechoslovakia was three years behind other Central European satellites like Poland and Hungary in going Communist. The Czech Lands were in many respects western. While part of the Habsburg territories, they had absorbed many German influences. A measure perhaps of Czechs' "Europeanness" was that they had endured only a limited Turkish invasion. The Turks were once at the gates of Vienna but not of Prague. The Christianity of the Czech Lands was Protestant and Catholic, not Orthodox. Politics there between the two World Wars had more in common with small, liberal democracies like Sweden, Holland and Belgium. Many of the reformist leaders in 1968 had either come of age during the First Republic or were children and so were open to the collective memories of a civil society recalled by their parents. For example, the fourteen contributors to the impressive collection of essays edited by Liehm, *The Politics of Culture* (New York, 1970) had an average age of 47 in 1968. Several of them, though not all, were convinced socialists. Yet others represented direct experience of liberal, European influences; Milan Kundera pleaded for a Czech culture joined to Europe; Josef

Škvorecký spoke of Christian democracy; Jiří Mucha had spent his childhood in Paris with his famous father and had been correspondent there for *Lidové noviny*; and Eduard Goldstücker had been in Britain during the Second World War.

The cultural disposition of the Czech intelligentsia is important because the Prague Spring movement was very much an affair of the intellectuals. The workers were only marginally involved and the army and the state apparatus remained under the control of the government. Dissidents came overwhelmingly from the universities and the writers' and journalists' unions. Indeed the central demands of the whole movement of 1968 may be thought to have been intellectual liberties: freedom of speech and opinion, and an end to censorship (Skilling, 1976, p. 572; Kusin, 1971b, p. 247). Such claims clearly entailed political pluralism and multi-partyism. The impetus here came from Liehm, Ludvík Vaculík and Ivan Klíma and others in the Union of Czechoslovak Writers (SCSS) and the dozens of writers and journalists who wrote and worked particularly for *Literární noviny* before September 1967, *Literární listy* after March 1968 and, more generally, the established newspapers and media. Milan Šimečka put it well: "(There was) the new look of the newspapers, radio and TV. This was the most striking sign of disorder. People queued up at kiosks every morning and bought three or as many as five daily newspapers: that was probably the worst sign of all. In existing socialism one of the signs of order is that citizens buy only one paper since they know all too well that all the others will say very much the same" (Šimečka, 1984, p. 25). To use Liehm's terminology, in 1968 the transmission belts of writers' unions and media, created to carry out orders from above, developed a spontaneous life of their own and made "horizontal" contact not just with each other but with an increasingly enthusiastic general public.

After 1969 there occurred what Šimečka calls the "civilized violence" of the "existing socialism" of Gustav Husák. Control by the party apparat was re-established over media, culture and universities. Not only were traditional party hierarchies re-constituted but explicit policies of discrimination and punishment were imposed on dissidents, actual and suspected. The Czechoslovak Communist Party (CzCP) was purged of as many as 500,000 members; personnel in media, the universities and the cultural industries were dismissed. The Writers' Union, which had had about 400 members in 1968, was dissolved and re-organized. But its new membership was only 50 and even in 1977 only 165 (Skilling, 1981, Document 12). Many writers were banned; dissenters were put under surveillance and in some cases imprisoned.

Modern Czech history, then, is a story of recurring disruption and dissonance. A new, sudden and largely unanticipated transition began in November 1989. The CzCP abdicated any claim to a "leading role" and suddenly there were no obstacles in the way of re-establishing a civil society. Unlike in 1968 the emphasis was not upon a pluralist socialism but upon a pluralist liberalism: privatization, the restitution of confiscated property and the advantages of the market.[2] Several parties ran in the first election of 1990, an election conducted once more according to proportional representation so that it might easily have been believed that the multiple political divisions of the First Republic had only slept and never gone away. (If there is discontinuity in Czech history there is also persistence!) Political fragmentation continued in 1992 with the splintering of the Civic Reform umbrella group and next year Czechoslovakia itself split apart.

In the media, too, changes were apparent. But the brave, new world of the Velvet Revolution was not without its anxieties and failures.[3] The newest technologies have become more widely available: Internet, fax, satellite TV reception. *Blesk*, a tabloid, and *Lidové noviny* were, however, the only new newspapers, the latter soon to disappear and re-appear, and *Nova*, a new TV station. Otherwise the names at least of the established organs of opinion remain in place. Of course they have adapted. For example, *Rudé právo*, the execrable, official voice of the old party-state was privatized and fell under the majority ownership of its former associate editor, Zdeněk Porybný. It publishes a TV guide and an auto magazine in its Saturday edition, has dropped *Rudé* from its title and has become a modest critic of the Klaus government and a supporter of the Social Democrats.

The Czech Lands continue to be extensive consumers of print media. There are by western standards still many newspapers, dailies and weeklies, with a relatively high circulation. The top ten dailies published in Prague had a combined circulation of over 1,593,000 in June 1997 and the ten most popular weeklies over 1,169,000.[4] *Dnes,* the former *Mladá fronta Dnes*, once the newspaper of the Communist youth movement, has the largest circulation, followed by *Právo*. Most newspapers have been privatized but there are now concerns over the takeover of local media by foreign corporate interests, especially the Ringier consortium in Switzerland and the German company, Neue Passau Press. German ownership of provincial Czech newspapers has been particularly numerous so that the overall German presence in the media market raises perplexing questions of Czech media's objectivity on issues such as the role of Germany as a regional power and the unresolved issue of the restitution of the lands of Sudeten Germans expelled from Czechoslovakia at war's end, not to mention unsettled Czech claims over Nazi atrocities between 1938 and 1945.

Some observers are critical of post-Communist media. Journalists are young, untrained, poorly paid and lacking in commitment to "objective" and investigative standards. Critics talk of the dominant type of the journalist as a sort of *engagé,* literary figure who proffers "opinion" in his stories and whose inspiration has more to do with partisan commitment and aesthetic elegance than factual reportage. Czech journalists, it is said, prefer to identify with a leader, a cause or a hero rather than participate in the mundane world of facts and investigation. Again, as if the First Republic and Communism, for that matter, had never gone away, there has re-appeared a tradition of media as politically partisan organizations, with editors-in-chief establishing a party line and journalists required to fall into step. In this way, if there is to be investigative journalism, it must be set loose on all political parties and leaders, except those favored by the newspaper or TV station that the reporter happens to work for. There is concern that journalists are compromised in other ways; that most business journalists in Czech Republic receive *sub rosa* rewards from sources favored in their stories and that the same is true of a minority of political journalists. Also, the banks, still state-owned and indirectly under the control of the government, have or have had ownership interests in some newspapers and magazines. Banks own about 40% of the weekly, *Ekonom*, and Investicni a postovni banka had an interest in *Telegraf*, historically a mouthpiece of Václav Klaus's Civic Democratic Party (ODS) though, proof perhaps that even power has its limits, the latter is now a defunct newspaper. Journalists and editors talk of heavy-handed political pressure from the former prime minister who would intimidate TV stations and newspapers to have them cancel a particular programme or re-orient a given story; Klaus it was who castigated Munro Luther, owner of *The Prague Post*, as "his worst enemy" (Levy, 1995).

Similar incidents are, of course, not unknown in other accredited, civil societies. And it can be expected that other features of *normal* western experience will be replicated: newspaper circulation will likely continue to decline, some newspapers will go out of business; (*Práce*, a newspaper sponsored by trade unions, went bankrupt in 1997;) TV will probably become the major source of the public's information and opinions; and media will become more sensationalist and superficial in their coverage. But, that said, it is difficult to conclude that contemporary media in Czech Republic are in any definitive way so inferior in democracy, diversity, and informational and libertarian zeal that they do not fit the designation of a civil society. Much of political life, perhaps like life itself, is a judicious estimate of the degree to which the glass is half full or half empty. Czech media exhibit features of democratic immaturity and insufficiency. (The same can after all be said of media in the West.) In other respects they demonstrate attributes to be expected in a society struggling to transcend the submerged and compromised journalistic traditions of its past but open to the intimations of a civil-social order that are also part of its cultural inheritance. The story of the collapse of the Klaus government illustrates this incomplete, mixed picture.

In late 1997 a story was leaked to the media by a member of the government, Josef Zieleniec, the Minister of Foreign Affairs. He had been a founder of the Civic Democratic Party in the early 1990s, indeed some claim that he was its principal founder. He and other cabinet members such as Jan Ruml and Ivan Pilip had had disagreements with Klaus over the pace and extent of economic reform, especially privatization; probably Zieleniec was also offended at the moral compromises that the government had tolerated, especially in the privatization process; and there was, no doubt, personal rivalry and disappointment. The story that was leaked involved financial contributions to the ODS of one, Milan Šrejber, a businessman, who had successfully obtained ownership of a steel mill in northern Bohemia after a privatization decision in 1995. The contributions, made afterwards, were reported as being from two foreign donors, one a Hungarian and the other, curiously, a Mauritian. *Dnes* and *Právo* particularly developed the leaked story and the former was instrumental in exposing the fact that the two contributors were fictitious. *Lidové noviny* also played a large role in pursuing the story as did *Nova* TV. In the end the smell of scandal was sufficient to bring down Klaus and lead to a change of government. Much of this speaks well of the idea of a free press that holds leaders accountable. *Dnes* and *Lidové noviny* had had reputations as newspapers that were partial to Klaus's government. Their loyalty to the truth trumped their political partisanship in this case and this is positive.

The other side of the picture is less encouraging. The story was disclosed by politically connected insiders; and while the government fell, to date no-one has been charged with any infringement of electoral or privatization laws; and the story was allowed by the media to be buried and fade away after the initial disclosure. Klaus appointed an independent accounting firm to examine the ODS's books but its findings were limited by the audit's terms of reference. The audit did not vindicate the party; neither did it get to the bottom of things. What it did achieve was the political management of the scandal by the ODS and the limiting of political damage. After a spell in the dog-house, Klaus and his party came roaring back in the election of June 1998, gaining 27.5% of the popular vote. Of course, it is not required that a democratic electorate reject outright an ostensibly corrupt government and party. But there is a common view among opinion leaders in Prague that the media should have done a better job in pursuing and developing this story after it was handed to them on a plate.

III. Gellner and Civil Society

Ernest Gellner developed his theory of civil society in his last major work, *Conditions of Liberty: Civil Society and Its Rivals* (London, 1994). His theory of "Civil Society", as he puts it, nonetheless depends on his earlier account of nationalism in *Nations and Nationalism* (Ithaca and London, 1983). In traditional, agricultural societies, he says, people are governed by a ruling class of warrior and scribe, soldier and priest, military and clerisy. At this time only the rulers have what Gellner calls a "High Culture"; that is, an education that provides training in formulating and understanding "context-free messages in a shared idiom" (Gellner, 1994b, p. viii). Rulership is typically local but priest and ruler belong to a High Culture that is international. Status in this society is, of course, ascribed and everything is done to differentiate between classes. There is little mobility, either vertically or horizontally. Beneath the ruler extends a peasant class of serfs and laborers who are illiterate. Typically the bonds of social unity are provided by a religion of some kind. Political power is authoritarian and usually decentralized. If by chance political authority is weak, communal conformity will, anyway, typically be strong.

Afterwards, says Gellner, arises industrial society which places an imperative importance on "rational knowledge": knowledge that is coherent and consistent and which works to promote technical efficiency. Industrialism emphasizes economic growth; it extends the division of labor although specialization's are much more permeable and permit a "mutual affinity of style". That is to say, specialization's are much more mutually intelligible. At the heart of industrial society is education. Scientific and technical innovation, successfully organized, lies at the back of economic productivity. Effective industrial societies are those that provide extensive mass education and training in literacy, numeracy, basic work habits and skills, and familiarity with basic technical and social skills. Education in industrial society is "universal, standardized and generic" (Gellner, 1994b, p. 27). The provision of this education is too large and expensive to be provided by anything other than a centralized state. Government becomes the political protector, paymaster and quality-controller of education (Gellner, 1994a, p. 107).

Inevitably, then, according to Gellner, the modern industrial state becomes the national state. Industrialism pries workers free from locale and class; it makes labor mobile and workers interchangeable. Contract and market create an economic world of anonymity. A traditional, agricultural society is culturally differentiated; an industrial society is, typically, culturally homogeneous. The state, as an educator of everyone, becomes willy nilly a fabricator of culture. Normally the state will organize a new, universal High Culture on the basis of a shared language, religion or ethnicity: the nation in other words. Thus the nation is co-extensive with culture and culture is organized through education provided by a national state. This is the norm of the modern world. Yet Gellner is only too well aware of an abnormal kind of nationalism. This is ethnic or folk nationalism based on the appeal by an insurgent elite to revive and consolidate the folk culture of a pre-industrial peasantry. This type, he claims, is an epiphenomenon or a "pretence"; *really*, nationalism is the organizing of an anonymous High Culture suitable to industrialism.

Various parts of Europe experienced nationalism differently (Gellner, 1994a, pp. 113-124). In the Atlantic area, Gellner says, medieval, dynastic regimes especially in France and England consolidated themselves early as efficient, central administrations and governed culturally homogeneous societies. In the Middle Zone, Italy and Germany had well formalized High Cultures but weak institutions of political centralization. And so nationalism there was more concerned to create a strong central state in order to advance an already constituted culture. In central and Eastern Europe, in the main the Habsburg lands, multi-ethnicity prevailed; there were many peasant cultures and they lacked the character of High Cultures. Here, therefore, both ethnically based states and local High Cultures were absent and must needs be created. Nationalism, Gellner seems to say, understandably emphasized Folk Culture: "Notwithstanding the fact that its real social roots lay in the emergence of a mass anonymous society, destined to use a shared and standardized culture, (nationalism here) adopted the pretence...that it was defending and perpetuating a village, folk culture. It had to do so: defending a newly created High Culture against the expansionism of the old one [i.e. German-Habsburg culture], it had to borrow the themes from local Folk Culture" (Gellner, 1994a, p. 111). Here by implication speaks Gellner on Czech nationalism in the 19th and early 20th centuries. Clearly for him folk nationalism is at best an illusion and a distortion; it is a version of false consciousness and an unstable basis of rule. The new national states that emerged in 1918 "had all the weaknesses of the old empires- they were just as haunted by minorities." As well they had weaknesses of their own: they were small, new, governed by "inexperienced, greedy and incautious ruling classes and their ethnic minorities were frequently drawn from hitherto dominant groups, with consequent instability" (Gellner, 1994a, p.120). We assume that Gellner includes Czechoslovakia in this general condemnation.

What of Civil Society? It was, Gellner says, a "miracle" and a "mystery", appearing in England in the 17th century (Gellner, 1994a, pp. 32, 86). Here was its first appearance historically. Its coming was so significant that it may be said to have made the modern world possible; it was the breach in the wall that brought about the overcoming of authoritarian regimes, the normal historical pattern of state systems (Gellner, 1994a, p. 51).

Civil Society, he says, presupposes the existence of a coercive, efficient, central state able to provide security and the adjudication of competing private interests (Gellner,1994a, pp.1, 2, 31, 93). It is, in other words, the liberal state, traditionally understood. As we have seen Civil Society also builds on the cultural homogeneity and High Culture which nationalism normally brings about. Civil Society is dominated by science and technology and, to realize their potential as agents for economic growth, a Civil Society will organize a market open to all and an educational system denied to none. Civil Society, driven by the imperatives of technical inventiveness and exponential growth, brings about astounding internal mobility and interchangeability. Historically, Gellner says, societies have been static, differentiated and hierarchical affairs; their social structure has been unchanging and inflexible and unified by force and religious dogma. Civil Societies achieve the astounding innovation of being relatively structureless, flexible and variable though sufficiently stable and unified to survive. The secret here is what Gellner calls "modularity": "Modular man (sic) is capable of combining into effective associations and institutions, *without* these being total, many-stranded, underwritten by ritual and made stable through being linked to a whole inside set of relationships, all of these being tied in with each other and so immobilized. He can combine into specific-purpose, *ad hoc*, limited association, without binding himself by some blood ritual. He can leave an association when he comes to disagree with its policy, without being open to an accusation of treason...It is *this* which makes Civil Society: the forging of links which are effective even though they are flexible, specific, instrumental. It does indeed depend on a move from Status to Contract: it means that men honor contracts even when they are not linked to ritualized status and group membership. Society is still a structure, it is not atomized, helpless and supine, and yet the structure is readily adjustable and responds to rational criteria of improvement. Modularity of man is the main answer to the question: how can there be countervailing institutions or associations which at the same time are not also stifling?" (Gellner, 1994a, pp.99-100).

Civil Society is, to repeat, according to Gellner, an arrangement in which there is a strong state providing public order and liberal, procedural justice; it entails also an autonomous, pluralistic, private economic sector which prevents state power exceeding its proper bounds. The emphasis is upon balance and countervailing power: a strong state but an independent, economic sector producing an offsetting equilibrium. Gellner is *not* a devotee of the liberal, minimal, "nightwatchman" state. His views on state-managed education I have already detailed. He believes as well that the dangers inherent in modern technology and the passing of the family's traditional role as provider of last resort require an interventionist, welfare state, albeit one more limited and smaller than most post-war liberal democracies provide (Gellner, 1994a, p. 90).

He continues: the structure of the state under Civil Society should be *democratic* in the specific sense that the government should be "accountable"; there should be arrangements ensuring a rotation of personnel and parties in office. Remuneration for politicians should be relatively low (Gellner, 1994a, pp. 93, 184-9). Civil Society is, socially, individualistic-modular: open, mobile, flexible, meritocratic, instrumentalist and anonymous. Ideologically too it will be diverse and varied, without a dominant system of dogma or religious belief: secular and unsacramental, desacralised and given to "ambiguity, irony and nuance": "The political centralism is essential for in the modern world economic and social units simply cannot double up as order-maintaining ones. Economic pluralism, far from total, is compatible with political control over strategic economic issues (indeed, requires this). The autonomy of the economy is needed not merely in the name of efficiency, but so as to provide pluralism with a social base which it cannot any longer find anywhere else. It requires intellectual or ideological pluralism: the growing economy which is indispensable to the system is impossible without science, and science is incompatible with a cognitive picture of the world which is socially sustained, enforced and endowed with *a priori* authority" (Gellner, 1994a, p. 212).

Finally, Gellner distinguishes Civil Society from three other modern alternatives: the *Umma* of the Moslem world with its strong central state, suffocating religious uniformity, politically dependent economic institutions and extensive social atomization (Gellner,1994a, pp. 15-29). Also, there is the failed *Umma* of Marxism with its autocratic central state, pervasive, secular, religion-like conformity and non-existent economic pluralism (Gellner, 1994a, pp. 30-43). And, lastly, Civil Society differs from "segmentary" societies - tribal and class-dominated - which lack strong, central, coercive arrangements but which subject their citizens to extensive communal uniformity (Gellner, 1994a, pp. 8-12).

Gellner is not an historicist. The emergence of Civil Society was not inevitable; it defied the normal pattern of history; its appearance was possibly adventitious. But, having come into existence, it possesses great expansionary power because it emits strong, inherent appeal and because it rides the powerful waves of technological innovation and economic growth. The proof of its uniqueness, Gellner claims, lies in its defiance of an age-old social rule: that if rulers/warriors are separated from producers/workers, the latter will be despoiled by the former. How did it come to pass that soldiers were convinced to remain in their barracks, obedient to civilian rule and respectful of the independence of the economy? (Gellner, 1994a, pp. 61-88). It all began in England in the 17th century, he repeats. Several reasons explain its rise there (Gellner, 1994a, pp. 73-8). First, England was the pioneer in the use of science and technology for economic purposes and was the first to produce a regime of continuing and exponential growth. This created, he says, an "unlimited Social Bribery Fund" that was used to buy off discontent. Also, superiority in science and technology brought technical mastery on the battlefield. A nation of veritable shopkeepers effectively defended itself against its enemies. Secondly, north-Western Europe was at this time a multi-state system so that throttling Civil Society simultaneously in several places was impossible to achieve. Thirdly, because of continuing exponential growth, a balance was tipped in England and it became established for all to see that production was a surer path to personal wealth and status than coercion and rapine. Fourthly, the division of labor is different in the modern era. There *are* distinct and separate jobs but underlying the division of labor is a spreading homogeneity: "every job is carried out in the same style and in much the same spirit" (Gellner, 1994a, p.75). This affects the military's role as well. The soldier, instead of being a ritualized, honor-laden warrior, becomes a sober professional like everyone else. Fifthly, the individualism of Protestantism in England and elsewhere, for example the United States, established the individual's right to commune with God directly. Priestly elites were displaced and the individual pursued virtue, alone: "Virtue, freely practiced between consenting adults, may be a great boon to Civil Society, or even its essential pre-condition. Concern with virtue led men to a disinterested pursuit of interest - accumulation without enjoyment, hence to re-investment, hence continuous growth - rather than transformation of wealth into power, status, pleasure or salvation, as is more common among men" (Gellner, 1994a, p. 77).

The sixth factor making possible Civil Society was what Gellner calls the "ideological stalemate" (Gellner, 1994a, p. 78). The English Reformation produced two types of Protestantism: an Anglican Church that, although Protestant, was official, established and priestly; and a variety of dissenting groups and sects, loosely called Puritans. The latter particularly emphasized the individual's unobstructed communion with God. If the Puritans had had their way, they would have imposed the rule of the saints, a theocracy. However historical contingencies forced them to compete with Anglicanism. What was set up, says Gellner, was a contest between "a socially rooted...ritualistic religion" and "the preachers of uncompromising, absolute and enforced virtue", the enthusiasts. In the 17th century the contest resulted in an ecclesiastical stalemate. The enthusiast-puritans were denied a chance to found a theocracy, turned inward and pursued virtue through economic activity. Finally, there was a political stalemate. The struggle of king and parliament produced an offsetting balance: a strong central government but a mixed constitution of monarch and parliament.

To repeat, Gellner is no historicist. The triumph of Civil Society was not inevitable. It happened to occur in England in the early modern period. But having emerged there it launched other societies on the same course, notably the Dutch and the Americans. What Gellner claims is that a Civil Society can be established through "emulation"; it is a moral ideal that other people will wish to imitate. But not all societies can expect to become Civil Societies just through will and choice. There must be suitable cultural preconditions and the evolution of a Civil Society is a long process. Evidently it is also his view that no given society can necessarily attain Civil Society status in precisely the same way as England in the 17th century. If we can accept that the Czech Lands are a Civil Society of sorts, and if Gellner's theory is to have any comparative significance for democracy and liberty in this part of Central Europe, it will be because the reasons causing the English to become a Civil Society cannot be applied literally but *functionally.* I mean by this that the particular circumstances of 17th century England were specific and unique but that the social *processes* that produced a Civil Society there will have some general applicability. In this way Gellner's *Conditions of Liberty* will have heuristic value for understanding another society. His book offers, then, the following propositions about what a Civil Society is and how it comes about:

1) A Civil Society depends on scientific and technological innovation and the availability of a universal education;
2) A Civil Society is best secured in a poly-centric world order. Such an international system permits "natural selection" and emulation by other aspiring Civil Societies;
3) An economy of high productivity helps produce a Civil Society because it allows social conflict to be more easily contained;
4) For a Civil Social culture to emerge the military must be subjected to civilian rule and military office made open to all the talents; it becomes a career whose norms are bureaucratized and professionalized;
5) Crucial to the development of a Civil Society is the existence of a healthy individualism devoid of what Gellner calls "atomization." That is, an individualism unaffected by cynicism, opportunism and spurious enterprise.

It will, however, be an individualism content to engage in mundane, unheroic activities like money-making and trade;

6) Civil Society results from an inter-play of socio-economic forces that produce an equilibrium. The state will be strong, the economy independent, plural and enterprising but not so independent as to render the state impotent. The emphasis is upon separateness but as well balance, compromise and stalemate;
7) Representative government must offset overweening executive authority or there can be no accountability of government to the public. Elections will ensure a rotation of office-holders; and political life should be rewarded modestly. Not all citizens need be politically participant. For most citizens personal fulfillment will be better realized in private activities rather than within the public or political realm.

IV. Conclusion

Gellner's theory re-tells many of the established insights of political sociology and anthropology: that economic growth mutes social conflict and that the co-existence of liberty and order requires a delimited state. But his particular virtue is that he re-combines these with a special insight to produce his compelling account of Civil Society. The mood of his book is mildly celebratory: arguments he has had with Marxists he clearly enjoys having won; there is an almost Churchillian celebration of Atlantic civilization and its winning of Civil Society in the beginnings of the modern world. However, his account is not uncritical nor static; he discusses anxiously the future of Civil Society; he worries that its dependence on productivity may bring its demise if economic growth stumbles (Gellner, 1994a, pp. 202-3). Gellner's strength lies in the coherence and historicity of his account. He offers a powerful explanation of how Civil Society came about and he provides a systematic list of the elements of a Civil Social order: a strong but limited state; cultural homogeneity in aid of a High Culture of technical-instrumental knowledge; modularity or individualism; a private economy separate, independent and offsetting of government; political accountability; and, ideological variety. As a heuristic device his theory orients the scholar to the historical origins and evolution of a Civil Society culture. He emphasizes the genetic and the cultural; and in the early part of this essay I have attempted to emphasize similar themes and processes with regards to civil society in the Czech Lands: viz., the absence of an indigenous aristocracy and its replacement by liberal intellectuals; the Czech Lands as a cockpit of diversity; the early Czech nationalist emphasis upon education; the modern attaining of a technological and industrial order; the recurring Czech intellectual passion for individuality and free speech, and so on.

No society is ever a completely realized paragon of civil social order or of the specific type that is Gellner's. Czech Republic has set its course by some version or other of this ideal. Yet it carries within it cultural and historical deficits: the residue of Habsburg autocracy; a tendency towards ethnic nationalism; and towards atomization, "moral torpor, mediocrity, and an exclusive concern with minding one's own business, the result of close to fifty years of authoritarian subjection" (Keane, 1988, p. 4). Jiří Mucha is no doubt correct when he says that the political culture of the Czech Lands was adversely affected by that veritable absent indigenous aristocracy. Czechs, he says, learned to wear the loyal mask and secretly kicked their masters' furniture. This "concierge syndrome" led to a "cringing respect for authority" (Liehm, 1970, pp., 225-9). The syndrome did not go away. If anything authoritarian rule accentuated it. I have noted that the consociational politics of the First Republic were made possible by extensive deference towards leaders; and in 1938/9 and 1968 military invasion was countered by something less than official, military resistance.

Singling out some of the important hallmarks of a civil social order - ideological diversity and a free press - contemporary Czech media could well increase their investigative and critical orientation towards public authorities. The fall of the Klaus government in late 1997 is instructive. A civil society is a delicate balancing act. The economy is to be privatized. But privatization can lead to new injustices and new forms of hegemony. Privately owned economies require sensitive supervision by government. (Remember Gellner's dictum: the state in a free society is to be strong and off-setting, albeit limited.) If the Czech banks continue to be largely owned by the state and if they exercise a large sway over a number of firms and enterprises through the conversion of outstanding loans into debt equity and through their holdings of investment fund portfolios, there is an imperative to privatize further or the government will continue to preside over a statist economy. Yet even privatized financial and monetary markets cry out for necessary public regulation. Equity markets, for example, must establish a scheme of rules that permit investors' confidence in the integrity of transactions; otherwise insider trading will become endemic and investment dry up. Klaus's government failed to provide the right policy regime in these areas. Also, it evidently avoided addressing the important issue of election finance legislation. In the end it was chased from office by among others a persistent, critical media. Here are signs of the maturing of a civil society; the glass is half full.

ENDNOTES

1. Jan Patočka, the moving spirit behind the Charter 77 movement, had the interesting idea of what he called a "moral foundation:" "The concept of *human rights* is nothing but the conviction that states and society as a whole also consider themselves to be subject to the sovereignty of moral sentiment, that they recognize something unqualified above them, something that is blindingly sacred and inviolable even for them, and that they intend to contribute to this

end, with the power by which they create and ensure the *legal* norms" (Skilling, 1981, 218).

2. F. M. Barnard established definitively the socialist credentials of the 1968 reformers. What they wanted, he concludes, was pluralist socialism (Barnard, 1991).
3. My perspective on contemporary Czech media is based on some thirty interviews with editors, journalists and political scientists in Prague, February 1995, August 1996 and June 1998.
4. Information on circulation figures is derived from *The Prague Post Book of Lists*.

References

Anderson, B., (1983), *Imagined Communities*, London: Verso Books.

Anderson, P., (1974), *Lineages of the Absolutist State*, London: New Left Books.

Barnard, F.M., (1991), *Pluralism, socialism, and political legitimacy: reflections on opening up communism*, Cambridge: Cambridge University Press.

Gellner, E., (1983), *Nations and Nationalism*, Ithaca and London: Cornell University Press.

Gellner, E., (1994a), *Conditions of Liberty: Civil Society and its Rivals,* London: Hamish Hamilton.

Gellner, E., (1994b), *Encounters With Nationalism*, Oxford: Basil Blackwell.

Golan, G., (1971), *The Czechoslovak Reform Movement: Communism in Crisis, 1962-1968*, Cambridge: Cambridge University Press.

Havel, V., (1991), *Open Letters*, London: Faber and Faber.

Havel, V., (1997), *The Art of the Impossible*, New York: Alfred A. Knopf.

Interviews with: Bohuslav Blažek, Dean Calbreath, Miloš Calda, Jiří Dolák, Petr Dudek, Vladimira Dvořáková, Alex Friedrich, Jiří Holub, Vladimír Jaroš, Miroslav Jindra, Terezie Jungrová, Jiří Komínek, Daniel Kumermann, Ross Larsen, Alan Levy, Michelle Legge, Siegfried Mortkowitz, Vladímír Mlynář, Jaroslav Plesl, Zdeněk Porybný, Jan Přikryl, Lubomír Sedlák, Jaroslav Veis, Jaromír Vepřek and Zdeněk Zbořil; Prague, 1995, 1996 and 1998.

Keane, J., editor (1988), *Civil Society and the State: New European Perspectives*, London: Verso Books.

Kusin, V.V., (1971a), *The Intellectual Origins of the Prague Spring*, Cambridge: Cambridge University Press.

Kusin, V.V., editor, (1971b), *The Czechoslovak Reform Movement, 1968*, Oxford: Oxford University Press.

Liehm, A.J., editor, (1970), *The Politics of Culture*, New York: The Free Press.

Seton-Watson, R.W., (1943), *A History of the Czechs and Slovaks*, London: Hutchinson and Co.

Šimečka, M., (1984), *The Restoration of Order: The Normalization of Czechoslovakia 1969-1976*, London: Verso Books.

Skilling, H.G., (1976),*Czechoslovakia's Interrupted Revolution*, Princeton: Princeton University Press.

Skilling H.G., (1981), *Charter 77 and Human Rights in Czechoslovakia*, London, Allen and Unwin.

Táborský, E., (1945), *Czechoslovak Democracy at Work*, London

Táborský, E., (1961), *Communism in Czechoslovakia*, Princeton: Princeton University Press.

About the Authors and Contributors

Sohrab Abizadeh is a Professor of Economics at The University of Winnipeg in Manitoba, Canada. He served for five years as Associate Dean of Arts and Science and was a Senior Tax Policy Advisor to the Government of Alberta. Sohrab Abizadeh's recent published works have appeared in *Public Choice, Atlantic Economic Journal, Public Finance* and *Public Finance Quarterly*. He is the Co-editor of *Fiscal Systems and Economic Development: Case Studies of Selected Countries*, (1996), Nova Science Publishers, Inc., New York. Abizadeh's main areas of research are public finance, economic development and growth and transition economies. He has made three research trips to Central and Eastern Europe since 1992.

Sheena Gardner is an Applied Linguist at CELTE, the University of Warwick, UK. She was previously an Associate Professor in Education at The University of Winnipeg; Research Fellow in Islamic and Middle Eastern Studies at Edinburgh University, UK; Lecturer in English at Gezira University, Sudan; Lektor at Albert Ludwig's University, Freiburg, Germany; and Teaching Fellow in Linguistics at St. Andrews University, UK. Her current research interests include, among other, Anthroponymy in Arabic and in Botswana. She has published in different areas in a variety of local, national and international journals, and was recently co-editor of the *TESL Canada Journal*.

Annabelle Mays is an Associate Professor and the Director of the Education Program at The University of Winnipeg in Manitoba, Canada. From 1992-97 she was also an Associate Dean of Arts and Science. Her recent publications includes articles in B.T. Peck (ed.) *Teaching and Learning in Lithuania Since "Rebirth": A Challenge for School Directors and Teachers*, Part 2, New York: Nova Science, 1998 (forthcoming) and the *Journal of Canadian and International Education*. The major focus of her research and publications is the study of educational change and transformation in Eastern and Central Europe.

Allen Mills is a Professor of Political Science at The University of Winnipeg in Manitoba, Canada. His area of specialty has been Canadian political thought, particularly the ideas of the non-Marxist Left. His major publication is *Fool for Christ; the Political Thought of J.S. Woodsworth*, (Toronto, 1991). He was visiting lecturer in Canadian Studies at Charles University, Prague in 1992. An early interest in consociational theories in Canada led to an interest in Czech politics. He has made three research trips to Czech Republic.

Joel Novek is currently Professor and has been Chair of the Sociology Department at The University of Winnipeg. He has been a Visiting Research Associate at the Massachusetts Institute of Technology and the University of Paris. His major research interest focuses on the social and environmental impact of technological change. Among his most important recent publications are articles in the *International Journal of Health Services, Society and Natural Resources, Canadian Review of Sociology and Anthropology* and *Canadian Journal of Sociology.*

Eleoussa Polyzoi is currently an Associate Professor of Education and Coordinator of Developmental Studies at The University of Winnipeg in Manitoba, Canada. Her research interests include the development of conversational skills among preschool children, comparative special education and education transformation in Eastern and Central Europe. Her articles have appeared in the *Journal of Canadian and International Education, Canadian Journal of Research in Early Childhood Education,* and *Canadian Journal of Special Education.*

Dan Stone is a Professor of History at The University of Winnipeg in Manitoba, Canada. He is the author of *The Polish-Lithuanian State, 1386-1795* (forthcoming), *Polish Politics and National Reform, 1775-1778* and *The Polish Memoirs of William John Rose* (as editor). He has published articles in *Slavic Review, Canadian Slavonic Papers, Polin: A Journal of Polish and Jewish History, Polish Review* and *Annales historiques de la Révolution* as well as chapters in books such as *Polish-Americans and Their History: Community, Culture, and Politics* and *Polish Democratic Thought from the Renaissance to the Great Emigration.* He has been visiting East Central Europe since 1963.

Karen S. Vorst is a Professor of Economics at Indiana University, Bloomington, Indiana, USA. She was a Fulbright Scholar in 1996. Her recent publications have appeared in *The Journal of Economics* and *The Journal of Economic Issues.* She is the co-editor of a book on *Financial Market Restructuring in Selected Central European Countries* (1998, Ashgate Publishing Co., England). Vorst's areas of research includes monetary theory and policy, banking and financial systems and transition economies of Central and Eastern Europe.

Willadee Wehmeyer is a Professor of Economics at MidAmerica Nazarene University, Olathe, Kansas, USA. She has worked as a consultant and an independent researcher for two years. Professor Wehmeyer is the co-editor of *Financial Market Restructuring in Selected Central European Countries* published by Ashgate Publishing Ltd. Her recent publications have appeared in *The Journal of Economics*. She has traveled to Central and Eastern Europe to present papers and to do research.

INDEX

O

P

Q

R

S

T

U

V

W

Y